Lexical Change and Variation
in the Southeastern United States,
1930–1990

To Bill —
"Close the language door.
And open the love window."
The moon won't use the
door, only the window.
(Rumi) Love & Blessings,
Ellen

Lexical Change and Variation in the Southeastern United States, 1930–1990

Ellen Johnson

The University of Alabama Press

Tuscaloosa and London

Copyright © 1996
The University of Alabama Press
Tuscaloosa, Alabama 35487-0380
All rights reserved
Manufactured in the United States of America

∞
The paper on which this book is printed meets the minimum requirements of American National Standard for Information Science-Permanence of Paper for Printed Library Materials, ANSI Z39.48-1984.

Map 6, on p. 54, is from Hans Kurath, *A Word Geography of the Eastern United States* (Ann Arbor: University of Michigan Press, 1949). Used by permission.

Library of Congress Cataloging-in-Publication Data

Johnson, Ellen, 1959–
    Lexical change and variation in the southeastern United States, 1930–1990 / Ellen Johnson
       p.   cm.
    Includes bibliographical references and index.
    ISBN 0-8173-0794-X (alk. paper)
       1. English language—Southern States—Lexicology.   2. English language—Variation—Southern States.   3. English language—Dialects—Southern States.   4. Language and culture—Southern States.   5. Americanisms—Southern States.   6. Linguistic change.
I. Title.
PE2924.J64   1996
427'.975—dc20   95-31808

British Library Cataloguing-in-Publication Data available

This book is dedicated to Thomas.

Contents

List of Tables	viii
List of Maps	x
Acknowledgments	xi
Introduction	1
1 Collection and Categorization of the Data	5
The Linguistic Variables and the Interview	5
The Social and Regional Variables	13
2 Variation	29
Patterns of Variation	31
Statistical Methods	35
Special Topics	42
3 Change	61
Statistical Methods	62
Change and Variation	65
Change in the Lexicon	73
4 Culture and the Lexicon	79
The Lexicon as an Object of Study	80
Cultural Change and Lexical Change	85
Society and Language Variation	92
Appendix 1: Biographical Sketches	114
Appendix 2: Variants Associated with Regional or Social Groups	137
Appendix 3: Variants Exhibiting Diachronic Change	146
Appendix 4: Tallies and Selected Commentary	153
Appendix 5: Index of Variants by Question Number	285
References	294
Index	303

Tables

1	Questionnaire topics	6
2	Informant characteristics and communities	15
3	Summary of informant characteristics	18
4	Population compared to sample	24
5	Educational levels by group	27
6	Percent/Number of statistically significant tests by variable	31
7	Percentage of variants linked to each non-linguistic variable	32
8	'Sofa', 1990 (stage 1)	38
9	'Sofa', 1990 (stage 2)	39
10	*Sofa*, 1990	40
11	*Shell* (beans), 1990	48
12	*Firedogs*, 1990	49
13	Words whose distributions match those reported in Kurath (1949)	51
14	Some words from the *Word Geography* whose distributions are not substantiated here	52
15	*Snake Feeder*, 1930s	53
16	Items associated with more than one socio-regional category	57
17	Questions with 'No Response' linked to a non-linguistic variable	59
18	*Couch* data	63
19	*Couch* results	64
20	Variants with significant differences by both time and region	66
21	Variants with significant differences by both time and rurality	67
22	Variants with significant differences by both time and education	68

23	Variants with significant differences by both time and sex	69
24	Variants with significant differences by both time and race	69
25	Variants with significant differences by both time and age	71
26	Lexical change and number of responses per question	77
27	Lexical variation and number of responses per question	78
28	Questions with 'No Response' occurring more frequently in 1990	86
29	Questions with 'No Response' occurring more frequently in the 1930s	87
30	Percent of questions by type of referent that show diachronic change	87
31	Average number of variants by type of referent	88
32	Words associated with urban and rural groups due to cultural differences	108
33	Words associated with regional groups due to geographical differences	109
34	Percentage of questions exhibiting variation linked to social or regional variables that denote obsolete or agricultural referents	110

Maps

1	Location of communities	14
2	*Snake Feeder*, 1930s	44
3	*Mosquito Hawk*, 1990	45
4	(Peach) *Seed*, 1930s	46
5	(Peach) *Kernel*, 1930s	47
6	Kurath 1949, figure 15	54
7	*Soo(k)-Cow!*, 1930s	55

Acknowledgments

I began working part time at the Linguistic Atlas of the Middle and South Atlantic States (LAMSAS) in the summer of 1987, following my first year of graduate studies at the University of Georgia. I knew very little about dialectology, but by the end of the first two weeks, my head was already full of potential research projects based on this huge quantity of data. This volume is the result of making some of those ideas a reality. My continuing work for the atlas project is still inspired by possiblities for applying modern theories and methods to this historical database. These new ideas, however, take their place within a long tradition of scholars who have come before and who will come after. It is a unique intellectual experience to have become part of the community of language researchers who have participated in this project. Its membership includes many of the foremost practitioners of sociolinguistics today, and I am proud to be a part of it. Some of the staff members who have belonged to this team during my tenure are: Judy Blankenship, Nancy Condon, Nellie Felder, Barbara Ferré, Rafal Konopka, Deanna Light, Tim Marsh, and Debbie Vaughn. The collaborative atmosphere in the LAMSAS office is a fertile source of feedback and insights.

The editor-in-chief of LAMSAS, William A. Kretzschmar, Jr., a.k.a. "Dr. K.", has provided an abundant measure of support and guidance from the beginning of this project. This volume was originally prepared as my Ph.D. dissertation, Lexical Change and Variation in the Southeastern United States in the Twentieth Century (1992), under his direction. He has gone far beyond the requirements of dissertation advisor to become a mentor in many ways. He taught me to look beyond the confines of the university to my colleagues within the field of dialectology. Learning the tacit conventions of the academic world of conferences, publishing, editing, and fundraising is not an easy task, but Bill Kretzschmar has always been there to answer my questions and encourage me to try things on my own. I appreciate his willingness to allow me to follow my own direction. I alone bear responsibility for any shortcomings of this work.

Others have kindly offered constructive criticism and support to this work. I received helpful advice from Guy Bailey, Cindy Bernstein, Larry Davis, Virginia McDavid, Mike Miller, Michael Montgomery, Salikoko Mufwene, David Sankoff, and those who commented on the work in progress presented at conferences, as well as two anonymous reviewers for The University of Alabama Press and *Language Variation and Change*. Portions of this volume were presented at the American Dialect Society session held at New Ways of Analyzing Variation (NWAV) 20 ("Lexical Variation in the Southeastern US in the 1930s"), the 1992 spring meeting of the Southeastern Conference on Linguistics ("Lexical Variation in the Southeastern US, 1990"), and NWAV 21 ("Change and Variation in the Lexicon: A Study in Real Time"). Excerpts have appeared in the journal *Language Variation and Change* ("The Relationship between Lexical Variation and Lexical Change" [5: 285–303, 1993]) and in *Language Variety in the South, II*, ed. by Cynthia Bernstein, Tom Nunnally, and Robin Sabino ("Geographical Influence on Language Choice: Changes in the Twentieth Century," [in press]).

The members of my Ph.D. committee at the University of Georgia were Ben Blount, Renate Born, Jared Klein, and Don McCreary. I would like to thank them all for their encouragement and advice. Ben Blount, especially, contributed to my understanding of language and culture both through his courses and through hours of discussion; he served as my advisor while the linguistics program was part of the Department of Anthropology and Linguistics. John Algeo introduced me both to the degree program and the atlas project and has been a continuing source of support. Lynn Berk at Florida International University initially motivated me to enter a Ph.D. program; I found her course on language contact so fascinating that I wanted more.

Finally, I owe an intellectual debt to two men I have never met, but whose meticulous and exuberant legacies, respectively, have been a continual presence while I worked on this project: Guy Lowman and Raven McDavid. Both of them did an enormous amount of work for LAMSAS. Lowman brought a level of phonetic skill and precision to the atlas project that is unmatched. As I traveled to the places he had visited sixty years before, I often wondered how they had appeared to him. Some remain virtually unchanged, others would be unrecognizable. McDavid brought the atlas data to life. I only hope that I can convey here a small part of the sense of familiarity and understanding of the culture and the language of the South that he was able to impart in his writing.

This book would not have been possible without the help of numerous people in the thirty counties where I did my fieldwork in 1990. My experiences in the field were so rich and varied that an entire chapter could have been devoted to them. The fieldwork was in many ways the most enjoyable part of the project. The informants remain anonymous and depersonalized in this quantitative analysis, but they are quite real in my memory. I appreciate the welcome I received in so many places and the sacrifice people made of their time to help me with my research.

The American Association of University Women provided assistance so that I could devote a year to this project with few other responsibilities. I am truly thankful to them, both for their support and their faith in me. Their American Fellowship came at a time when I needed some assurance that this project was a worthwhile one. The Fulbright Commission of Chile and the Universidad Arturo Prat in Iquique provided me with time and space to work on revisions. The material from LAMSAS was collected and edited with the aid of funding from the American Council of Learned Societies and the National Endowment for the Humanities.

Ray Frasure unfailingly stood behind me while I was working on this project, giving it material, emotional, and even linguistic support. My parents, Charles and Rebecca Johnson, are at least partly responsible for the values of commitment and perseverance that were necessary for the completion of this project. Other members of my families have also been very generous with their love and support, especially Karen Aubrey-Garrett. I had hoped to birth my son, Thomas Johnson Frasure, and the dissertation at about the same time, but alas, the dissertation required about nine more months. I dedicate this book to Thomas, now a wonderful child who can't wait to be four.

E. J.
Clarkesville, Georgia

Lexical Change and Variation
in the Southeastern United States,
1930–1990

Introduction

This is the report of a project designed to measure change and variation in the lexicon by contrasting data collected in the mid-1930s with comparable data collected in 1990. It is a broad study, spread across 62,500 square miles and encompassing 78 speakers with birthdates ranging from 1847 to 1959. Responses to one hundred and fifty different questions, or **linguistic variables**, are tabulated for each speaker. The result are analyzed separately for the two sets of data collected in different decades in order to reveal synchronic patterns of variation by the **social** and **regional variables** of age, sex, race, education, rurality, and region. These two analyses are then compared to see how such patterns have changed. Finally, the words, or **variants**, used in the 1930s are compared to those given in 1990 in order to determine change in the vocabulary across the 55-year time span. Linguistic change can then be checked against the language variation observed previously in order to better understand the relationship between variation and change.

Several issues of theoretical interest are explored. Among these are questions about the role of social groups in linguistic change and the amount of variation attributable to each of the categorizing variables. The amount of change that may be attributed to sociolinguistic variation and the efficacy of social and regional variables in explaining language difference will be explored as well. One corollary to the former is the question of the utility of an analysis of variation across age groups for studying change. Lastly, there are questions about characteristics of the lexicon, as opposed to syntax and phonology.

Previous studies have shown that particular social groups seem to lead in linguistic change while others are more conservative. By noting which groups of speakers are associated with new words and which with older words, this study may provide additional evidence for the relationship betweeen variation and change. Since this project analyzes variation for similar populations at two distinct points in time, it may shed light on how the influence of particular non-linguistic variables can differ over time. Speaker characteristics, such as ethnicity, may change in their relative importance to language variation, reflecting an increase or decrease in social polarization along those lines. Such changes have been the topic of much heated debate, notably the convergence/divergence controversy with regard to Black Vernacular English. The testimony of cultural historians is important in explaining why certain social and regional variables are more important than others. Also, cultural factors are often linked to preferences for older or newer words.

One issue that has not been widely discussed is the amount of variation that is attributable to any of the standard sociolinguistic variables and whether it may increase or decrease. Many sociolinguists are inspired by the hope that they can provide evidence of systematic order for speech differences that seem to vary chaotically. The questions for this study were selected because they would each provide evidence of variation, i.e. there was more than one possible response for each item. It was not known at the outset of the project whether any of this variation was linked to specific groups of speakers. The entire range of responses can thus be compared to those that do show such a link with a particular group, as evidence for what percentage of variation in the lexicon can be explained through an analysis using the most common demographic variables. This is not possible for studies which examine only those language features that are known to correlate to such variables. The question of how much language variation can be explained by group-based differences is akin to the question of how much language change is revealed by age-based differences. A comparison of the total set of lexical changes to those suggested by apparent time results within each data set will be of interest in examining the question of which age-related differences are actually indications of linguistic change.

The amount of differentiation in language as a whole can also be studied using this data. By comparing the number of responses to the same questions at different times, growth and decline in specific areas of the vocabulary and in the entire set of lexical items analyzed here can be delimited. The ability to assess the amount of variation at different points in time by examining the size of the vocabulary raises questions about how the lexicon is unique. Whether differentiation proliferates in the same way for pronunciation and grammatical features is far from clear. Of particular interest is the question of how the language acquisition process differs for phonology, syntax, and lexical and pragmatic levels. There are both pros and cons in choosing the lexicon as a way to reveal patterns of linguistic behavior. Cultural influences on lexical change are ubiquitous; some of these are obvious, while some will require further study.

The first chapter describes the experimental design and methodology for fieldwork and data organization. It includes a discussion of which speakers were chosen as informants and why, with a table comparing relevant characteristics of those interviewed in 1990 and in the 1930s as well as a related appendix containing a brief biographical sketch of each person. Principles governing both the inclusion of items in the questionnaire and the categorization of informants are also included here.

Chapter 2 provides a discussion of the synchronic variation that exists for each set of data, along with a description of statistical methods used in the analysis. The relative importance of the six variables and changes in their importance will be covered here. Appendix Two lists all the terms that proved to be associated with particular social and regional groups.

Chapter 3 and Appendix Three contain the results of the analysis of diachronic differences in the frequency of words. A test appropriate for paired samples was used to reveal vocabulary changes during the course of the century. There is some discussion of aspects of semantic change as revealed in the data, as well as a section on the relationship of change to variation.

The last chapter presents cultural evidence that can enhance an understanding of the differences across time and across groups that were found in the study. The links between vocabulary change and particular social groups are discussed within a language contact framework. The role of culture in shaping the lexicon is another theme explored in this chapter.

Some specific questions addressed by this research project are: Does linguistic variation between different social and regional groups of speakers persist today as it was documented in the 1930s, or are there different differences? Are the speech communities more like one another, or are they more divergent and/or fragmented than ever? How is change in culture reflected in semantic change? And, does sociolinguistic change appear to be the result of specific social and cultural changes, especially those entailing increased cultural and dialect contact?

This book is truly a product of the hybrid sort of dialectology described in Chambers and Trudgill 1980. It applies methods and concepts developed by urban sociolinguists to data collected in the rural dialectology tradition. No one today can convincingly speak of the regional distribution of linguistic features without taking the social status of these features into account, nor can anyone discuss social factors influencing language without locating them in geographical space. The two fields have become intertwined, with a consequent decrease in the importance of disciplinary roots. For example, William Kretzschmar and William Labov are both working on spatial statistics, and Guy Bailey and John Baugh are both experts on Black Vernacular English. If there are statements here that seem to revive the old confrontational attitude of dialectology vs. sociolinguistics, they are the unintentional reflexes of conflicts passed down through generations of scholars that can persist long after their basis has disappeared. This study draws upon insights from researchers in both fields. Though there always will, and should, be disagreements, these should serve as a motivation for further research activity, not as an excuse for a refusal to learn from one another.

1

Collection and Categorization of the Data

The conclusions of this project are based on an examination of two sets of data: one collected in the late 1930s as part of the Linguistic Atlas of the Middle and South Atlantic States (LAMSAS), and one collected by the present researcher in 1990. These sets include pairs of informants matched according to personal characteristics and living in the same Georgia, South Carolina, and North Carolina communities. This chapter will describe the survey design and methodology under two major headings: linguistic variables and demographic variables. The first covers the items chosen for the analysis and the ways they were elicited and recorded; the second discusses the choice of informants and the ways they were categorized.

The terms **question**, survey **item**, and **linguistic variable** are used interchangeably to refer to a cue designed to elicit an array of words that designate more or less the same object. Likewise, **word, synonym, term, response,** and especially, **variant** are used to designate the members of a set of verbal responses to each cue. **Social variables** refer to age, sex, race, and education as grouping devices for categorizing speakers, while the **regional variables** are rurality and region.

The Linguistic Variables and the Interview

The 150 linguistic variables chosen for the analysis are all lexical items. They form a subset of items included in the LAMSAS questionnaire, and cover topics such as farm animals, household items, clothing, food, greetings, weather, and other everyday terms. The responses for each question have been grouped into eleven databases according to their typical order in the interview and their topic or semantic field. These are listed in Table 1.

Table 1: Questionnaire topics

1) rooms, furniture
2) milking-related terms, other calls to animals
3) outbuildings, architectural features, kitchen utensils
4) modes of transportation, tools
5) domestic animals and sounds they make, weather terms
6) corn, breads, snacks
7) meats, fruits, vegetables
8) insects, wild animals, plants
9) kinship terms, items related to childbirth
10) marriage, death and illness
11) school-related terms, holidays, clothing

Items chosen from the LAMSAS worksheets fit the following guidelines: (1) If the compilation of linguistic atlas worksheets by Davis et al. (1969) listed several possible responses (e.g. *fire dogs, dog irons,* and *andirons*) to the question, it was assumed the question would be productive in eliciting synonyms, thus providing a range of lexical variation; (2) Some items that were less productive of lexical variation were included because it seemed likely that they would have changed in distribution by the late-twentieth century, e.g., words like *clabber* (thick sour milk), and *singletree* and other words referring to aspects of horse-drawn transportation. The amount of change documented in this study is thus not representative of the proportion of items likely to change in the lexicon as a whole; and (3) A number of items were chosen because they were analyzed by Hans Kurath in his *Word Geography of the Eastern United States (Word Geography)* (1949). This gives the added aspect to the study of verifying by computer the distributions of lexical items claimed by Kurath—and long assumed by others—to reveal the major dialect boundaries of the United States. Following these guidelines, 240 questions were considered for inclusion because they were likely to produce evidence of either variation or change, or because they were responses that could be used to replicate Kurath's study.

Even though an item fulfilled one or more of the above conditions, it still may have been excluded. Sixty-one items, especially adjectives, that were included in the original plan proved in three trial interviews to be difficult to elicit without breaking up the flow of the questioning by focusing on words rather than content or by using an awkward "fill in the blank" type of strategy. Even without these items, the interviews averaged three hours in length, and the volunteer informants often ran out of patience by the end of the sessions.

Of the 179 remaining items, problems of comparability between data sets, incompleteness of the LAMSAS data, or complete lack of any variation in the responses necessitated discarding 29 additional questions. Though many of these had been included in the 1990 interviews, it became obvious after listing the responses that the two sets were not comparable, either because the questions as asked by Lowman and Johnson were different or because the fieldworkers perceived the target responses differently and thus counted different items as appropriate answers. For example, Lowman recorded only variants such as *string bean, snap bean,* and *green bean* for the 'green bean' question, while Johnson also included words referring to the way the beans are grown, e.g., *bush bean, half runner,* and *pole bean*.

The relevant LAMSAS records were not closely examined before the interviews took place in an effort to minimize the influence that knowledge of previous responses to the questions might have on fieldworker expectations. Thus, discoveries like the 'green bean' problem, and the fact that although 'grits' was listed as a question in the worksheets it was rarely asked by Lowman, occurred after the design phase of the project. These changes in the original questionnaire did not have any effect on the outcome of the analyses, since the linguistic variables were never considered to represent a comprehensive set. If an item did not meet the selection criteria, it was discarded, whether before or after the interviews. Only a few items turned out to show neither synchronic nor diachronic variation (e.g., 'whoa') and were dropped following the fieldwork. A few items that were listed originally as separate questions were found to be indistinguishable from one another in the LAMSAS field records and so were combined in the present study (e.g., both jocular and neutral terms for 'vomit', and male and female 'attendants at a wedding').

Eighty-three percent of the final set of linguistic variables are nouns, with the remainder about evenly divided between verbs and interjections. Linguistic variables are generalized concepts that are realized in speech in different ways. In this case, the variant realizations are sets of responses to the same question. Most questions were intended to produce synonymous responses, and 67 percent did yield what could be called synonyms, although the concept of synonymity is a complex topic (cf. Algeo 1989). Some of the questions clearly produced variants with different referents, while responses to many questions (27 percent) describe things that could be categorized as the same but might also reflect subtle differences. For example, *sweet potatoes* and *yams* are used in a restricted way by some informants to refer to specific types of sweet potatoes, while other speakers use the terms interchangeably to refer to all varieties. Some use only one term, and it is not possible to determine whether they are referring to only one particular variety or not. Likewise, some people make a distinction between the loud and soft noises a cow makes and reserve the use of *hum* for the soft one, while others do not seem to make this distinction. A living room is different depending on the type of house it is in, and one might argue that the referent of *drawing room* is different from that of *front room*. Pancakes come in varying sizes and are cooked in different amounts of grease, and large cakes of cornbread may be of different shapes.

Are words for these items truly synonyms? Some are; others exhibit the full range of dialect polysemy and analogy outlined by Algeo (1989) in his typology of dialect differences, and the term *heteronymy* may also apply (Görlach 1990). The important point is that we have no way of knowing the exact referent of any of the terms. They were all produced as responses to particular worksheet questions which, since informality was valued in the interview, were not rigorously stated in the same way every time but varied from situation to situation. We must rely on the fieldworkers' judgments that they are equivalent, with special usage sometimes noted in the commentary. This still leaves some room for misinterpretation by the fieldworker, and requires the assumption that the interviewer shares or understands enough about the cultural and cognitive models held by informants to avoid categorization errors. The diverse nature of the variables studied here does not pose a problem as a tool for investigation so long as one accepts Wolfram's idea (1991) that the linguistic variable is "a convenient construct employed to unite a class of fluctuating variants" rather than a set of variants with the same meaning that fit neatly into a predetermined structuralist framework as interchangeable parts of a linguistic rule.

This type of linguistic variable will require a more complex interpretation of the results. Since the variants may differ in referential meaning as well as social meaning, semantic and cultural differences must be considered along with the preferences of social and regional groups as explanations of variation. The different variants produced by the speakers are not simply differences in language. As noted above, for most of the variables in the study it is likely that the denotational meaning is the same, e.g., for *midwife, wishbone,* and *clouding up*. However, variables like *baby carriage/wagon/stroller* and *rye bread/sourdough bread/whole wheat bread/light bread*, which produce responses with clearly different referents, are problematic.

The question arises as to whether these items should be included in the study or not. Consider the third, intermediate, category. For this category, which comprises one-fourth of the variables, the variants are sometimes synonymous and sometimes not. This includes pairs like *britches/trousers*, which may or may not refer to the same style of pants, depending on individual usage; cases where the same word may be used to denote items that differ materially, like *siding* to refer variously to wooden clapboards, aluminum siding, and "brick siding" (tarpaper printed with a brick pattern); and even traditional favorites like *mosquito hawk/ snake feeder*, for which there is evidence to suspect that different insects may be involved for some speakers. Since the six percent of variables that definitely subsume different things differ only in degree, not in kind, from this intermediate type, it seems best to include all of them, with the caveat that not all variants of a variable are synonymous, although they all share a "functional comparability" (Lavandera 1978: 181).

This discussion has not even begun to explore other factors that might determine the choice of variants, including connotational meaning, the effect of linguistic context, and subtle stylistic differences, all of which could affect variation. The interview was structured so as to minimize the latter, but personality differences, switches between discourse styles within the same speech situation, and even the location of the interview certainly resulted in some style-shifting both within and between interviews. Johnstone's work (e.g., in press) has discussed many of these factors affecting variation as aspects of individual choice. She states that "social, psychological, and rhetorical facts are mediated by the individual", who selects variants from the linguistic resources available for reasons that include personal history and individual personality characteristics. Thus, there are many types of meaning associated with the variants recorded in this study, though the analysis is limited to social meanings: how the use of a certain feature may be connected with belonging to a particular social or regional group. Lavandera notes that the notion of linguistic variable in quantitative studies is not as easily applied to lexical and syntactic data as to (non-referential) phonological data, and this is indeed the case. Because of a lack of psychological and contextual evidence, especially in the LAMSAS data, this study necessarily confines itself for the most part to commenting upon only one "of the kinds of information that differences in form may be conveying"

(Lavandera 1978: 171). In future studies, the 1990 data may provide further insights to the semantic differences embodied within the linguistic variables.

Once the questions were chosen, the next step was to decide how to ask them. The essentially ethnographic interview technique used by both fieldworkers (i.e., Lowman and Johnson) was developed in Europe, by Edmont in France (Gilliéron 1902-10) and Jaberg and Jud (1928-40) in Switzerland and Italy. Jaberg and Jud, in particular, acknowledged that language cannot be understood in isolation but must be studied in its cultural milieu. Their *Wörter und Sachen* technique relies on an investigation of cultural artifacts together with their names, to ensure semantic comparability. Thus, when it is not clear what item an informant is referring to, speakers may be asked to describe it, and when apparent synonyms are offered, they may be asked whether these refer to the same thing, as well as about their reasons for choosing the different terms according to context.

To prepare for the interviews, Johnson studied a tape-recording done by Raven McDavid, drawing upon McDavid's experience as a LAMSAS fieldworker (McDaniel, ms.). In it, he performs a sample interview to demonstrate how the questions were typically worded. Instructions to fieldworkers found in Pederson, McDavid, Foster, and Billiard 1974 and Kretzschmar, McDavid, Lerud, and Johnson 1994 were also consulted. Johnson then conducted three pilot interviews to familiarize herself with the worksheet, identify problematic items, and avoid awkward ways of phrasing the questions. Both Lowman and Johnson attempted to conduct the sessions in an informal way. In the 1990 interviews, informants seemed to be at ease with the technique, having viewed numerous such speech situations on television in news broadcasts, talk shows, etc. The questions were purposely worded to call attention to their informational rather than linguistic content. Questions such as "What do you call the place where the pigs stayed?" were avoided in favor of questions like "Where did you keep the pigs?" Although speakers were openly informed of the purpose of the interview, they still tended to assume the fieldworker was interested in what they had to say rather than how they were saying it.

Informants often gave more than one response per question. For the above example, a speaker may have provided an answer such as, "In the hog pen. These days we call them pig parlors and they're indoors, but we used to have a floored pen we put them in to fatten them up." This hypothetical response includes three different variants: *hog pen, pig parlors*, and *floored pen*. In some cases, additional names were specifically elicited with a question like, "Did you ever call it anything else?" At other times, the fieldworker simply recorded a word that was used in conversation and went on to another topic without requesting synonyms or otherwise drawing attention to the item in question.

Lowman had two notebooks, one listing the questions and one in which he recorded the responses, page by page, in fine phonetic notation. Johnson had a tape recorder and a computer printout of questions with a list of common synonyms which she circled during the interview. Her responses were first entered into a database from the field notes, with a table for each informant. The tapes were checked to verify the responses and add commentary. The LAMSAS responses were entered from the "list manuscripts", collations giving all responses to each question. Since this organization of data by linguistic variable was the most useful format for analysis, Johnson's responses were re-sorted into this format as well.

Three types of responses were marked as doubtful and excluded from the statistical analyses: responses which the fieldworker had reason to believe might not be normal usage, responses given by someone other than the informant, and responses that are doubtful because either the fieldworker or the informant was confused about the response. All have comment codes associated with them in the databases.

The first category includes suggested (SUG) and heard (HRD) responses. These are doubtful because the response may not be the speaker's natural, normal usage. Sometimes a word was suggested by the interviewer if indirect questioning failed to produce a response or if the fieldworkers were interested in whether a particular word was used in a locality or not. The "heard" category includes words that speakers report they have heard from speakers of other races or age groups, "Yankees", in a song or movie, etc.

Another reason to mark an item doubtful was that it was not offered by the primary informant (the one whose social characteristics are coded into the database) but by someone else present at the interview (AUX). These auxiliary informants were usually wives of men who were interviewed. Two LAMSAS records, those of SC11I and NC23B, included responses from auxiliary informants that have not been marked as doubtful. These speakers shared all of the same social and regional variables as the corresponding main informants and were thus considered equivalent for the type of analysis used in this project.

For the last type of dubious response, the code FDT is used to indicate that the fieldworker was unsure of the response, as when the referent is unclear or there has been some other communication problem. DBT indicates that the speaker was hesitant about using the word, unsure of its definition or pronunciation.

In the same way that subsuming a group of variants under the rubric of a linguistic variable involved choices by the fieldworker, grouping of responses with minimal differences into variants for testing required choices by the analyst. To make hard and fast rules about grouping procedures seemed to violate the nature of the data, which was more amenable to a case-by-case determination. Inflectional suffixes such as plurals and tense markings were disregarded so that *frogstool* and *frogstools*, *spew* and *spewed*, were treated as the same. More troublesome were cases of compound nouns combining words for basic-level categories with words for super-ordinate categories. For example, *clingstone* and *clingstone peach* were treated as the same variant, although *stud* and *stud horse* and *blinds* and *window blinds* were analyzed separately. The choice was sometimes made on practical grounds: at least three instances of a variant were needed for the statistical tests used here, so less frequent responses were more likely to be combined. All the responses for any given question were treated in the same way.

The same held true for deciding whether different pronunciations count as the same word or different words. This choice was often guided by consulting *Webster's Third New International Dictionary* (1971) or the *Linguistic Atlas of the Gulf States General Index* (LAGS, Pederson, McDaniel, and Adams 1988) to see if phonological differences were reflected in different spellings. Since the materials from the LAMSAS data were encoded in phonetics only, and the other field records were on tape, these decisions had to be made at the stage of entering the forms in the database in normal orthography. Two categories of items defied grouping by standard spellings: animal calls and terms for 'mother', 'father', 'grandmother', and 'grandfather'. For example, /kwop/ and /kwʊp/ (calls to horses) were combined, collapsing the vowels but leaving consonantal differences, as between *kope* and *kwope*, to mark different variants. Vowel differences were retained as separate forms, however, in 'father' words, hence *pae* (with [æ]), *pa*, and *paw*, although *grandpa* and *grandpaw* were combined. The rationale behind some of these choices was, as noted above, an attempt to have as many items as possible qualify for inclusion in the analysis (i.e. by occurring at least three times). For example, *pae*, *pa*, and *paw* occurred often enough to test without combining them, while *grandpaw* didn't. Such differences, especially those involving vowels, are not categorical. Many items could be reanalyzed in different combinations, but the amount of time involved to test all the possibilities would be prohibitive.

The Social and Regional Variables

LAMSAS fieldworkers typically went to rural communities and sought out the oldest locally-born speaker they could find, usually with limited education and travel experience, as representative of the speech of that community. Next, however, they would usually interview another person in the same area who was younger or better educated; perhaps several more, depending on the size of the town. Nevertheless, the informants are disproportionately old, white, rural, and male. The LAMSAS sample is analyzed in detail in Kretzschmar et al. (1994). The subset of LAMSAS informants chosen for this study is an attempt to overcome the statistical bias inherent in atlas sampling by balancing informants according to social characteristics as evenly as possible.

This survey includes 39 speakers from 30 counties ("communities" in atlas terminology) in Georgia, South Carolina, and North Carolina (Map 1). The area includes three geographical regions that have previously been considered important in demarcating dialect areas—the Atlantic Coastal Plain, the Piedmont, and the Appalachians—and was designed to include five communities in each of the six LAMSAS grid areas in this region, though these categories were later abandoned (see discussion below).

Almost all the fieldwork for LAMSAS was done by two fieldworkers. All the LAMSAS records chosen for this study were completed before 1940 by Guy S. Lowman; thus discrepancy between fieldworkers and dates of interviews is not a problem. By choosing only Lowman records, however, the survey is limited in ways that make north/south comparisons inappropriate. The only interviews Lowman did in Georgia and South Carolina were those he did as part of a Preliminary South Atlantic States survey designed to refine the questionnaire to be used in the rest of the South Atlantic area. In contrast, he completed all of the 156 LAMSAS interviews conducted in North Carolina. This study includes all nine of the people he interviewed in Georgia and eleven of his nineteen records from South Carolina. Since the preliminary questionnaire was used to establish a baseline dialect believed to be best represented by older folk speakers, this type of speaker was overwhelmingly chosen by him in these two states. To compensate for this, most of the speakers from North Carolina who were chosen for this project were

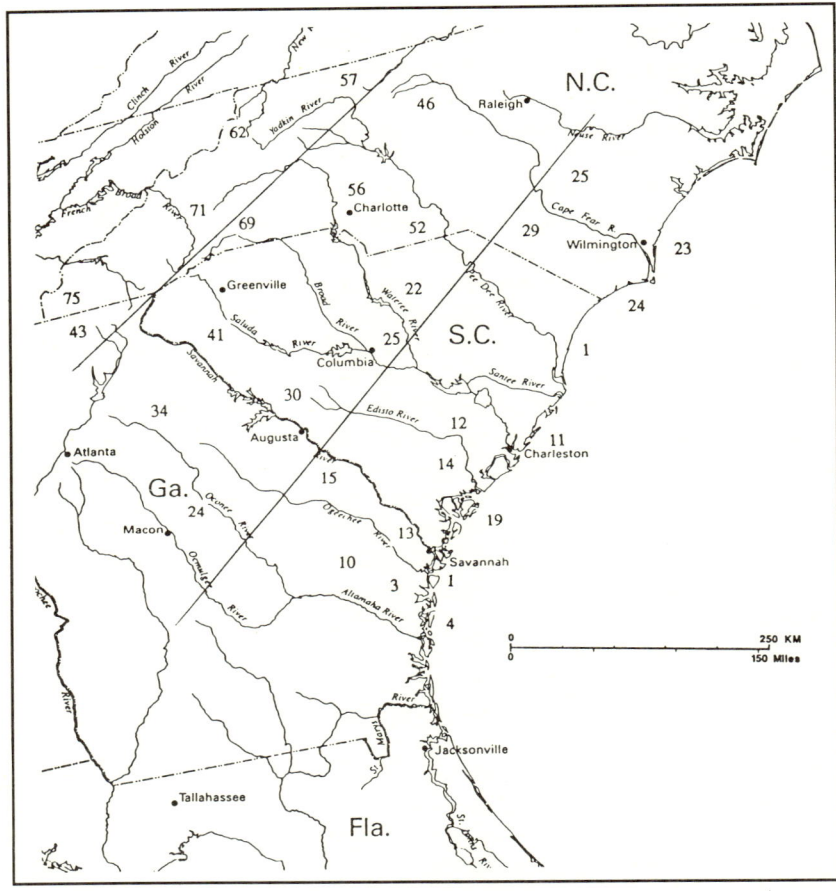

Map 1: Location of communities*

*Maps are adapted from Kretzschmar et al. (1994:6)

younger, and they included more urban, educated, and female speakers.

A biographical sketch of each of the LAMSAS respondents was available, and an attempt was made to control for as many variables as possible in choosing the matching second sample, so that any differences that occur can be accounted for by change in the language rather than by the type of informant chosen. Biographical sketches for all 78 informants are given in Appendix 1. Johnson was successful at finding speakers of the same sex and race in each location, with the exception of Shallotte, N.C., where a black woman and a white man were interviewed instead of a black man and a white woman. The totals for the categories of region, sex, and race are thus equal for both data sets. Groups by age, education, and rurality are slightly different in this phase of the project, as described below. As often as possible (contingent upon finding suitable contacts), the 1990 fieldwork was done in the same neighborhoods where interviews were conducted for LAMSAS. Contacts were made in 1990, as they were earlier, by inquiring at the county courthouse, post office, or library—or from previous acquaintances—about people of the type sought who might be willing to answer questions. Table 2 gives the most pertinent characteristics of each informant. Identification numbers are the same as for LAMSAS, with the 1990 speakers having a 2 at the end.

Table 2: Informant characteristics and communities

Informant	County	Town	Born	Ed.	Race	Sex	Rurality
GA1F	Chatham	Savannah	1856	3	W	F	U
GA1F2	Chatham	Savannah	1900	3	W	F	U
GA3A	Liberty	Flemington	1854	2	W	M	R
GA3A2	Liberty	Fleming	1910	1	W	M	R
GA4N	McIntosh	Crescent	1881	1	B	M	R
GA4N2	McIntosh	Meridian	1944	2	B	M	R
GA10A	Evans	Manassas	1867	2	W	M	R
GA10A2	Evans	Claxton	1905	1	W	M	R
GA13A	Effingham	Rincon	1865	1	W	M	R
GA13A2	Effingham	Springfield	1919	2	W	M	R
GA15A	Burke	Alexander	1851	1	W	M	R
GA15A2	Burke	Girard	1913	2	W	M	R

Data

Informant	County	Town	Born	Ed.	Race	Sex	Rurality
GA24A	Baldwin	Mt. Pleasant	1870	1	W	M	R
GA24A2	Baldwin	Mt. Pleasant	1912	1	W	M	R
GA34A	Clarke	Bogart	1869	2	W	F	R
GA34A2	Oconee	Bogart	1922	2	W	F	U
GA43	Union	Lonesome Cove	1849	1	W	M	R
GA432	Union	Gaddistown	1916	1	W	M	R
SC1A	Horry	Burgess	1856	1	W	F	R
SC1A2	Horry	Good Hope	1909	1	W	F	R
SC11N	Charleston	Charleston	1876	2	B	M	U
SC11N2	Charleston	Charleston	1928	3	B	M	U
SC11I	Charleston	Charleston	1883	3	W	F	U
SC11I2	Charleston	Charleston	1943	3	W	F	U
SC12B	Dorchester	St. George	1864	2	W	F	R
SC12B2	Dorchester	St. George	1919	2	W	F	R
SC14A	Colleton	Hendersonville	1850	2	W	M	R
SC14A2	Colleton	Ehrhardt	1916	1	W	M	R
SC19N	Beaufort	Hilton Head	1881	–	B	M	R
SC19N2	Beaufort	Hilton Head	1928	3	B	M	U
SC22N	Kershaw	Camden	1869	1	B	F	U
SC22N2	Kershaw	Galloway Hill	1916	1	B	F	R
SC22B	Kershaw	Camden	1869	2	W	F	U
SC22B2	Kershaw	Camden	1925	2	W	F	U
SC25A	Richland	Lykesland	1856	1	W	F	R
SC25A2	Richland	Olympia Village	1908	2	W	F	U
SC30A	Edgefield	Johnston	1871	1	W	M	R
SC30A2	Edgefield	Johnston	1925	2	W	M	R
SC41A	Anderson	Anderson	1855	2	W	F	U
SC41A2	Anderson	Williamston	1906	2	W	F	U
NC23B	New Hanover	Myrtle Grove Sound	1891	2	W	F	R
NC23B2	New Hanover	Myrtle Grove Sound	1938	2	W	F	U
NC24N	Brunswick	Shallotte	1848	1	B	M	R
NC24N2	Brunswick	Longwood	1910	1	B	F	R
NC24A	Brunswick	Freeland	1867	1	W	F	R
NC24A2	Brunswick	Saspan Neck	1926	1	W	M	R
NC24B	Brunswick	Supply	1892	3	W	M	R
NC24B2	Brunswick	Shallotte	1954	2	W	M	R

Informant	County	Town	Born	Ed.	Race	Sex	Rurality
NC25A	Sampson	Clinton	1864	1	W	M	R
NC25A2	Sampson	Clinton	1916	1	W	M	R
NC25B	Sampson	Turkey	1866	2	W	M	R
NC25B2	Sampson	Turkey	1916	3	W	M	R
NC29B	Robeson	Lumberton	1894	3	W	F	R
NC29B2	Robeson	Lumberton	1952	2	W	F	U
NC46B	Guilford	Guilford College	1893	3	W	M	R
NC46B2	Guilford	Greensboro	1947	3	W	M	U
NC46C	Guilford	Greensboro	1889	3	W	F	U
NC46C2	Guilford	Greensboro	1947	3	W	F	U
NC52N	Anson	Wadesboro	1847	1	B	F	U
NC52N2	Anson	Morven	1900	1	B	F	R
NC52B	Anson	Morven	1889	2	W	M	R
NC52B2	Anson	Morven	1933	2	W	M	R
NC56A	Mecklenburg	Huntersville	1877	2	W	F	R
NC56A2	Mecklenburg	Huntersville	1935	2	W	F	U
NC57B	Stokes	Danbury	1901	2	W	M	R
NC57B2	Stokes	Walnut Cove	1959	2	W	M	R
NC62B	Ashe	W. Jefferson	1884	2	W	F	R
NC62B2	Ashe	W. Jefferson	1931	2	W	F	R
NC69A	Polk	Mill Springs	1860	1	W	M	R
NC69A2	Polk	Mill Springs	1923	2	W	M	R
NC71B	Buncombe	Candler	1882	3	W	M	R
NC71B2	Buncombe	Leicester	1928	3	W	M	R
NC71C	Buncombe	Asheville	1887	3	W	F	U
NC71C2	Buncombe	Black Mtn.	1944	3	W	F	U
NC75A	Cherokee	Grandview	1853	1	W	M	R
NC75A2	Cherokee	Murphy	1907	1	W	M	R
NC75B	Cherokee	Murphy	1884	2	W	F	R
NC75B2	Cherokee	Murphy	1940	2	W	F	R

This type of purposive, rather than random, sampling gives first preference to the comparability between the two sets of data, so caution must be exercised in extrapolating the results to the general population. This calls for more conservative statistical tests, especially when testing for variation within samples. One must keep in mind that this is a historical study using methods that were developed to describe the more conservative linguistic features of a given geographical area; thus one requirement for respondents was that they (and preferably their parents also) were natives of the community. Procedures for choosing LAMSAS informants are carefully described in Kretzschmar et al. (1994). Barring a sudden and quite large influx of immigrants to the area who all share the same dialect, the speech of the native-born seems likely to continue to exert the strongest influence on new generations, despite demographic change.

The informants in this study have been categorized according to four social variables (age, race, sex, and education) and two regional variables (region and rurality). Their characteristics are summarized in Table 3 below. The number of categories has been limited to those for which evidence was available in the biographical sketches of informants found in the LAMSAS handbook (Kretzschmar et al. 1994).

Table 3: Summary of informant characteristics

	1930s Data Set	1990 Data Set
Female (F)	18	18
Male (M)	21	21
College Graduate	—	9 (H)
High School Graduate	8 (H)	18 (M)
Elementary School	15 (Graduate) (M)	12 (or Less) (L)
Less than Elementary	16 (L)	—
Black (B)	6	6
White (W)	33	33
1847–1860 / 1900–1913 (O)	12	11
1864–1876 / 1916–1928 (M)	13	15
1882–1901 / 1931–1959 (Y)	14	13
Rural (R)	30	25
Urban (U)	9	14
Mountain (M)	7	7
Piedmont (P)	13	13
Coastal (C)	19	19

The traditional atlas system for classifying informants collapses the qualities of old-fashioned or modern, less-educated or better-educated, and less or more contact with people outside the community into categories A and B; and "folk" versus "common" versus "cultivated" into categories I, II, and III. These classifications were rejected for this study because of their subjective nature and because people were grouped into these categories based partly on their speech, causing assertions about their associations with language forms to be a case of circular reasoning. (Surprisingly enough, however, an analysis of diphthongs in Johnson [1994a] did not reveal more correspondences with these categories than others.) Occupation was also encoded in the LAMSAS databases but not used in this project, since the same occupation, e.g., farmer or housewife, includes individuals of widely differing social class. The principles that were followed in grouping the informants according to the six non-linguistic variables are described below.

Age. Informants in each data set were classed into three groups by age. The birthdates of the first set of speakers span 54 years and those of the second set encompass 59 years, thus each set includes three generations. Though the speakers are all adults, the differences in their ages are just as great as between the subjects in many other sociolinguistic studies that include an analysis of change in apparent time (e.g., the New York department store survey, as reported in Labov 1972).

The ranking of LAMSAS informants by age at the time of the interview did not coincide exactly with a ranking by year of birth, since the interviews were conducted over a four-year period, from 1933 to 1937. The year of birth of each informant was calculated as the basis for grouping. The youngest group was younger than 55 when interviewed, and the oldest older than 75.

The division between the two youngest groups was clear, since a gap of six years existed between the date of birth of the oldest member of the first group and that of the youngest member of the second group. (This is the largest gap between dates of birth in the data set, except for that between the youngest informant, born in 1901, and the second youngest, born in 1894.) The division between the second and third groups was made with the goal of keeping the size of the groups fairly equal (Young n=14, Middle n=13, and Old n=12).

Years of birth match up nicely to events in U.S. history. The oldest group was born from 1847 to 1860, before the Civil War; the middle group was born during the war and the Reconstruction period, spanning the years 1864 to 1876; and the youngest group was born after Reconstruction, from 1882 through 1901.

For the second sample, the youngest group was between the ages of 30 and 60 (n=11), the middle group 60–75 years old (n=15), and the oldest group between 75 and 90 (n=13). Ranked by year of birth, the oldest group was born from 1900 to 1913, before World War I; the middle group was born before the Great Depression, spanning the years 1916 to 1928; and the youngest group was born from 1931 through 1959. For the 1990 fieldwork, the criterion for matching age was to find someone within ten years of the age of the LAMSAS informant.

The time depth of this study can be viewed in two ways. In real time the comparison would span fifty years, but in apparent time, adjusted for the age of first language acquisition, the difference between a 31-year-old in 1990 (NC57B2) and someone who was 90 in 1937 (NC52N) would be more than a century. With regard to the lexicon, language learning is cumulative and continual. The vocabulary of each informant, then, would not accurately reflect the state of the language at the time informants first acquired it (as may arguably be the case with pronunciation), but includes words in use throughout their lifetimes. We may thus find in the data, as in the above example, a 143-year span, from vocabulary that was current in 1847 to vocabulary of 1990.

Education. The three classifications of speakers by education in the first data set are high school graduates (n=8), elementary school graduates who did not finish high school (n=15), and those who did not finish elementary school or who had no education at all (n=16). These are based on LAMSAS categories which were not defined at the time of the interviews, but which were created post-hoc from information about years of schooling found in the informant biographies (see Appendix 1).

The LAMSAS categories for education are thus necessarily disputable. Most of the informants would have finished school before 1915, i.e., before free, public, compulsory education was widespread. School systems between, and even within, states were far from standardized, and statements such as "graduated from Jones Academy" are impossible to classify exactly without researching each institution and determining what grades were taught there during the particular years the informant attended. In addition, grade levels themselves may have been nonexistent in some schools, and students went to school for varying time periods in a year, owing to agricultural or other responsibilities. This means someone who was "educated through age eighteen" may conceivably not even have finished grammar school. Generally, those who attended past the age of thirteen, or for 5-8 years, are considered elementary school graduates and those who went past the age of seventeen, or for twelve years, are considered high school graduates.

There are four speakers who are not assigned an educational category in the LAMSAS database. The LAMSAS classification contains seven groups by education, and there was not enough information about these people to confidently place them in one of these groups. Since this study has only three educational divisions, less information was needed in order to assign them to one of these broader groups. Three of these informants—SC22N, a domestic worker; NC24N, a former slave; and NC25A, a sawmill worker—have been assigned here to the lowest educational group based on biographical information (included in Appendix 1) and their IA folk speaker designation in LAMSAS. The remaining informant, SC19N, could not be classified for education.

The three classifications of speakers by education in the second sample are college graduates ($n=9$), high school graduates who did not finish college ($n=18$), and those who did not finish high school or who had no education at all ($n=12$). Educational groups have changed from those analyzed for LAMSAS, since the population is generally more educated today, although the proportion of informants in the high, middle, and low educational groups is about the same.

Education is the closest variable to social class. Class is defined by different researchers in different ways, but it is usually a combination of scores based on education, income, occupation, and residence. For the speakers interviewed for LAMSAS, such scores cannot be obtained because of a lack of information on key indicators. For example, the occupations of LAMSAS informants that are by far the most common are "housewife" and "farmer", neither of which offers a clue to income or status in the community. Studies such as Nichols 1983 have brought up serious questions about the validity of classification principles employed in the past to assign social class, especially to women (i.e. based on their husbands' occupations), which possibly produce skewed results. By stating results based on education only, rather than a combined score, informants are classified according to individual rather than family characteristics. The subjective classifications made by LAMSAS fieldworkers into the traditional classes I, II, and III were avoided here in favor of a more objective measurement, but it is reasonable to expect that these categories might provide additional evidence of social class membership, despite their qualitative rather than quantitative basis. They will likely be utilized more in future research.

Race. Informants were grouped by race into two groups, black and white, with only 6 black speakers and 33 white ones. African American speakers were not represented in LAMSAS proportionate to their distribution in the population. Limiting the set of informants to those interviewed by Lowman further reduced the pool of African American informants. It should be noted that racial designation here is social, not genetic, since people of mixed ancestry are typically considered to be black by the larger society, and previously by law in the South. This conforms to the LAGS practice of designating black and white "castes" rather than racial groups (Pederson, McDaniel, Bailey, and Bassett 1986:287). There is not enough information in the LAMSAS records to determine the degree of participation by individuals in the African American community, as in e.g., Baugh 1983, thus the classification must remain a simplistic one. The term *African American* is not used exclusively. A recent poll by the *Atlanta Journal-Constitution* indicated that Southern blacks still prefer *black* as a group designation. Similar results were also reported by both Smitherman (1991) and Baugh (1991), although these authors advocate a change to *African American*.

Sex. Like race, this classification of informants was adopted directly from LAMSAS. Unlike race, however, this category is a biological one rather than a social designation for gender that might more directly correspond to language differences. Thus the limitations of this type of classification, pointed out e.g. by Eckert (1989b), must be kept in mind. Measures of masculinity and femininity would have been difficult to incorporate into an atlas-type interview. The 1990 set of informants included three people who might well have been homosexual, though they did not explicitly state their sexual preference. It is not unlikely that this was also the case for some of the earlier informants. Sexual preference is not the only factor which may indicate disparity between biological sex and gender identity, since personality traits in general make gender a continuous variable, while sex is binary. Even though gender is thus preferable as a social variable, many other studies have also had to settle for an analysis by sex instead, with interesting results. Women are better represented in the sample chosen for this survey than in LAMSAS as a whole, with 18 women and 21 men in each data set.

Region. The category region represents a major change from the original research design. Eighteen grid units were devised for LAMSAS as a way to make statistical comparisons between areas. The sample included five counties from each of the six grid units in the Southeast.

These boundaries were drawn to include equal numbers of informants without regard to historical and political considerations. This was part of a plan for measuring quantitative regional dialect differences using only linguistic features as evidence, without the influence of predetermined, culturally defined areas. The equal numbers of informants in each grid unit could also be used for a quick visual check of the evidence without having to calculate percentages, as described in Schneider and Kretzschmar 1989 and Kretzschmar 1992a.

Currently, LAMSAS is moving away from this type of measurement of regional variation to more sophisticated inductive methods used by geographers (Lee and Kretzschmar, 1993). For the present study, working deductively from predefined categories works best, since this treats the variable region the same way as other variables of race, sex, age, and education. By dividing speakers into groups based on socially salient features, we can look at how social identity is encoded in language.

The division chosen for informants by location, then, is the familiar coastal, piedmont, and mountain configuration that stretches across the southeastern United States and has become associated with cultural characteristics as well as geological features. Speakers were assigned a region based on whether their county was located in the coastal plain (n=19), the piedmont (n=13), or the Blue Ridge (n=7) (as shown by the three diagonal bands on Map 1). Boundaries are those given by the U.S. Geological Survey on their map of "Fold and Thrust Belts of the United States" (1984, Reston, Va.). Three counties were located partially in the coastal plain and partially in the piedmont: Baldwin Co., Ga. (GA24A), Richland Co., S.C. (SC25A), and Kershaw Co., S.C. (SC22N and SC22B). These were assigned to the piedmont. All the other counties fell clearly within one region.

Rurality. Informants in LAMSAS were grouped based on U.S. Census criteria into Urban (population greater than 2500) and Rural categories. These designations were sometimes based upon the population of the actual locality, whether town or neighborhood, of the person's residence. If this information was not available from census records, the status of the nearest post office was used as the basis for classification. Thirty speakers represented by the 1930s data are rural and only nine are urban. Five of the places where both 1930s and 1990 informants lived changed from rural to urban in the 55 intervening years between Lowman's and Johnson's interviews. Other differences in rurality between the two data sets come from Johnson's selection of informants who were from a different part of the county than the previous informants. Although she tried to match the speaker characteristics as closely as possible, she was not always able to find a volunteer in the exact locality. All pairs of speakers but one did come from the same county. The exception resulted from the fact that the town of Bogart, Georgia, straddles the county line. Two of the 1990 speakers came from more urban areas, while two came from more rural ones. Twenty-five of the second set of speakers are rural, and fourteen are urban.

Urban speakers are underrepresented relative to the total current population of the area, particularly for the second sample. The counties in these states did not necessarily become urbanized at the same rate as the population. Urbanization results as much or more from movement of people to urban areas from rural ones as from an increase in population in formerly rural areas. Since the sampling procedure was based on finding informants in the same counties, the 1990 sample is less like the general population in terms of rurality. This is unfortunate, though not insurmountable, if one wishes to extrapolate from these results facts about the speech of the Southeast in general. This skewing is one reason for the stringent significance level used to evaluate the statistical analysis, and is further discussed in Kretzschmar et al. 1994.

Comparison with Actual Population Characteristics. As might be expected from the LAMSAS sampling practices, some types of speakers are overrepresented in the samples. The disparity between the number of African Americans in the sample and the number in the population is not as great for the second data set (see Table 4), since the black population has continued to decline in the South until just recently.

Table 4: Population compared to sample

	Census Yr./ Data Set	Percent of GA/SC/NC pop.	Percent of sample
White	1940/1	66.2	84.6
	1990/2	72.4	84.6
Black	1940/1	33.5	15.4
	1990/2	25.6	15.4
Male	1940/1	49.4	53.8
	1990/2	48.5	53.8

	Census Yr./ Data Set	Percent of GA/SC/NC pop.	Percent of sample
Age 25–44	1940/1	27.8	7.7
	1990/2	32.9	12.8
Over age 75	1940/1	1.2	30.1
	1990/2	4.5	28.2
Ed. < 7 yrs.	1940/1	76.2	41.0
elem grad	1940/1	15.4	38.5
hs grad	1940/1	8.4	20.5
Ed. < hs	1990/2	22.2	30.8
hs grad	1990/2	60.0	46.1
coll grad	1990/2	17.8	23.1
Urban	1940/1	28.7	23.1
	1990/2	56.1	35.9

(All education figures from the census are for population age 25 and older.)

The biggest discrepancy is in age, with the speakers included in this project being much older than the general adult population. Thus we must recognize the historical character of such a study and assume that the speech recorded is probably not typical for the year it was recorded, but would be considered somewhat old-fashioned. This does not affect the comparability of the two samples. The most surprising difference is that the LAMSAS speakers, especially, are much more educated than the population they were drawn from. The LAMSAS sample is apparently not as biased toward uneducated speakers as we have assumed it is. This is probably because of the selection of Type III informants in twenty percent of the communities. The problem is not with the selection of the subset of LAMSAS informants, since the total group is also better educated than the population. For all LAMSAS informants from North Carolina south, one-third fall into each of the three educational groups. Compare this to the figures for the general population given in Table 4. This table compares percentages from the U.S. Census data to percentages for the sample, according to age, sex, education, race, and rurality. (No figures were available for population by region as it is used in the study.) The census figures are from the totals for Georgia, South Carolina, and North Carolina.

<u>Interaction between Categories</u>. This project was carefully designed to be appropriate for univariate testing. Multivariate testing has not yet been applied to the data, though it will be a necessary tool for future research attempting to provide a more sophisticated explanation of the results that are discussed here. There is certainly some influence of the variables upon one another, especially since the makeup of each category is not balanced with regard to the other variables. The imbalance can sometimes be attributed to demographics, especially in the following cases: (1) All but one of the blacks in the first sample were in the lowest educational group; (2) No African American informants live in the mountain region; (3) Speakers having the highest educational level are disproportionately young; (4) Half of the speakers from the piedmont area are urban, as are one-third from the coast (in sample 2, increased from one-seventh in the first sample) but only one-seventh in the mountain area; and (5) None of the least-educated speakers live in urban areas in the second sample.

Some skewing within categories is related to sampling problems inherited from LAMSAS. This poses a different problem than imbalance corresponding to asymmetry in the population as noted above. For example, all the college graduates that Lowman interviewed in the three states were female, and all but one of his urban informants were female. This led to the following results: half of the males in the first sample were in the lowest educational group; most of the urban informants are female; and almost all of the males live in rural areas. Also, the piedmont region has more females, the coastal region has more males, and the urban speakers tend to be younger. It is clear that Lowman was unaware of the requirements of modern sampling procedures. This survey was designed to minimize problems resulting from such skewing but they could not be eliminated entirely.

A detailed analysis by educational group is given in Table 5. It reveals one source of possible interaction between variables attributable to features of the sample population. For example, ten of the males, but only five of the females that Lowman interviewed were in the lowest educational group. Only one speaker from the youngest age group fell into the lowest educational bracket, while most of the older speakers did. Two of 25 rural speakers in 1990 were college graduates, compared to half of the 14 urban informants. The imbalance of variables within categories could lead to errors in interpretation of language use. It is wise to remember, for example, that variation by sex, rurality, or race could be partially attributable to educational level. The consequences of the skewed data turn out to be less serious than expected, however, as will be seen in the following chapter.

Table 5: Educational levels by group

		Low	Mid	High	Missing
Blacks	1930s	4	1	—	1
	1990	3	1	2	
Whites	1930s	11	14	8	
	1990	9	17	7	
Females	1930s	5	8	5	
	1990	4	10	4	
Males	1930s	10	7	3	1
	1990	8	8	5	
Urban	1930s	2	3	4	
	1990	—	7	7	
Rural	1930s	13	12	4	1
	1990	12	11	2	
Young	1930s	1	5	7	1
	1990	—	9	4	
Middle	1930s	6	7	—	
	1990	5	6	4	
Old	1930s	8	3	1	
	1990	7	3	1	
Mountain	1930s	2	3	2	
	1990	2	3	2	
Piedmont	1930s	6	5	2	
	1990	3	8	2	
Coastal	1930s	7	7	4	1
	1990	7	7	5	

* * * * *

    This type of wide-meshed non-community-based survey differs in many ways from participant-observer type studies done within a particular community. Both types of study can reduce individual speakers to conglomerates of sociological categories. Statistical analysis requires measures that can be represented in computer files by numbers. Such measures entail the loss of information about speakers and the speech event that might provide further clues to linguistic behavior, as well as a loss of information on linguistic features that do not occur frequently enough to be analyzed quantitatively. All the (non-dubious) responses to the questions and some of the speakers' comments about particular terms are included in Appendix 4. This should give the reader a clue to the wealth of details in the databases that may be examined at length at some point. The tape recordings of the interviews will also be available for future studies of a more ethnographic type. Works by Eckert (1989a) and Feagin (1979), in particular, provide a model for including the voices of the speakers themselves in order to better understand the social structure of the community. Other researchers (e.g., Labov 1972, Preston 1989) have given extensive consideration to the language attitudes and perceptions of speakers. In the case of lexical data, speakers sometimes offer overt reasons for their linguistic choices. The interview tapes are full of anecdotes such as McDavid often used to illustrate his descriptions of language behavior. The short amount of time spent with each speaker does limit the type of interpretation that is possible from this data, but insights gained from this project can be followed up by further research in the same communities. Such a combined approach would lead to a more holistic perspective on language use and is the goal of a long-range plan of research utilizing the data from this study.

2

Variation

The 150 questions from the LAMSAS worksheets yielded 1,007 variants, while the 1990 interviews produced 1,402 different terms, an average of 6.7 and 9.4 different responses, respectively, for each linguistic variable. This tremendous amount of variety in the speech of only 78 informants underscores the richness and complexity of language variation in the speech of the southeastern United States, a region that Raven McDavid claimed contained more language variety than any other part of the country (1979 [1970]). Dialectologists have long been wary of terms that make the speech of a group or region seem to be monolithic (e.g., "American English", "Black English", or "Southern English"), and variation on this scale shows why.

About half of the words from the first sample and two thirds of those from the second sample occurred only once or twice or were dubious for some reason, leaving 488 and 484 variants, respectively, to be subjected to statistical tests, one test for each of the six social and geographic categories. Of these, 94 words from the first set and 63 from the second set of speakers were indeed used more often by at least one group of speakers. The statistical tests thus revealed associations for only 19.3 percent and 13 percent of the lexical items tested.

Appendix 2 contains a list of the items that were linked to each of the non-linguistic variables. The number of the question is given first, followed by the particular variant that is linked to the group. A list of other variants given as answers to the same question follows. Along with presenting the results of the analysis of variation, this chapter compares the patterns of variation exhibited in the 1930s to those for 1990. This project has a goal similar to that of Preston 1991 in ranking variables by the amount of influence they exert on speech, though it does not go as far as either Preston 1991 or Bell 1984 in considering the influence of linguistic and stylistic factors. The non-linguistic variables included here do not show equal effects, and their relative importance changes over time. Change in the overall amount of variation and in the amount that can be linked to the social and regional groups will also be considered.

Following a presentation of the overall findings is a description of the statistical methods used to arrive at these results. The remainder of the chapter covers a variety of topics related to variation between groups: transition patterns, a comparison to the patterns depicted in Kurath's *Word Geography*, interaction between the demographic variables, and the distribution of the incidence of 'No Response'.

This project, in its broad application of categories, treats its informants in the Southeast as though they all belong to one "speech community", even though this community is far from being homogeneous. Labov states that "a speech community cannot be conceived as a group of speakers who all use the same forms" (1972:158) and Hymes (1972) likewise does not base his definition of a speech community on linguistic homogeneity but on shared social attitudes toward language. A more recent definition of speech community by Labov states that the community norm does "normally rest on a uniform structural base" (1989:2). This project did not rigorously investigate language attitudes, nor does it attempt to describe an underlying vocabulary structure shared by all the informants. Thus these data do not provide the evidence needed to confirm the participation of speakers in a single speech community based on either shared attitudes or a shared grammar.

The present study takes a "polysystemic" view of communities that is similar to that of Hudson (1980) and LePage and Tabouret-Keller (1985). It is thus at odds with Labov, who rejects "the illusion that the linguistic community is an aggregate of individuals with an unlimited number of different systems in their heads" (1989:2). From the perspective adopted here, individual speakers belong to more than one community. One way their membership in these communities is revealed is by the features of their speech that are linked with the groups to which they belong. The psychological construction of identity is important for the definition: "the individual creates for himself the patterns of his linguistic behaviour so as to resemble those of the group or groups with which from time to time he wishes to be identified, or so as to be unlike those from whom he wishes to be distinguished" (LePage and Tabouret-Keller 1985:181). People who identify themselves as Southerners form the Southern (U.S.) English speech community. Most people who live in the South do identify with the region, even a high percentage of those who were not born there, despite the negative stereotypes about the region which persist in other parts of the country (*Atlanta Journal-Constitution*, 1992).

Patterns of Variation

The analysis of the first set of data shows that there was good justification for linguistic geographers like Kurath to focus solely on region as a factor influencing language variation, since region does account for the largest percentage of relationships between language and non-linguistic characteristics. The percentage of statistically significant tests that are linked to each factor are summarized below in Table 6. During the course of the twentieth century, however, variation based on region of residence has declined, while age, sex, and race have become relatively more important. Education and rural versus urban residence each continue to account for about twenty percent of the variation that is linked to non-linguistic variables. Note that this table only serves to rank the variables relative to one another for the set of words that showed a significant connection to one of the groups, not by overall importance for the entire data set.

Table 6: Percent/Number of statistically significant tests by variable

	1930s	1990
Total	100% / 103	100% / 70
Region	30% / 31	10% / 7
Rurality	21% / 22	20% / 14
Education	19% / 20	20% / 14
Race	13% / 13	20% / 14
Age	10% / 10	19% / 13
Sex	7% / 7	11% / 8

These results clearly show that the importance of geography as a factor in explaining linguistic variation is diminishing. It is important to note, however, that the apparent increase in the influence of race, sex, and age is only relative to the amount of variation that can be explained by any of the variables. Table 7 shows the percent of all the words tested from each set that can be linked to each non-linguistic variable. Race, sex, and age are not much more important overall in lexical choice for the 1990 data. For example, thirteen variants (2.7 percent) in the 1930s and only fourteen (2.9 percent) in 1990 are linked to race, even though race now accounts for 20 percent of the demographically-related variation instead of 13 percent. The effects of rurality and education on speech have declined, as well as that of region, though not as markedly.

Table 7: Percentage of variants linked to each non-linguistic variable

	1930s	1990
Number of Variants Tested	488	484
Region	6.35	1.45
Rurality	4.51	2.89
Education	4.10	2.89
Race	2.66	2.89
Age	2.05	2.69
Sex	1.43	1.65

Instead of leading to an absolute increase in the effect of other variables, the decline in regional variation contributed to a surprising decline in the total amount of lexical variation that can be tied to non-linguistic variables. Nineteen percent of the 488 items tested from the first data set, but only 13 percent of the 484 items from the second set had any statistically significant patterning.

When there is less variation linked to particular groups, the variation that remains may take on increased importance to speakers. Hence, over time, one may perceive greater differentiation by race if one hears fewer identifiable regionalisms, but continues to observe speech differences between the races. The amount of difference has not increased, but there may be a perception that it has, since this difference remains while other differences diminish. This possibility, that emerges by looking at the relative importance of a number of variables over time, may shed some light on the divergence/convergence controversy regarding Black Vernacular English (cf. e.g., Bailey and Maynor, 1989). This would be an interesting topic to research using the model developed in Preston 1989 for measuring perceptions of differences and similarities. Chapter Four will provide further discussion of the change in patterns of variation and its relationship to demographic trends.

Sixty-seven percent of the 150 questions yielded at least one variant that showed a distribution associated with a particular group of speakers. As mentioned above, only 19 percent of the earlier and 13 percent of the later data sets showed a statistically significant connection with any group. This small number of associations means that age, for example, plays a role for less than three percent of the total number of variants in 1990, and sex is a factor for just over one percent of the words collected in the 1930s (see Table 7). Analyses on larger samples (e.g., McDavid 1989 and Allen 1985, 1986a, 1986b on the variable sex) seem to reveal more associations than this relatively small sample can support. However, even if more tests had been significant, there is no reason to assume that they would be different in kind from those validated here.

One issue that has not been widely discussed in the literature is the amount of variation that is attributable to any of the standard variables used in sociolinguistic studies and whether it may increase or decrease. No one, as yet, has quantitatively determined just how much variation is inherently unexplainable. The questions for this study were selected because they would each provide several synonyms; they were not chosen on the basis of previously determined links to social or regional groups. By comparing the entire range of variants to those that do show such linkage, this study provides evidence for the amount of variation in the lexicon that can be explained by sociolinguistic analysis. Studies which examine only those variables that are known to correlate to social variables cannot show this as clearly. Bernstein (1993) addresses the same question with similar results. Using the variables sex, ethnicity, age, education, income, number of years in Texas, region, and rurality, she was able to account for between 9 percent and 27 percent of the variation in data from the Phonological Survey of Texas.

Many sociolinguists are inspired by the hope that they can provide evidence of systematic order for speech differences that seem at first glance to vary chaotically. A widespread assumption in the past two decades or more among linguists has been that most of the variety that exists in language that cannot be attributed to linguistic factors can be explained on the basis of either differential behavior of groups within a language community or stylistic differences. Such an assumption allows the belief that the facts of language which do not seem to be governed by linguistic rules are still governed by variable stylistic or social psychological rules that we can discover, as exemplified in Guy 1988 (52) and elsewhere. This study does not offer support for such an assumption, though it doesn't require us to abandon it either, since it does not speak directly to the question of linguistic explanation. The analysis by six of the most salient socially identifying variables fails to account for over 80 percent of the lexical variation observed. The small amount of variation linked to social differences speaks to the fluidity and relative lack of polarization within this society, but does not contribute greatly to an understanding of the basis for lexical choice in general. A comprehensive theory of socially informed lexical meaning might be able to contribute to such an understanding by providing a measure of the influence of low-level semantic distinctions. Linguistic motivation might thus serve to explain a large proportion of the variation, though it is hard to know where to begin to look for the general properties of semantic or contextual influences that will apply to a wide range of terms. Work such as Johnstone's (in press) on individual choice mediated by personal history might also provide further explanation. The previous section covering the choice of linguistic variables includes further discussion of these points, as does the following section on the relationship of change to variation.

Differences in amount of variation by different groups (i.e., which groups use the most words) cannot be compared here due to an unanticipated differentiation that occurs in Guy Lowman's interviews. The number of speakers giving multiple responses is fewer in North Carolina than in the other states, because these interviews were done later using the standard South Atlantic States version of the worksheet. Lowman used a preliminary version of the worksheet in Georgia and South Carolina, where he made a greater effort to elicit as many forms as possible in order to determine which questions would be most productive for the final version of the questionnaire. The forms are not different in type but they are in number, possibly creating the appearance of more homogeneity in the North Carolina communities than actually exists.

The increase in the amount of variation unrelated to any of the social or regional variables in the intervening years between Lowman's and Johnson's fieldwork is an unexpected and interesting result. Although Johnson recorded more different words, the average number of responses per informant in 1990 was not higher than in the 1930s. The database tables for each question from the first set contained an average of 55 rows, and those from the later set had an average of 52. Each table included the responses for 39 speakers. This means that Lowman recorded an average of 1.4 responses per informant to Johnson's 1.3 per informant, a negligible difference. Thus, although people seem to be using more different vocabulary items, many of them are not marked for a particular region or social group.

Statistical Methods

It will be helpful to keep in mind that frequency in this study is not equivalent to frequency in studies that count occurrences of a variant from an extended recording of an individual's speech. Here, frequency refers to the number of informants in the sample who mentioned a particular term in response to a question. Kretzschmar and Lee have noted in a related study on linguistic atlas data (1991) that "the calculation does not predict that the variant word will be used in conversation at the same rate that we elicited it." Follow-up studies in the standard sociolinguistic paradigm will be needed to establish the probability of occurrence.

Due to the possibility of one informant offering more than one response to a question (as about a third of them did for each question) the variation is not complementary. Use of one form from a set more often by one group does not mean the other form will be used more by the other group in the category, nor does it mean that the form is the most common one for the group with which it is associated. For example, the question 'named for' in the 1930s data produced two main responses: *named for* and *named after*. Eight women and one man used the phrase *named for*, while 16 women and 21 men said *named after*. The difference by sex for *named after* is not large enough to be statistically significant, hence *named after* is not linked to males. *Named for*, however, is linked to females although more females used *named after* than *named for*.

This feature of multiple responses is important in determining appropriate testing methods. Typical chi-square contingency tables (listing each variant and the number of informants who used it from each social group), although found in many sociolinguistic studies, have limited application for linguistic atlas data. Because each informant often gave more than one response to a question, the total number of responses is greater than the number of informants, thus invalidating the principles used to determine expected frequencies for chi-square tests. These issues are discussed further in Schneider and Kretzschmar (1989) and Johnson (1994a).

Not every variant was tested. Cases where too few or too many informants used the variant were not analyzed. Although very low frequency forms are often of linguistic interest (cf. the infamous *hapax legomenon*) and are counted as contributing to the overall amount of variation, they cannot be subjected to the type of quantitative analysis performed here. Of the different words that occurred, 670 were used by at least three, but no more than 36, of the 39 informants in a data set, making them suitable candidates for analysis. Variants were not tested if they were the sole response that occurred more than twice to a question; such worksheet items were considered to display no lexical variation. The maximum number of acceptable occurrences varied, since the amount of missing data varied for each question. There had to be at least three speakers who did not use the form, as well as at least three who did. For example, in the case of an item for which four speakers did not complete the question, no more than 32 of the remaining 35 speakers could have used the form for it to be testable. Consider the four responses to the question about 'pants' from the 1930s data: *pants, britches, trousers*, and *pantaloons. Pantaloons* occurred only three times, and one occurrence was dubious, being suggested by the fieldworker. *Pants* was used by 37 speakers, too many for analysis (all informants answered this question). Thus only *britches* and *trousers* were tested for variation. The significance of responses does not seem to be tied to frequency; counts range from 3 to 36 instances for those words that exhibited significant variation, with an average of 11 but a standard deviation of 8, showing that the tests were effective for a wide range of frequencies.

If informants were asked a question but did not answer, whether it was because they did not know or remember the term, the community had no term for the referent, or the referent was unknown, they received a score of NR (No Response). This was considered an acceptable response to a question and was, like the lexical items, subjected to tests for associations with particular groups of speakers.

In contrast to the NR category, two types of individual responses were excluded from the tests as missing data. The first was truly missing, that is, the informant did not complete the part of the interview that included the relevant question (coded with NA). The second case coded as missing data for the analysis of specific lexical variants included occurrences of the variant that were judged as doubtful. In such cases, it could not be said that the informants did not use the form, but it was dubious to claim that they did, so they were discarded from the analysis. Reasons to consider a response doubtful were discussed in the section on the interview in Chapter One. If a speaker's only response to a question was a doubtful one, it was counted as an instance of "No Response" for the NR analysis and as missing data for the analysis of the particular lexical item. Instances of the NR and NA codes may be seen in Appendix 4, which gives a tally of all the non-dubious responses to each question.

The analysis required several steps. The first was to extract the information for the relevant 39 informants from the LAMSAS databases with 1,162 informants, and to construct comparable database tables for the 1990 interviews. This resulted in a set of eleven databases, as listed in Table 1. Each database contains the results for approximately 14 questions. There are two tables for each question, one for each data set. Each table includes the following columns: "inumber" and "informid" (informant identification codes); "comnt" and "comtext" for comment codes and longer commentary, respectively; "doubtflg" to flag doubtful responses (Y or -0-); and "item" for the response to the question, with one row per response. A portion of one of the tables is given in Table 8 for illustration.

Table 8: 'Sofa', 1990 (stage 1)

inumber	informid	item	comnt	doubtflg	comtext
1.	GA1F2	settee			
2.	GA3A2	sofa	AUX/NEW	Y	wouldn't call it that in past
2.	GA3A2	davenport	AUX/SUG	Y	
3.	GA4N2	settee			
3.	GA4N2	loveseat			
4.	GA10A2	couch			
5.	GA13A2	NA			
6.	GA15A2	sofa			
7.	GA24A2	sofa			
8.	GA34A2	davenport			leather, opened into a bed
8.	GA34A2	sofa	SUG	Y	
9.	GA432	benches			not upholstered

In order to calculate the statistics, separate tables had to be created for each variant, with one row only per speaker. A binary score was assigned to speakers depending on whether or not they used the particular variant. In preparation for creating these smaller tables, columns were created for each word to be tested in the main table of responses to a question. These were then filled in with a 1 whenever the variant appeared and a 9 for missing data. Table 9 shows the columns "inumber" and "item" from the 'sofa' table for the same informants that were presented in Table 8. The five added columns are shown with values corresponding to the terms used by each speaker (each ends in 2 to identify it as the results for the 1990 data set). "Ou" stands for *couch*, "lo" for *lounge*, "so" for *sofa*, "tt" for *settee*, and "be" for *bench*.

A new table was then projected for each variant. It contained only those rows that had been marked with a 1 or a 9 for that particular

Table 9: 'Sofa', 1990 (stage 2)

inumber	item	ou2	lo2	so2	tt2	be2
1.	settee				1	
2.	sofa			9		
2.	davenport					
3.	settee				1	
3.	loveseat					
4.	couch	1				
5.	NA	9	9	9	9	9
6.	sofa			1		
7.	sofa			1		
8.	davenport					
8.	sofa			9		
9.	benches					1

column. This was combined with a table listing all of the informant numbers, since these had been lost for rows that did not contain either the pertinent response or the missing data code. Next, this temporary table with one row per informant was further combined with a table containing the information on non-linguistic variables for each speaker. Speakers who did not use the variant in question were given a score of 2 where the new column was empty.

For the example below, the first temporary table for the *sofa* variant would contain only the informant number and the column "so2" for speakers 2, 5, 6, 7, and 8. The second temporary table would add informant numbers for speakers 1, 3, 4, and 9, who would have a null value for the "so2" column. The final table used for the analysis converted these nulls to a score of 2, meaning those speakers did not use the term *sofa*. Those who did use it received a score of 1, and 9 was entered for those with missing data or a dubious use of the term. A portion of this table is shown in Table 10.

Table 10: Sofa, 1990

inumber	so2	sex	age	region	educ.	race	rurality
1	2	1	1	1	3	2	1
2	9	2	1	1	1	2	2
3	2	2	3	1	2	1	2
4	2	2	1	1	1	2	2
5	9	2	2	1	2	2	2
6	1	2	1	1	2	2	2
7	1	2	1	2	1	2	2
8	9	1	2	2	2	2	1
9	2	2	2	3	1	2	2

In the column "sex", 1 denotes female and 2 denotes male. A 1 indicates the oldest age group and a 3 the youngest, while a 1 under "region" stands for Coastal, a 2 for Piedmont, and a 3 for Mountain. The highest educational level is 3. The codes for the "race" column are 1 for blacks and 2 for whites. For "rurality", 1 means urban and 2 means rural.

The table was then exported from R:Base in DBase format and imported to SPSSPC+, the microcomputer version of the SPSS statistical software. A batch file was executed in SPSS that would retrieve the .DBF file from the database directory; recognize data coded with a 9 as missing data; save the file as an SPSS system file; retrieve it; and run the six statistical tests, one for each non-linguistic variable. The batch file had to be changed using a search and replace command for each variant.

The actual test used to compare the lexical choices across social and regional groupings of informants was the Kruskal-Wallis statistic. This is a non-parametric test based on rank rather than frequency. It is equivalent to the Wilcoxon Rank Sum Test, differing only in that it can compare scores for more than two groups. The SPSS program gives significance levels both adjusted and not adjusted for ties. The dichotomous nature of the data means that many cases will be tied, so the adjusted figure was used. Lehmann (1975) discusses the appropriateness of the Kruskal-Wallis statistic for 2 x n tables (as found in this study). Its use of rank makes it preferable to Chi-Square in this situation, since it is not subject to the Cochran Restriction on empty cells and low frequencies, both of which are common in a data set this small. Kretzschmar (1992) and Miller (in press) include further discussion on these matters.

For now, only univariate testing has been applied to the data, as intended in the project design. At some future point multivariate testing to sort out interaction between variables will be attempted. Such testing is difficult with samples of this size, since the type of information on frequency of occurrence that is found in variation studies that count expected and realized instances of a form in a sample of conversation is not available. Interaction between variables was potentially a major source of error, since the informants are not evenly distributed across the groups. If several factors had influenced lexical choice for each item, variation could easily have been attributed to the wrong variable without special care and additional testing, but 90 percent of the variants with a significant link to one of the non-linguistic variables were associated with only one category.

Only variants showing a significance level with a p-value of less than one percent ($p < .01$) were accepted as revealing differential language use between groups. This is stricter than the standard p-value of .05 used in most of the linguistic studies that validate findings with statistical evidence, and it means that the probability for an alpha error, or claiming a difference where none actually exists, is only allowed to be less than one percent. This low p-value is necessary due to the non-random, non-normal distribution of the sample. While selection of informants for this study tried to minimize the sampling bias that exists in atlas surveys, it could not entirely eliminate it. The unevenness of the sample was discussed above and it must be acknowledged, but the strict application of statistical criteria to validate claims based on the data should more than compensate for its shortcomings. This procedure is much more statistically sound than the use of percentages and frequencies as evidence without testing whether differences in percentages are real evidence of differences in the population or whether they could be due to chance.

As Davis 1983 discusses in some detail, new methods from sociology that were introduced into variation studies in the 1960s initiated a great deal of criticism of the decidedly non-random atlas sampling techniques used to collect the data in the 1930s and 1940s. Nevertheless, the use of truly random sampling never really caught on in sociolinguistics or dialectology, and most studies continue to use data collected from speakers chosen because of availability and convenience to the fieldworker. Studies such as the one utilizing the services of the Texas Poll reported in Bailey and Bernstein (1989) come close to random sampling, but only of the population with telephones in their homes (less than 80 percent in some Texas counties [Doyle 1993]). Cogent criticisms of weakness in previous quantitative techniques used with LAMSAS materials were taken to heart by the current editor, William A. Kretzschmar, resulting in derivative research from these materials that is now at least as scrupulous in its methods as that of most other projects studying language variation.

Special Topics

The analysis of variation illuminates several facets of dialect study; this section mainly concerns transitions and questions related to the nature of the sample. Types of transition zones have always been of interest to dialectologists. The subsection on the tripartite variables discusses the different patterns of lexical distribution that categories with three-way distinctions, like education, display. Some of these patterns suggest a gradual transition between dialects; others do not. Features of geographical transition are especially noted. The geographical distribution of lexical items is then compared to the dialect areas delineated by Kurath. The enduring contribution of his work is shown by a comparison of words that were included both here and in the *Word Geography* (Kurath 1949). Other issues raised here focus on the interactions between variables that are a natural consequence of the sample characteristics; the patterning of 'No Response' instances most clearly displays such interaction. 'No Response' is analyzed here as a response type and is shown to be linked fairly frequently to social or regional categories. The chapter will conclude with results from this analysis.

Tripartite Variables. Those categories containing three groups each—age, education, and region—are separated in Appendix 2 on the basis of whether the form is used by one or two groups only, with a clear distinction from the remaining group(s), or whether there is a gradual differentiation between the groups. If there is a continuum of usage, all three categories are included in the heading, showing that the variant is used mostly by the first group listed, somewhat less by the second group, and much less for the third group.

For example, the items listed as "Mountain" show a large difference in the statistical scores between that region and the other two. Those listed as "Coastal and Piedmont" have a complementary distribution to the "Mountain" forms, being used in both the coastal and piedmont regions, but not in the mountain region. Those listed under "Mountain, Piedmont, Coastal continuum" show a continuum of usage led by speakers in the mountain areas. The various types of distribution may

Variation 43

be illustrated with maps. Map 2 (*Snake feeder*: 1930s) and Map 3 (*Mosquito hawk*: 1990) show items that are significantly linked to only one region each, mountain and coastal, respectively. Map 4, showing the occurrence of (peach) *seed* in the LAMSAS sample, is an example of a variant used widely in both the mountain and piedmont areas but not on the coast, while Map 5 for (peach) *kernel* (also from the earlier sample) illustrates a continuum from frequent use in the coastal area to infrequent use in the mountains.

44   *Variation*

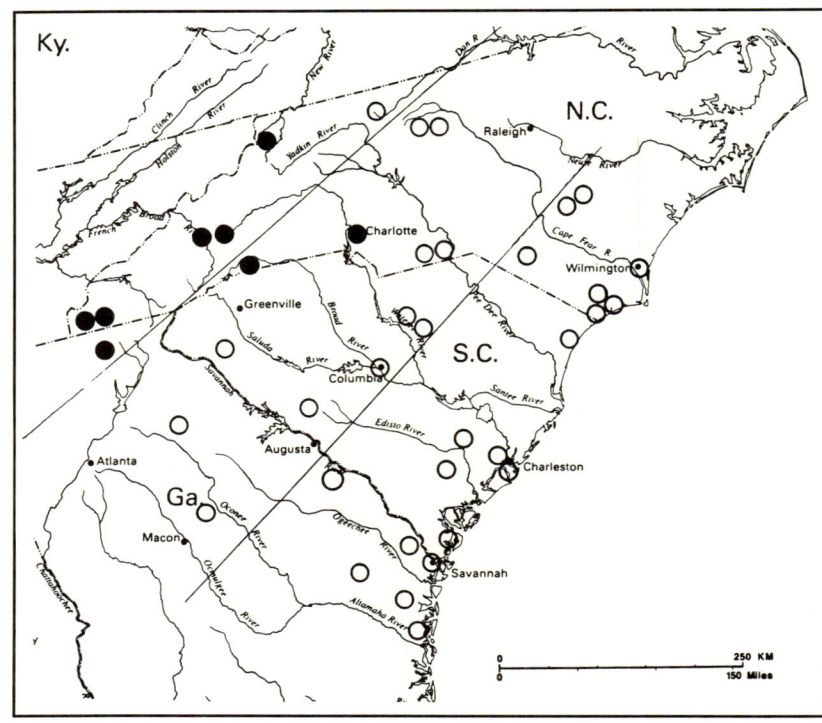

Map 2: *Snake Feeder,* 1930s

Variation 45

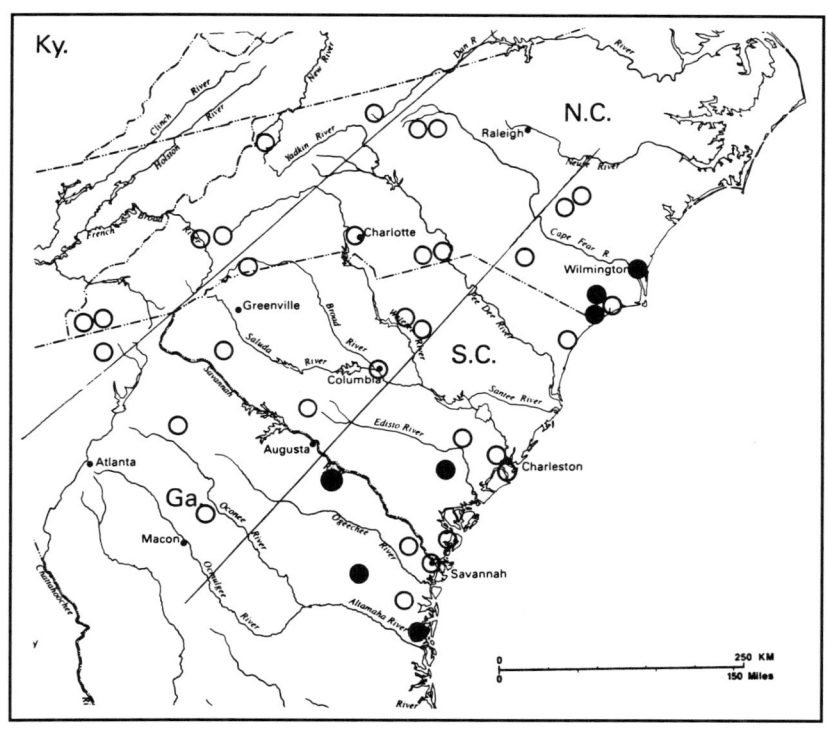

Map 3: *Mosquito Hawk,* 1990

46 *Variation*

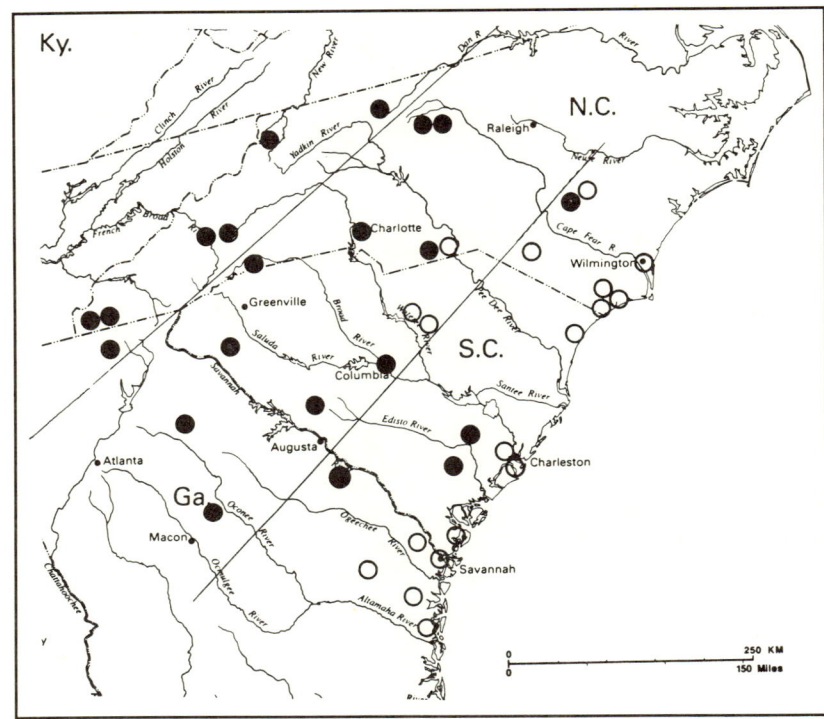

Map 4: (Peach) *Seed,* 1930s

Variation 47

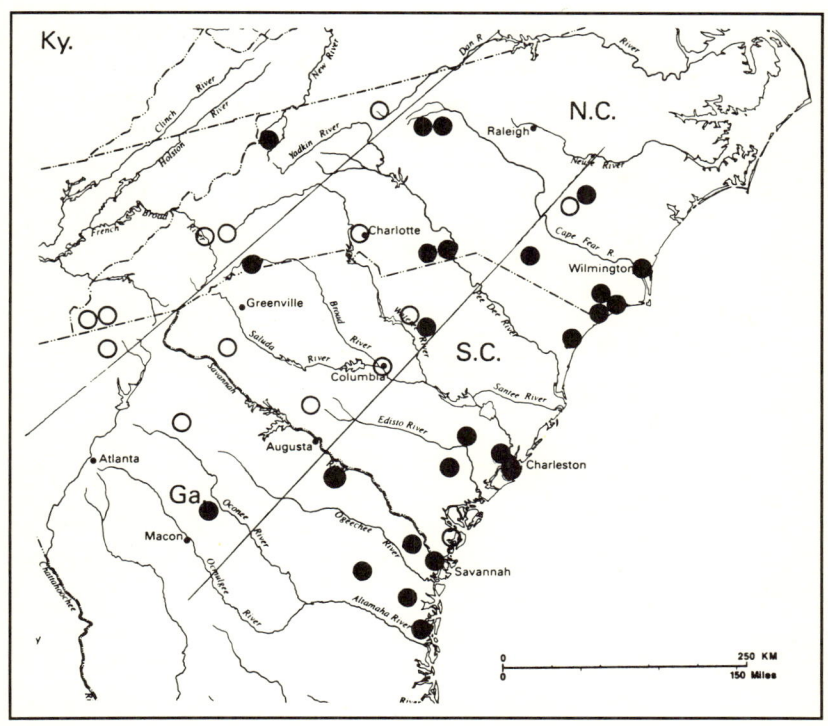

Map 5: (Peach) *Kernel,* 1930s

The assignment of distributions into dichotomous versus continuous types is based on the ranks shown in the results of the Kruskal-Wallis tests. Printouts of the statistical tests for *shell (beans)* and *firedogs* in the 1990 interviews (Tables 11 and 12) illustrate these two types of distribution by education. The lowest mean rank score indicates greater use of the variant, since speakers who used it received a score of 1 and those who did not were coded with a 2. The SPSS routine assigns ranks to each score based on the total number of valid cases. For the results exhibited in Table 11, 34 of the informants answered the questions, so each person would receive a rank between 1 and 34; these are averaged in the case of ties. In this case, 29 speakers used the term *shell* (indicated in the data set by a score of 1), so each of them was assigned the rank midway between 1 and 29, or 14.00. The speakers who had a higher score (2) because they didn't use the term were assigned the ranks 30–34, but since they were all tied, their ranks were the same: 32.00. When the informants are grouped by the demographic variables, the program averages the ranks for every person in the group and produces the figure labeled "mean rank". The p-value to check for significance is found at the bottom.

Table 11: *Shell* (beans), 1990

- - - - - Kruskal-Wallis 1-way ANOVA
ELL [*shell*] by EDUCATION

Mean Rank	Cases		
15.00	9	EDUCATE =	1
16.00	17	EDUCATE =	2
23.50	8	EDUCATE =	3
	34	Total	

CASES   Significance (Corrected for Ties)
34   .0060

Table 11 shows that the most educated informants did not know the most common verb for taking off the outside part of a bean, as compared to the other two groups (which show equivalent usage). On the other hand, *firedogs*, a term for andirons, was commonly used by the lowest educational group and rarely by the highest, with the middle group showing an intermediate degree of use.

Table 12: *Firedogs*, 1990

```
- - - - - Kruskal-Wallis 1-way ANOVA
          FD [firedogs] by EDUCATION

Mean Rank  Cases
    9.00     9   EDUCATE =   1
   17.25    16   EDUCATE =   2
   25.50     8   EDUCATE =   3
            --
            33   Total

              Significance
              (Corrected for Ties)
CASES
 33             .0003
```

Categories with three divisions can provide further insight into transition areas. The middle groups for education and age sometimes lead in usage of particular variants, rather than always exhibiting a frequency of use intermediate between the highest and lowest groups. In this aspect, age and education behave differently than region, with the piedmont acting less like a cultural entity in its own right than the middle generation or middle education group.

The piedmont region shows no variant specifically linked to it, nor does it lead in using a term shared with other regions; thus it only serves as a transition area, though it may do this in two distinct ways. It can either side completely with one or the other of its neighbors or it can participate in a limited way with either. For *gully, soo-cow, soo-calf, seed*, and *carriage*, its speech is like that of the mountain area. *Cowpen* and *clabber* are shared with the coastal area. For all of these variants, speakers throughout the region use the word to the extent it is used in a neighboring region. The continuum situation for twelve variants shows a more gradual change, with some piedmont speakers using a variant that is more widespread in one or the other of the adjoining regions.

While the piedmont area never behaves independently, it does behave cohesively for some variants. Such variants would be more suited to charting dialect boundaries, though even with these, isoglosses imply a more abrupt change than that revealed by quantitative differences, as discussed in Chambers and Trudgill (1980) and Kretzschmar (1992). For the LAMSAS data set, there would be four isoglosses between the piedmont and the coast and one between the piedmont and the mountains. The second set shows only one of each. Kurath placed the boundary between the Midland and Southern dialect areas at the juncture of the piedmont and coastal regions, and these results seem to indicate that he was indeed justified in placing it there rather than between the mountain and piedmont regions. Six words associated with the coastal area are used to a lesser degree in the piedmont, the same number of variants that are shared in a continuum with the mountain region. A better representation of the boundary between Midland and South would have been one that showed a wide band across the piedmont area, acknowledging its status as a transition zone.

Although the Midland was at one time a distinct cultural area, its distinctiveness was already beginning to fade by the 1930s, due to influence from the coastal area. In 1990 few linguistic variants remain to distinguish its southern boundaries. Influence from the coastal focal areas has diminished, but new focal areas in the piedmont, where forms from both Midland and Southern regions were already mixed, will likely further erode the differences by spreading change both to the north/west and to the south/east. Further observations on the dwindling importance of region are discussed in Chapter Four. Davis and Houck (1992) discount entirely the notion of a Midland dialect area, believing there is only a gradual transition between Northern forms and Southern ones, though Kurath stated that "it has a considerable body of words that sets it off from the North and South" (1949: 27). Davis and Houck's methodology is based on the technique used in Carver 1987, whereby lexical items are grouped into sets, and the percentage of a set that occurs in a given locality is measured. This is a way to describe the degree of participation of a community in a particular dialect area. Because it measures this participation based on a percentage of a conglomerate of terms, this method obscures the way individual words are linked to an area. In theory, one community could use five words out of a set of ten, while a neighboring community used the other five. Both would receive a score of fifty percent, even though the residents apparently do not speak the same dialect. This question is explored more fully in Johnson (1994b). The present study does show a division between Kurath's Midland and South at the time the LAMSAS data were collected, since there were at least 38 words that showed a distinct difference in usage between the mountain areas (located in Kurath's Midland) and the coast (Kurath's South). This is larger than the number of words associated with any of the divisions by social groups. Only 2 of the 24 words that were more common in the mountains are shared with the North, according to Kurath 1949, so these differences are not due to the status of the Midland as simply a transition area between Northern and Southern speech areas.

Comparison to Kurath. One of the goals of this project was an attempted replication of Kurath's *Word Geography* (1949), which was based on a preliminary examination of the lexical variants in the LAMSAS files. Of the 94 significant variants from the LAMSAS data found in this study, Kurath mentions 37. For the 37 words that are both noted in Kurath 1949 and found to be significantly distributed in the earlier data by the present study, 20 corroborate Kurath's findings. These are listed in Table 13.

Table 13: Words whose distributions match those reported in Kurath (1949)

soo(k)-cow (cow call)	hull (beans)	fireboard
piggie (call to pigs)	paper poke	snake feeder
sheepie (call to sheep)	tow sack	milkgap
soo-calf (call to calf)	plum peach	corn dodger
liver and lights	press peach	earthworm
best man	living room	red worm
haslet	bawl (cow sound)	

Only three statements from the *Word Geography* are actually contradicted by this study. All concern variants (*mantelpiece, cowpen,* and *chick* (call to chickens)) that are said to occur throughout the region, though the statistical analysis shows they are associated especially with the coastal area. Kurath also notes that *mantel, doughnuts, back house,* and *midwife* occur throughout the eastern United States, without noting

52   *Variation*

that the first two are more common among educated speakers, that *back house* is used mostly by the middle educational group, and that *midwife* is used more by whites than blacks. Fourteen variants that showed significant associations with demographic variables did not reveal the regional patterns noted by Kurath. These are shown in Table 14 below. Kurath found these to be located in sub-regions which were not tested here.

There are many other terms included in the *Word Geography* whose distributions could not be verified by this analysis. Table 14 lists only those words that do show statistically significant distributions in the first data set, though not the pattern described by Kurath. The 394 words that were not linked to demographic variables were not compared to the *Word Geography*.

Table 14: Some words from the *Word Geography* whose distributions are not substantiated here

Variant	Distribution noted in Kurath 1949
moo	younger generation
spider	Tidewater north of Pee Dee River
clearstone	SC, eastern NC piedmont
biddie	NC, Pee Dee area
cottage cheese	urban trade name
freestone	Midland, NC coast
pail	South (not Midland) for wooden one
breakfast strips	Carolinas
cruller	Dutch settlement area
garden house	VA, northeastern NC

Fifty-three associations found in this study were not noted in the *Word Geography*. Most of these were linked to social variables. While there are scattered comments on social variation in Kurath's book, region was the only variable that was systematically analyzed. This earlier research, done with colored pencils and maps as tools rather than computers, proves to be remarkably correct as well as extremely detailed, revealing more geographical patterns than can be shown here and showing agreement with nearly all the regional patterns documented herein. Kurath did miss the following regional associations found here for the 1930s: *bring a calf* (mountain); *gully* and (peach) *pit* (mountain and piedmont);

family pie (mountain w/continuum); *threatening, sieva beans, spring frog(s),* and *relatives* (coastal); and *scholar* and (peach) *kernel* (coastal w/continuum).

Map 6 is from Kurath (1949) and shows isoglosses for two supposedly quintessentially Midland terms, *sook!* and *snake feeder*. This can be compared with the maps below for *soo(k)-cow!* and *snake feeder* from the LAMSAS subset analyzed here. The statistical tests for *soo(k)-cow!* (results depicted in Map 7) show that this was a good choice to demonstrate this dialect area, since it was used significantly more in both the piedmont and mountain areas. *Snake feeder*, on the other hand (Map 2 and Table 15, below), was shown to be associated with only the mountain area in this analysis. It is not such a good representative of the Midland area as a whole, since it is limited to a sub-region of the Midland.

Table 15: Snake Feeder, 1930s

- - - - - Kruskal-Wallis 1-way ANOVA

SNF [*snake feeder*] by LOCATION

Mean Rank Cases

23.00   18   LOCATE = 1
19.92   12   LOCATE = 2
7.14   7   LOCATE = 3
        --
        37   Total

Significance
(Corrected for Ties)

CASES
37   .0000

54 *Variation*

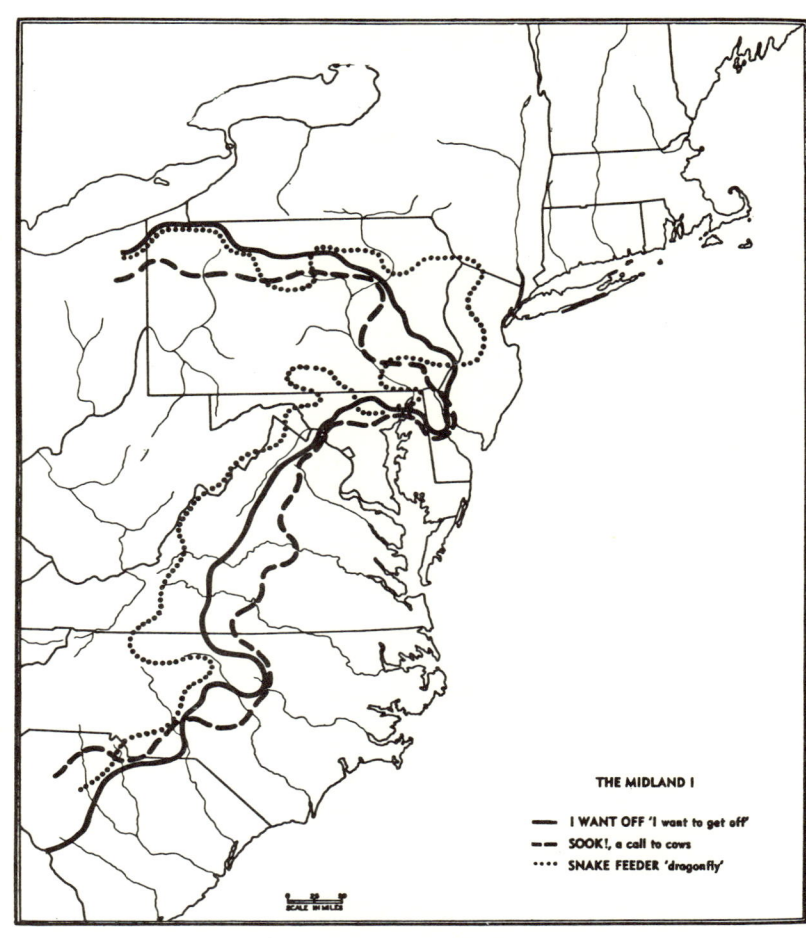

Map 6: Kurath 1949, figure 15

Variation 55

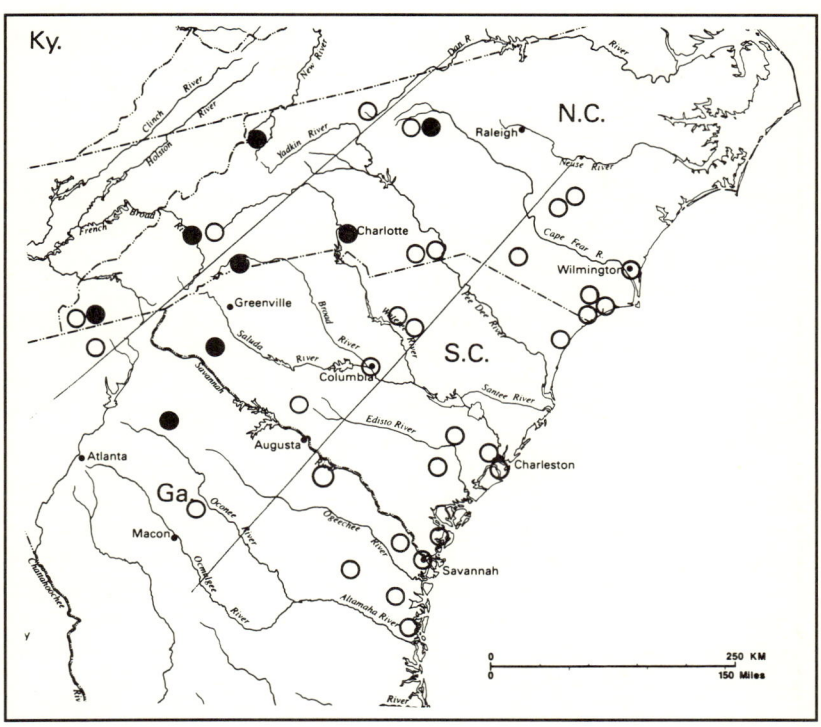

Map 7: *Soo(k)-Cow!*, 1930s

Interaction between Variables. As noted in Chapter One, the non-linguistic variables are not evenly balanced. Therefore, most of the results that show lexical choice linked to more than one group are probably not independent of one another. Connections between them are not surprising. What is surprising is that these links did not show up more often. Eighty-five of 94 significant variants in the first sample and 57 of 63 in the second sample were linked to only one non-linguistic variable. The statistical test used, and the low p-value deemed acceptable, served to validate perhaps fewer relationships than actually exist, but they also culled out only the most robust associations, thereby compensating for the shortcomings of the sample, and revealing one variable that is clearly the most salient for most of the variants tested. The unevenness of the sample does not invalidate those relationships that do show significance.

If an urban-rural difference is influenced by differentiation by sex, for example, because more women are urban, we must assume that sex would have been a significant factor overall. If more urban males had been included, it is possible that some variation by sex might show up that is not revealed here, assuming that sex as a variable behaves differently in urban than in rural areas. This does not mean that there would suddenly be no difference in the use of the form between the rural areas and the urban ones, although the difference might be less sharp. To take an extremely simplified example, if all the urban female informants for the LAMSAS sample used a word that none of the rural informants and no urban males used, there would be 8 who used it and 31 who did not. If five of the urban speakers (instead of one) were male, the difference would be 4 to 35, but the form would still only occur in the urban areas and the urban-rural distinction would still hold true. Sex, although important here for urban variation, would not be as important for the overall set of informants, since the rural females behaved like the rural males in this hypothetical example.

The fourteen items that were significant for more than one category are starred in Appendix 2 and summarized below in Table 16. Two variants, *attic* and *Happy New Year(s)*, were used more by both the younger informants and the better-educated ones. Of course, more younger speakers were better educated. *Woodpecker* was the only item to show significance both with females and with the middle and higher education groups. In this particular sample, this is not because women are more insecure and status-conscious and therefore prefer the presumably more prestigious form (Trudgill 1983, etc.). It reflects both the higher degree of education of the females in the sample and, possibly as well, an avoidance of the somewhat taboo alternate form, *peckerwood*, although this latter does not clearly show distribution by sex. It is important to note that even in a set with only two variants, because of multiple responses by the same informant, increased use of one variant by one group in a category, e.g., females (*woodpecker*), does not usually coincide with increased use of the other variant by the other grouping, e.g., males (*peckerwood*).

Table 16: Items associated with more than one socio-regional category

Variant	Categories
attic	young, high education (continuum)
Happy New Year(s)	young, high and middle education
woodpecker	female, middle and high education
living room	female, urban
Idaho potatoes	female, urban
rail fence(s)	male, rural
loft ('attic')	rural, low education
freestone	urban, high and middle education
shav(s)	rural, low education, old and middle age
polecat	rural, old (continuum)
pen(s) (for hogs)	low education, old (continuum)
doubletree	white, rural
student	white, high and middle education
foreigner ('stranger')	white, middle educ. (continuum w/low)
haslet	male, coastal (continuum)

Women in the sample are more urban, hence the dual patterning of the variables sex and rurality for *living room* (female and urban, set 1), *Idaho potatoes* (female and urban, set 2), and *rail fence(s)* (male and rural, set 2). Ties between rurality and lack of education result in the combinations associated with *loft* and *freestone* for the 1930s sample and *shav(s)* in 1990. The oldest speakers have lower average educational levels, and *pen(s)* ('hog pen') is associated with both the low educational and old age groups. The rural speakers in the sample are older than the urban ones, and *polecat* is linked to both rural and older speakers. Whites, especially in the first sample, are both more rural and more educated than blacks, hence the outcomes of *doubletree* and *student*. However, whites share the increased use of the term *foreigner* ('stranger') with the middle to low education groups in sample 2. Lastly, the coastal region has more males, and *haslet* is linked both to males and to this region.

All but one (*foreigner*) of the fifteen words used more frequently by more than one category of speakers can thus be explained by the characteristics of the sample. The asymmetry noted here has not been tested for significance; rather, statements about the sample are based on simple percentages obtained from crosstabulations. Sample characteristics are discussed in detail in Chapter 1, where it is noted that associations between groups in the sample are not always problematic, since many of the unbalanced groups got that way because they are not balanced in the general population. Ties between them in these cases represent demographic trends and are not due to poor sampling.

No Response. The variant 'No Response' was also tested for connections with the regional and social variables. It displayed the same type of interaction between variables noted above. NR was entered if informants did not answer the question because: (a) they did not know or remember the term, (b) the referent of the term did not occur locally, or (c) the only response to the question was a dubious one, e.g. provided by an auxiliary informant, suggested by the fieldworker, or reported as usage heard from other speakers. Johnson recorded more 'No Response' variants than Lowman, probably due to the choice of linguistic variables, which was biased toward terms for things that had become obsolete by 1990. For 28 questions in the first sample and 85 in the second, there were at least three occurrences of 'No Response'. These were subjected to the same type of recoding and testing used with the lexical variants to look for associations with social and regional categories. 'No Response' showed significant variation by non-linguistic variables for 15 and 17 questions from the first and second data sets, respectively. These are listed below in Table 17.

'No Response' answers are clearly related to the semantic field to which an item belongs and the amount of knowledge of that field possessed by different groups. For example, urban speakers gave no response more frequently than rural ones for 15 of the 26 questions, due to the rural bias of the questionnaire. Females and African Americans had significantly more 'No Responses' on 7 and 6 questions, respectively, a result that is of interest for studying language and power issues. Language and gender studies, such as Eckert 1989b, suggest that power (as instantiated in gender, among other things) may be a more salient predictor of language differences than gender is. The vocabulary that was investigated

Variation 59

for LAMSAS is in some ways the vocabulary that "belongs" to socially dominant groups. The above results could be interpreted as evidence that English (or at least the varieties of it that were of interest to earlier dialectologists) is a (white) "man-made language" (Spender 1980). However, the urban category does contain a higher percentage of both women and blacks than the rural category, so the results may have been influenced by the sampling bias. Groups that gave no response more often

Table 17: Questions with 'No Response' linked to a non-linguistic variable

Question	NR, 1930s	NR, 1990
andirons	Coastal	
attic		Old
cottage cheese	Black	
cow call when milking	High Education, Urban	Urban
cow call in pasture	Urban	Female, Urban
horse call in pasture	Urban	
mule to turn left		Female, Urban
mule to turn right		Female, Urban
call to pigs	Urban	
call to sheep	Urban	
valley (of roof)	Black	Female, Urban
cowpen		White
grindstone		Female
(wagon) tongue		Black, Urban
shafts (of buggy)		High-Mid-LowEd., Young, Urban
singletree		Urban
doubletree	Urban	Urban
bawl (of calf)	Urban	Female
peanuts		Black
chipmunk	Coast-Pied.-Mtn.	
green frog	Urban	
minnows		Black
terrapin		Female
sycamore	Old	
bastard	Urban	
Happy New Year	Black	

for just one or two questions were both old and young speakers, highly educated ones, white speakers, and those from the coastal area.

Ad hoc conjectures purporting to explain the reasons for particular forms being associated with particular groups could proliferate here, both for the 'No Response' results and for other variants. In the absence of data on cognitive associations or etymological evidence, such speculations are perhaps no more than folk etymologies offered by a linguist. Regardless of their tenuous nature, such hypotheses are quite interesting, and Chapter 4 will discuss cultural factors which could explain some of the findings, using evidence from historians. There are various social psychological theories, theories of communication, and theories of social class that fit more or less closely to the occurrence of group-based linguistic variation found in this study. The efficacy of such theories as explanatory devices will also be explored in Chapter 4, along with other cultural elements found to be reflected in language use.

3

Change

This study is unusual among sociolinguistic analyses because of its time span. Few variationist research projects have had truly comparable data spanning nearly sixty years available for analysis. Real time studies have an advantage over studies using change in apparent time (across age groups), since they do not have to rely on other sources of evidence to determine whether differences among age groups correlate with actual change in the language over time. Studies with teenage informants, in particular, run the risk that differential usage is a function of peer group identity rather than innovation that will have an impact on the language as a whole (Christian, Wolfram, and Dube 1988:139). This project will examine aspects of diachronic change that can be verified statistically. It will also investigate the relationship of change to variation.

Change in the lexicon could be statistically documented for 232 variants that were used more frequently in one or the other of the data sets. Tests were conducted on each of the 670 variants that occurred at least three times in one of the samples. One hundred forty-five words were used significantly more often in the earlier data collected by Lowman; 87 were more common in Johnson's interviews.

The variants that increased or decreased in usage during the century are listed in Appendix 3. [The "*x*" with some entries indicates that various contexts were combined. For example, "(*x*) bad weather" for the question 'clouding up' represents all of the following responses: *fixing to be bad weather, going to be bad weather, looks like bad weather.*] Twenty-two percent of the 670 variants subjected to statistical testing proved to be old; 13 percent of the words are new. In terms of which linguistic variables proved productive, 111 of the 150 interview questions (74 percent) exhibited at least one variant that was old and 67 (45 percent) had at least one new word as a response. Only 29 questions exhibited no change in their sets of lexical variants, while 33 had among their responses both old and new terms.

Speakers sometimes commented on words that they considered to be either modern or, especially, old-fashioned. Of the 670 variants that were tested with statistical methods, 113 (17 percent) were noted as old by at least one informant; 43 of these were documented as old by the analysis. Seventy-three variants were considered to be new by at least one speaker; only 16 of these were verified as new by the analysis. Thus, although speakers perceived many changes that were not documented, they do provide corroborating evidence for 30 percent of the old words and 18 percent of the new ones. It seems that speakers have more subtle knowledge about language change than could be verified quantitatively. Allen (1989) discusses such commentary at length.

This chapter will examine those vocabulary changes that have been documented diachronically. The first section covers statistical methods used to verify the changes. The 67 variants that changed and that were also significantly linked to one of the demographic variables in the earlier analysis will be discussed, and the overall relationship between change and variation assessed. Finally, theories of lexical and semantic change and their applicability to the results of this study will be examined. Meillet (1921) was one of the first historical linguists to study the role of sociological factors in linguistic change. His work, as interpreted in Nerlich (1992:177), explained semantic change based on (1) relationships between words and other words, (2) relationships between words and objects, and (3) relationships between words and the differential usage of them by speakers of different social groups. The dimension of change that is linked to social groups is discussed first in this chapter, followed by the topic of change based on relationships between words. The relationship between words and objects is a major focus of Chapter 4, which deals with the influence of cultural change.

Statistical Methods

The binomial principle continues to apply in this part of the study (Schneider and Kretzschmar 1989). This requires that each variant or member of a set of responses be tested separately, as opposed to a multinomial test of the whole set at once.

The database columns that were filled in with 1s and 9s for the first analysis were used again in this part of the project. A table was projected from the responses to a question from the first sample with only

Change   63

the rows where the relevant variant occurred (1) or the data were missing (9). Another was projected from the table for the second sample in a similar fashion. These two were combined with each other and then with a table containing all the informant numbers. Those informants who did not use the word received a score of 2. Table 18 shows the results for *couch* for the nine pairs of speakers from Georgia. (Information on how the preliminary tables were prepared was given in Chapter 2. Tables 8 and 9 in that chapter demonstrate the preparatory coding necessary for the creation of the table excerpted in Table 18.) Neither of the informants who share the designation as speaker number 1 in each set used the term *couch*. For the second pair of speakers, the 1930s informant said *couch*, but the 1990 informant did not. The data for the fifth pair indicate that the earlier speaker did not use the term, and the 1990 speaker either was not asked the question or used the term but in a doubtful way, i.e. it may have been suggested by the fieldworker, reported as heard elsewhere, or perhaps offered by another person present at the interview. The 9 simply signifies missing data.

Table 18: *Couch* data

inumber	ou	ou2
1.	2	2
2.	1	2
3.	2	2
4.	2	1
5.	2	9
6.	2	2
7.	2	2
8.	2	2
9.	2	2

The test chosen for the analysis was the Sign Test. It assigns a positive or negative value to the differences between pairs of data and checks to see whether there are equal numbers of each. For the data in Table 18, the second pair of speakers received a positive value, the fourth a negative value, the fifth pair was excluded from the test because of missing data, and the rest tied. The results for all 39 pairs of informants are shown below in Table 19.

Table 19: *Couch* results

NPAR TESTS /SIGN ou WITH ou2.

- - - - - Sign Test

OU with OU2

Cases		
13	— Diffs (OU2 Lt OU)	
1	+ Diffs (OU2 Gt OU)	
19	Ties	
--		
33	Total	(Binomial)
		2-tailed P = .0018

The term *couch* was used significantly more frequently in the later interviews. There were 13 negative differences, with values for the 1990 informants being lower than those of the earlier ones. A score of 1 signifies use of the term and 2 non-use; thus the lower the score, the greater the frequency of occurrence. Only one pair of speakers (the second pair in Table 18) produced a positive difference. For this pair, *couch* was used by the 1930s informant, but not in 1990. The p-value to determine statistical significance is found in the lower righthand corner. The term "2-tailed" means that the test was looking for a difference in either direction—whether the term was more common in either the first set or the second set of data—rather than only testing whether it was used more frequently in e.g. the first set or not.

The Sign Test is a non-parametric test appropriate for two related samples. A T-test for paired data would not have been suitable, since the data type is nominal, not ordinal. For the same reason, the Wilcoxon Test, which includes information on the magnitude of the differences, could not be used because the difference in the scores for the pairs of informants is always one or nothing. The acceptable p-level for the analysis of change was set at $p<.05$. This is a less stringent requirement than that chosen for the analysis of variation, since the paired sample design is more reliable than the quota sample used for LAMSAS. The 1990 informants were chosen according to strict criteria to fit a research model that is considered to be a standard statistical design. The previous informants were not chosen using techniques that are acceptable current practices in the social sciences, although there was a plan for selecting informants to fill a predetermined quota, as described in Kretzschmar et al. 1994.

The sample size determines how many more positive than negative differences (or vice versa) must occur before the difference is statistically significant. This varies due to missing data, but even if the variant does not occur in one sample at all, there must be at least six occurrences in the other set to document a change. This is an artifact of sample size rather than a requirement of the test, and was only determined through practical experience and an inspection of the data. Although the test was applied to the variants that occurred three, four, or five times (in one set), these variants could not be judged as either old or new because of the limitations of the Sign Test. That is, even if they did not occur at all in the other data set, it could not be considered as a statistically reliable indication of change.

Change and Variation

Previous studies have shown that particular social groups seem to lead in linguistic change while others are more conservative. By noting which groups of speakers are associated with new words and which with older words, this study provides additional evidence for, especially, which groups resist language change. Statements below about innovative groups must be viewed with caution, since there are fewer new terms which can serve as evidence. The research design was biased in its inclusion of more referents likely to have become obsolete during the course of the century. Thus the results speak more to what was lost from the vocabulary than what was gained.

More change than variation was documented, with 101 of the 150 questions displaying some significant social or regional variation compared with 121 questions demonstrating change in the lexicon. This breaks down to 232 words exhibiting change and 148 showing a relationship to a non-linguistic variable. Some of these are the same. Sixty-seven, or 29 percent, of the words that vary diachronically also show a link to one or more of the social and regional variables. The tables below list all the variants that were significant across both time and social/regional groups.

Table 20: Variants with significant differences by both time and region

Older Terms by Region		Newer Terms by Region	
fireboard (mantel)	M	chipmunk	MPC
soo-calf (call)	MP	carriage (for baby)	MP
tow sack (burlap)	M		
cowpen	CP		
milkgap (cowpen)	M	Listings with three letters denote
bawl (cow sound)	MPC	a continuum of usage.
threatening (weather)	C		
haslet (hog organs)	CPM	M = Mountain	
kernel (of peach)	CPM	P = Piedmont	
seed (of peach)	MP	C = Coastal	
plum peach	M		
press peach	CPM		
family pie	MPC		
spring frog	C		
scholar (elem. age)	CPM		

Region. The intersection with the largest number of members is that of older words with region, reflecting the importance of region as a non-linguistic variable for the 1930s data. In Chapter 2, it was noted that variation by region is decreasing. Table 20 shows that many of the terms that were associated with a particular region are declining in use.

Rurality. The concept of urban areas as focal points remains a viable one, as can be seen by the urban and rural affiliations of newer and older variants, respectively, in Table 21. It is interesting that these urban focal areas do not seem to contribute to regional differences. One would expect newer terms to be linked with the piedmont region (though few actually are), since this region includes the growing cities of Atlanta,

Greenville/Spartanburg, Charlotte, and Raleigh/Durham/Chapel Hill. If, however, changes are moving from one metropolitan area to another, as is the case for the Northern Cities Shift (Labov 1991), they might not affect the region as a whole. The heyday of Charleston as the most influential urban center is long since past, and, indeed, none of the newer terms are linked to the coastal area.

Table 21: Variants with significant differences by both time and rurality

Older Terms by Rurality		Newer Terms by Rurality	
loft (attic)	R	living room	U
kope (horse call)	R	new potatoes	U
weatherboarding	R		
rail fence	R	R = Rural	
lines (wagon or plow)	R	U = Urban	
shavs (on buggy)	R		
doubletree (on wagon)	R		
seed (of cherry)	R		
polecat	R		
turns out (school...)	R		

Education. Educational groups affiliated with older and newer terms reveal that lexical change is often led by the more highly educated speakers, with the terms that are declining in use more likely to be those that are linked to the lower and middle educational groups (see Table 22). This would be consistent with the idea that change from above, or more conscious change, is influenced by speakers with higher social status (as in, e.g., Labov 1990). Fieldwork experience indicates that speakers are generally more aware of vocabulary than phonetic differences, even though, as noted above, particular lexical forms are not often stigmatized to the same extent as variant grammatical features are (Wolfram 1991b: 45).

Table 22: Variants with significant differences by both time and education

Older Terms by Education		Newer Terms by Education	
garret	MHL	mantel	HM
loft ('attic')	L	woodpecker	MH
back house	MLH	turtle	H
hogpen	ML	stroller	MHL
shavs	L	truant	H
press peach	LMH	Happy New Year	HM
graveyard	HML		

Listings with three letters denote a continuum of usage.

H = High, M = Middle, L = Low level of education

Sex. Table 23 shows the relationship of change to variation by sex, with females associated more with newer terms and males with older ones. This is in agreement with the findings of Labov and others (summarized in Labov 1990) that women are more innovative than men in their speech, especially in change from above the level of conscious awareness. For change from below the level of awareness, such speech behavior is not at all consistent, as noted by e.g. Milroy (1987) and Johnson (a, in press). The results by educational groups, as well as overt commentary by informants, suggest that the changes found here are changes from above. Designation of a change as being above or below conscious awareness is usually based on stylistic differences, but such evidence is not available for this study. Social mores requiring feminine speech to be more "correct" (cf. McDavid 1989 and Allen 1986b) can result in conservative linguistic behavior by middle-class women (Cameron and Coates 1988). This seems not to be the case here, although informant characteristics are slightly skewed in the sample, so that the women are somewhat more educated and urban than the men. Urban, educated, young, and female speakers are all associated with newer words, and the opposite is true for their rural, less educated, older, and male counterparts. Although the sample is not balanced for these characteristics, neither is the population, so that the results may well be related to interaction between variables that is typical for this society.

Multivariate testing would be required to sort out the contributions of each variable, yet the different linguistic features associated with each suggest that they all play a role, whatever their combined influence.

Table 23: Variants with significant differences by both time and sex

Older Terms by Sex		Newer Terms by Sex	
rail fence	M	living room	F
doubletree	M	moo	F
haslet	M	woodpecker	F
rheumatism	M		
		M = Male, F = Female	

Race. Race is not strongly linked to the changes documented here, though the preponderance of older variants used by whites is perhaps indicative of a resistance to change that is not shared by blacks (see Table 24, below). This would seem to differ from the findings of Labov 1991 (38) and 1972 (318), which assert that it is African Americans who tend not to participate in overall local patterns of change, at least of vowel systems. In this case, however, although the black speakers do not use more old words, neither do they use many that are new, that is, words that show an increase in frequency for the entire set of 1990 speakers. Two of the three new variants linked to African American speakers are not truly variants, but rather indications of a gap in the lexicon, much as 'No Response' would be. That is, African American informants in 1990 knew the terms *gee* and *haw* (as, surprisingly, did most of the other informants), but did not know which was right and which was left.

Table 24: Variants with significant differences by both time and race

Older Terms by Race		Newer Terms by Race	
grindstone	W	daddy	W
doubletree	W	gee or haw (left)	B
mush	W	gee or haw (right)	B
grandfather	W		
		B = Black, W = White	

Blacks, females, and urban speakers were the most common sources of 'No Response' answers, and 'No Response' was much more common in the 1990 data. This is consistent with the conservatism of white, male, and rural speakers and the agricultural, historical orientation of the choice of linguistic variables, though both the 'No Response' results by race and those for change may be related to the fact that the urban category contains a higher percentage of African Americans than the rural category does. Despite the apparent linguistic conservatism of the white speakers, there is just not enough evidence here to make the complementary generalization that blacks are more innovative. In light of other studies that have found just the opposite (e.g., Kurath 1949, M. Miller 1978), it would be wise to refrain from making such a generalization on the basis of this scant evidence.

Age. The question of how much language variation can be explained by group-based differences is akin to the question of how much language change is revealed by age-based differences. A comparison of the total set of lexical changes to those suggested by apparent-time results within each data set will be of interest in examining the efficacy of apparent time as a heuristic device. As noted by Chambers and Trudgill 1980 and Labov 1981, dialectologists should not simply assume that studies of age-related differences are actually studies of linguistic change. Research on change based mostly on apparent-time effects is so common, however, that Bailey, Wikle, Tillery, and Sand state that, "If in fact apparent time differences cannot usually be equated with real time differences, the whole enterprise of studying linguistic change in progress rests on a shaky foundation at best" (1991: 243).

The correlation between variants associated both with age groups and with the older or newer data sets in Table 25 shows that language change can be reflected in variation across generations. This fits with evidence presented by Bailey, Wikle, Tillery, and Sand (1991) showing that changes measured by apparent time are usually accurate indications of change in real time. None of the age differences in either this study or theirs were contradicted by the diachronic data. The only older word in this data that is linked to a younger age group was used by the younger speakers in the 1930s and had disappeared from the lexicon by 1990. This speaks to the rapidity of change and is not evidence against the efficacy of the apparent-time construct. The only variant that presents a challenge is the older word *bureau*, which is associated with the middle age group in 1990, but not with the oldest speakers.

Table 25: Variants with significant differences both by time and age

Older Terms by Age

bureau (furniture)	M
shavs (on a buggy)	OM
low (cow sound)	O
bakery bread	Y†
middling	O
breakfast strip	OMY
polecat	OMY
youngun	OM

†From the 1930's data set.

Newer Terms by Age

fatback	Y
pit	Y
Happy New Year	Y

Listings with three letters denote a continuum of usage.

O = Old, M = Middle, Y = Young age groups

    The problem suggested by the results of this analysis is not that variation by age disagrees with diachronic change, but rather that if we study only changes that are pinpointed by age-group variation we may be missing many other changes that are occurring, at least in the lexicon. Only 5 percent of the variants undergoing diachronic change during the century, i.e., 11 of 232 words, showed a connection to one of the age groups in the study.

    Studies of sound change usually proceed under the assumption that a person's pronunciation reflects the language at the time of acquisition during their early childhood (cf. Bailey, Wikle, and Sand 1991, where changes have been dated on the basis of informants' years of birth). The lexicon is quite different in this respect, since people are continually learning and using new words throughout their lifetimes, as well as words they initially acquired. We cannot assume that this study presents a synchronic picture of the language either at the time of the interview or during the informants' childhoods. This may partially explain the lack of association of particular words with particular age groups within data sets, since their lifetimes overlapped considerably. Labov (1981: 180-181) specifically excludes vocabulary when outlining the basic assumption underlying the use of the apparent-time construct:

> . . . the individual acquires a certain system in the early years of language development, and keeps that system more or less intact throughout the rest of his or her life.

> There will be corrections to stigmatized patterns, new vocabulary, some borrowings from other speakers, but on the whole the phonetic and phonological pattern of the pre-adolescent and adolescent years is preserved. The 60 year old speaker in 1970 then gives us a fairly good representation of the system that was being acquired by youngsters in the 1920's.

Thibault and Daveluy (1989) note that apparent time as an indication of change in progress has worked best for phonological variables. Labov (1981) also questions whether syntactic change might not be invisible in apparent time due to change by individual speakers that parallels change in the community. The findings of this study indicate that numerous lexical changes are not reflected in differences among age groups.

Twelve of 22 variants linked to the oldest or youngest age groups (see Appendix 2) did not show up as having changed. Some of this age variation may have been age-grading as opposed to language change. This underscores the need to discriminate, as discussed in Milroy 1992a, between innovation (which is speaker-related) and change (which is system-related).

It should be stressed here that more frequent use of a new word by a particular group is not necessarily the cause of lexical change. Kroch (1989:238) notes that the assumption that "quantitative studies can be taken to provide direct evidence as to the causation of change, either regarding the origin of innovations or the functional pressures that favor their advance" has largely gone unexamined. For the vocabulary, innovation by one group of speakers and imitation by others is apparently not the only motivation for change.

Wolfram (1991:100) states that "change does not take place simultaneously on all different social strata; instead, it originates in particular social classes and then spreads from that point." Thibault and Daveluy also note that, "il est présumé que l'innovation se diffusera d'abord au sein d'un sous-groupe de locuteurs avant de se répandre à d'autres sous-groupes de la communauté" (1989:19). (It is presumed that innovation will first be diffused among a subgroup of speakers before expanding to other subgroups in the community.) The 71 percent of variants exhibiting change over the course of the twentieth century that are not associated with a particular social group challenge this presumption.

This is a serious charge, since an explanation of language change based on synchronic variation is the most important goal for many sociolinguists, and provides a major paradigm for the field. The failure to link change to variation for most changes documented by this study may be partially due to the unique acquisition patterns for the lexicon, as noted above, or to the breadth of the survey. Papers presented at the twenty-first conference on New Ways of Analyzing Variation in English by Milroy (1992b) and Eckert and McConnell-Ginet (1992) suggest that social variation has meaning for speakers only at the local level. Thus macro-level studies such as this one might miss associations that could be discovered by micro-level studies involving frequency counts within a single community.

A large majority of language changes could not be linked to social or regional groups in this study. This is a corollary to the fact that the majority of the total set of words recorded in the interviews were not linked to any of the non-linguistic variables. The non-parametric test required by the nature of the data thus revealed associations for only 19.3 percent and 13 percent of the lexical items tested. As noted above, these figures are consistent with those reported by Bernstein (1993) for Texas. These findings suggest that it is unlikely we will ever be able to link all cases of language change to demographic variation. As reported by Thibault and Daveluy (1989) from their longitudinal study in Montréal, and suggested by these findings as well, the possibility exists that some changes may indeed spread across the population without regard to social and regional groupings.

Change in the Lexicon

The search for a comprehensive and useful theory of words and their meanings that can encompass the types of changes found in this study has proved to be an ongoing challenge. Most current theories of lexical semantics focus on the syntactic roles of lexical items, adressing such issues as how to encode co-occurrence restrictions in a grammar. Theories of meaning that attempt to break down words into semantic primitives, much as one might divide them into phonemes, have gone in and out of fashion (cf. Lakoff 1987) and are based on a shaky epistemological foundation. Some authors (e.g., Sweetser 1990, Ruhl 1989, and Wierzbicka 1992) provide excellent analyses of specific lexical items, but their methodology requires an intensive study of particular terms that is not possible to accomplish within such a broad survey as this.

Much of the psycholinguistic and semiotic research into word meanings requires information of a different sort than can be derived from linguistic atlas-style interviews because it focuses mostly on semasiological features of words. A change in meaning alone, with the form remaining the same, is semasiological change, the type of change associated with semantics proper. On the other hand, there is onomasiological, or name, change in which the meaning remains the same but the word used to denote that meaning changes. Name and meaning changes, however, tend to occur in tandem, particularly when the lexicon as a whole is considered and not just one form or concept. Semasiological change is beyond the scope of the present study. As noted above, it is best discussed in a qualitative in-depth analysis using more psychological evidence than is available in the current database. The remainder of this section will be concerned with onomasiological change.

Most efforts by historical linguists in the area of lexical change have been in constructing taxonomies to describe the types of change undergone by specific words in the history of various languages. More work has been done on the implementation of new words and new uses of words than on loss of older terms. Stern (1931), Bréal (1964), and Ullmann (1962) describe the processes of nomination, borrowing, shortening, and metaphor, along with a host of author-specific taxonomic terms for various other mechanisms of lexical change. The rest of this chapter will be concerned with labeling the types of lexical changes that occur and noting the structural motivation underlying some of them. Thus it will be both an application of and an investigation of some of the concepts and questions proposed in the historical paradigm. Certain referents may be more or less likely to undergo name changes by virtue of the semantic field to which they belong or by the amount of variety in the set of terms used to describe them. Thus, one type of structurally motivated change may be related to the number of different words that refer to the same concept. This topic will be addressed in this section, while the question about the link between semantic field, or type of referent, and change will be examined in the next chapter.

Lexical and semantic change can be linguistically classified along several different parameters. Two types that have structural ramifications are semantic split and semantic merger. In these cases, the semantic range of a particular word is either extended or restricted. A semantic split occurs when two or more concepts embedded in one lexical form acquire their own separate words. Semantic restriction may result from a split when one or both of the new words denotes a narrower range of the original meaning. The term *loft* previously was used to refer to the upper level of either a house or a barn. It declined in the usage meaning 'attic' as its meaning was restricted. *Seed*, while still a general term, is no longer used to refer to seeds in peaches and cherries, but has been replaced by *pit* in that context. *Curd* has been narrowed in meaning so that it does not mean 'cottage cheese', but refers to the thick particles in cottage cheese. Meanings that were formerly subsumed under the term *rheumatism* are now divided between *neuritis* (not frequent enough to show up as new in the analysis), *bursitis*, and *arthritis*, with the latter frequently anthropomorphized as *Arthur-itis* (see Appendix 4 for commentary).

Semantic merger occurs when two or more formerly lexically distinct meanings are subsumed under one form. This seems to occur typically when detailed knowledge about a field is lost, so that distinctions are blurred, as in *peaches* in place of separate terms for freestone and clingstone varieties, *turtle* for species that live both in the water and on land (coinciding with a decline in *terrapin* for the land-based, inedible one), an increase in use of the simplex *hen* and concomitant decrease in *setting hen*, and the use of *kindling* to mean both 'lightwood' and other kinds of material used to kindle a fire. Semantic extension may be a result of a merger of the meanings of two forms or it may entail incorporation of an entirely new, but hitherto unacknowledged concept or feature. Thus *frying pan* now encompasses the electric version, and *siding* can now be made of aluminum or vinyl.

When metaphorical and metonymic uses become embedded in the lexicon, semantic extension results. If a particular metaphor is used often enough, the word used as vehicle may take on certain predicates of the topic. The comparison could then be literally true for the speakers, and the words would become synonymous. For example, if the words *hum* and *bawl* are extended metaphorically from human sounds to cow sounds to become the most common way of designating such sounds, they are no longer metaphorical: the equation "*moo* is like *hum*" becomes "*moo* equals *hum*". Simultaneously, the original meaning may fade from the language or become specialized while the derived meaning becomes the most common. The two meanings then split into homophonous words that are only minimally related. Two examples are found in the second data set: *den* (family room) and *kid* (child). On the other hand, the word may retain its metaphorical sense if the new usage remains secondary to the original meaning, e.g. *threatening* for 'clouding up'.

Sometimes the effect of change is increased iconicity, e.g. *chest of drawers* as opposed to the older form *bureau*, and *driveway* rather than *avenue* or *lane*. The principle of simplification as a natural process of language change, here by increasing transparency of meaning, does not always apply. Sometimes the new terms are less iconic, e.g., *cobbler* versus the older *family pie*, and replacement of *waiter* with the latinate (wedding) *attendant*. Other transparent terms that have declined in use are *spew* for 'vomit' and *falling weather* for rain or snow. Euphemism and dysphemism also play a role in vocabulary change, as in *dish cloth* for *dish rag* and *boogey man* for *devil*.

Structural relations within the lexicon may also effect changes. In such cases, change in vocabulary helps avoid confusion, as in *vest* rather than the older term *jacket*. *Breakfast bacon* as a compound was structurally required by the earlier use of *bacon* to refer to the unsliced cut of meat cooked with beans rather than the sliced, leaner portion of it eaten with eggs. A decline in usage for one referent allowed the shortened form to appear for the other object. Such ellipsis of compounds or phrases that commonly occur together may lead to semantic narrowing, as the surviving member of the compound takes on the full semantic meaning of just one of the previous senses and thus loses generality. *Baby carriage*, a metaphorical extension, was shortened as horse-drawn carriages disappeared and *carriage* was less likely to be misinterpreted, allowing more ambiguity. Shortening also occurred in *mantel(-piece)* and *(school) teacher*.

Due to the semasiological emphasis of most studies of the lexicon, many researchers have discussed the concept of "polysemy" (one word with many meanings), but few have explored the situation of "multiple synonymy" (one meaning to many words). Anttila (1972) implies that this situation is the primary cause for loss of vocabulary, so that when concepts have an excessive number of words that can be used to describe them, the set of synonyms becomes too crowded and some of them drop out of use. Table 26 below attempts to demonstrate the relationship between change and the amount of variation exhibited by a linguistic variable. It compares the average number of responses per question (from the earlier data set) for questions producing responses that were shown to be either old or new. If the above theory is correct, referents with large numbers of words to describe them should correlate with a loss of vocabulary, i.e., they should include variants that were verified as old. At the same time, one would expect to find that questions with a small number of responses might gain vocabulary, i.e., include variants documented as new.

Table 26: Lexical change and number of responses per question

	Average number of responses in 1930s	
All questions	6.7	n=150
Questions with no old or new variants	5.5	n=30
Questions with one old variant	6.3	n=84
Questions with two old variants	7.7	n=17
Questions with three old variants	12.6	n=9
Questions with one new variant	7.2	n=51
Questions with two new variants	7.0	n=14
Questions with three new variants	7.0	n=1
Questions with five new variants	7.0	n=1

The data show that, indeed, old lexical items are found in larger than average sets of terms for a single referent. The increase in the size of the sets of words as the number of older terms increases lends credence to the "lexical crowding" principle. The fact that the amount of variation shown by linguistic variables that have acquired new variants is greater than the amount shown by those with no new or old variants may be due to cases where the newer term was already present in the 1930s, though it gained in frequency by 1990.

The size of the set of words used to refer to the same concept is larger for questions that exhibit group-based variation as well. Table 27 shows the average number of responses per question for both data sets based on whether or not any of the responses showed social or regional variation.

Table 27: Lexical variation and number of responses per question

	Average number of responses		
	1930s	1990	n
All questions	6.7	9.4	150
Questions with no social/regional variation	5.8	7.6	49
Questions with variation in data set 1	7.7	9.5	70
Questions with variation in data set 2	6.3	10.4	54

For both the 1930s and the 1990 data, questions without variants linked to non-linguistic categories had the fewest responses per question. The items that showed variation in the earlier data set had a higher number of responses in that data set. Those questions that had responses connected to social or regional groups in 1990 produced more responses in the 1990 interviews. Although further statistical validation of these patterns is needed, these results seem to suggest that when there are a greater number of choices available to speakers, some of these alternatives are free to become marked for use by a particular group.

* * * * *

This chapter has explored a number of aspects of linguistic change, from structural descriptions of lexical change to its degree of association with particular groups. Vocabulary is constantly in a state of flux, with many words being lost and gained during the span of an average lifetime. The rapidity of change is especially evident in such cases as *bakery bread*, which was more common among younger speakers in the 1930s. When its overall use then is compared to its occurrence in 1990, it is shown to be old already. Likewise, *electric storm* did not occur at all among the earlier speakers, but was mostly used by old people in 1990. Changes in the lexicon may be influenced by a change in relationships between words in a set or by differential usage by social group. They may also be associated with cultural change. Ties between vocabulary and culture will be examined in Chapter 4.

4

Culture and the Lexicon

The lexicon of a language tells the story of the culture of those who speak the language. Jaberg and Jud, who came to the United States to train fieldworkers for the Linguistic Atlas of the U.S. and Canada project (of which LAMSAS is a part), were proponents of a research interest focused on *Wörter und Sachen*, or words and things, that was rooted in the relationship between language and culture. Linguists have long realized the importance of the connection between language and culture. Schuchardt said that "Alle Genealogie müß sich in Kulturgeschichte umsetzen" (All genealogy translates itself into cultural history), and Grimm noted that "Unsere Sprache ist auch unsere Geschichte" (Our language is also our history) (Wagner, forthcoming [1920]). Finally, as Johnson says in the preface to his 1755 dictionary (1979, cited in Aitchison 1991): "As any custom is disused, the words that expressed it must perish with it; as any opinion grows popular, it will innovate speech in the same proportion as it alters practice."

The present study offers a description of the vocabulary of the southeastern United States from two different eras of the twentieth century. Social, demographic, and technological changes between these two periods in time that have contributed to lexical change and variation will be described below. Cultural forces determine the strength of associations between words and particular social and regional groups. Changes in material culture, in lifestyles, and in institutions have led to losses and gains in the lexicon.

The region has changed from one that was predominantly rural, with an economy based almost solely on agriculture, to one with a majority of its population in urban areas. According to Daniel 1986, in 1900 only 18 percent of Southerners lived in urban areas, compared to 40 percent of the nation as a whole. In contrast, urban residents made up

56 percent of the Southern population in the 1990 Census. Women now participate in the workforce and other areas of public life that were closed to them at the beginning of the century, and African Americans continue to struggle for a "second chance at reconstruction" (Daniel 1986). While full equality has not yet been achieved, many barriers have fallen, barriers that were imposed on all areas of society by legally mandated racial segregation. Public education was virtually unknown in the Southeast prior to this century. A revolution in transportation and communication technology has affected the daily lives of the entire population.

This century has been one of unprecedented change in the world and in this part of the United States. Of all the linguistic levels, vocabulary is the most sensitive to such change since it is tied referentially to the culture. In this and other ways it differs from phonology and grammar. Certain aspects of language, such as its property of being rule-governed, are difficult to study with lexical evidence, while other features, such as its referential function, are ideally suited for analysis via the lexicon. This chapter will begin with a discussion of lexical variables as objects of study. This will be followed by an assessment of the relationship between cultural change and vocabulary change, which serves as the final part of a description of lexical change that was begun in the preceding chapter. The concluding section considers reasons for change in variation patterns by examining demographic trends.

This research project was conceived as an attempt to describe patterns and change in the lexicon. The results of the analysis can now be examined in the light of varying perspectives on language change and cultural change to see which of these best fit the facts. Social and cultural situations that seem promising as plausible explanatory mechanisms for why the language has changed in the ways it has will be explored. In some cases, work by historians can be adduced to verify claims made here, though in other cases ideas are presented that will remain speculative until further research can be undertaken.

The Lexicon as an Object of Study

This study differs from most other sociolinguistic analyses by the choice of lexical items rather than phonological or grammatical features as variables. Lexical items are perceived as behaving in different ways from other levels of language, and as being less amenable to structural analysis (e.g., Kurath 1972:25). The lexicon is different in several ways.

For example, speakers can freely acquire new vocabulary throughout their lifetimes, and they may be more aware of lexical choices than of phonological or syntactic ones.

The ongoing process of vocabulary acquisition by speakers of a language was discussed in the previous chapter as a possible factor influencing the relationship of change in real time to change in apparent time. New words may be acquired simultaneously by people of different ages to an extent that does not seem to be true of phonological differences. Chambers (1992:679) found that in dialect acquisition "lexical replacements are acquired faster than pronunciation and phonological variants". The following section on culture and changes in the vocabulary will further explore the question of whether the lexicon is more open than other levels of language to influence from language contact experience that does not involve speaker interaction, such as television. If so, the distinction may be due to differential acquisition patterns.

Vocabulary is perhaps more available for conscious reflection by speakers than are grammatical processes or pronunciation differences. This is evidenced by the way people will often hesitate in the middle of a conversation to try to find the right word (but usually not the right sound) to use. The introduction of new words into the community is often noticed and commented upon. As discussed in later sections, lexical items can also be marked as taboo. Taboo words are socially stigmatized because of their referent or the force they carry as a speech act. However, words rarely are subject to stigmatization based upon a stereotypical association with the speech of lower status social groups (Wolfram 1991a:45). Further evidence will be needed to determine whether lexical items are inherently less subject to stigmatization and, if so, why. One possibility that must be addressed is whether lexical variation is less socially and regionally stratified than other types of linguistic differences. Less stratification could contribute to fewer stigmatized forms. This study does show that only a small amount of the variety in the lexicon is due to demographic divisions, though more might be explained by semantic differences, local norms, or even individual preference. The relative infrequency of variation based on demographic variables may be attributable in part to the stringent statistical requirements for proving the existence of differences based on non-linguistic variables, though it is probably due to the inclusion of questionnaire items without regard to whether they exhibited previously determined patterned variation, as noted in Chapter Two. In any case, comparable evidence for the percent of grammatical variation that may be attributable to the variables studied here is not available. Bernstein's (1993) study, which explained about the same percentage of variation as this one, was based on phonological variables. Though these are more often stigmatized than lexical features, they are not as often subject to negative social evaluation as are grammatical features.

Awareness of lexical difference without stigmatization may be a contributory factor in the blurring of group distinctions. Thus, items appropriate to various styles may have been freely offered by speakers during the interviews. The data used in this study were all collected in a similar informal interview context, so the use of both casual and more formal terms by the same speaker is not the result of switching between different social situations or verbal tasks. What did happen, however, is that informants would offer forms used in many contexts with the understanding that the fieldworker would know that they were not always appropriate for any situation. The speakers knew that the fieldworker was interested in language, though an emphasis on content often minimized this focus. People find vocabulary interesting and so would often offer up all the forms they knew, even if that meant using some they considered dialectal. Sometimes informants would note that they themselves did not use a term but they had heard it elsewhere, as a way of distancing themselves from nonstandard items, but just as often they would explicitly state that, even though they knew it, they would not use the standard term in everyday speech. (If the term was clearly reported as heard from others, it was considered doubtful and not included in the compilations for analysis.)

Some questionnaire referents are mostly a part of private home life rather than a matter for public or printed discussion. For this reason, a local term may be used by all social classes rather than its Standard English equivalent known only from literary contexts, e.g. *lot* instead of *barnyard,* and *cur dog* or *feist* for *mongrel*. Usually there will be one or more variants that are in general use throughout the U.S. alongside others that are less frequent and/or limited to particular stylistic usage or use by certain geographical or social groups. Often, a speaker would offer both types of words. McDavid (1979 [1951]:219) said about the vocabulary of New York state that: "All Americans have in common most of their grammar and vocabulary, even when dealing with the simple things of everyday life that are learned from contacts within one's own community rather than from books . . . Even if some other local term is most frequently used in the community, the general term is recognized."

The inclusion of many non-public words in the questionnaire highlights one feature the lexicon shares with pronunciation: that regionally marked items can occur in the speech even of the upper social classes. The study of such words has at times, however, brought ridicule to dialectologists. Some of the vocabulary items found in a linguistic atlas are indeed marginal, purposefully so. Research into language variation, as opposed to the search for language universals, focuses on differences in language, not on similarities. That is one reason for studying actual speech rather than abstracted models. This search for differences is the basis for many of the items found on a linguistic atlas questionnaire that seem marginal. The theory is that words that are not used often in the public domain, but that remain within the home or local community only, will show a multiplicity of local variants. Many terms listed in a linguistic atlas are not often found in the newspaper, much less in scholarly treatises. This is not to say that they are not used much in everyday life. Words for 'andirons', 'bullfrogs', and 'dragonflies' may not be a frequent part of modern and/or urban speech, but what of 'pants', 'children', and 'living room'?

Studies in the field of traditional dialectology have received a great deal of criticism for focusing on the petty task of word collecting. In the variationist marketplace, it would seem that not much linguistic profit (Butters 1989a and 1989b) is to be gained from the study of lexical items, as the dominant paradigm in language variation studies is concerned almost exclusively with sound change. Linguists have generally tended to regard content words as unworthy of study as part of language, preferring to study the phonological components of words or the behavior of function words and morphemes. The great majority of the lexicon, if studied at all, is usually only studied for the combinatorial aspects which determine how words may be used in a sentence. Lexical meaning, because of its close relationship inwardly to thought and outwardly to culture, is often considered outside the realm of linguistics, and its study relegated to philosophy, psychology, literary criticism, and anthropology.

This view has arisen from a structuralist framework that views paradigmatic relations between grammatical functions and systems of vowels and consonants as paramount. Its proponents, as Doe (1988) contends, seek primarily to explain mental processes through the workings of language systems. Vocabulary items, being less systematic in their relations to one another, thus seem of little importance. In truth, the overlapping possibilities for choosing a particular lexical item from a semantic set and the many still-unknown factors, many of them admittedly extralinguistic, influencing this choice provide fascinating opportunities for study. As Guy puts it (1988:38), "language is quintessentially a social product and a social tool, and our understanding of any tool will be immeasurably enhanced by a knowledge of its makers and users and uses". The fact that the choice of words seems to defy the type of rules linguists have been able to define makes the lexicon even more intriguing. As Butters (1989:184) suggests, to label an item of little importance in defining a dialect based solely on the fact that it is not part of a phonological or grammatical system is a questionable practice that may result from a narrow perspective focusing on certain aspects of language to the exclusion of others. Kurath found that the lexical isoglosses that geographically divide groups of speakers are essentially in agreement with the morphological and phonological differences, and thus of equal value in determining dialect boundaries, at least in the Eastern United States (1972:38).

As noted in the introduction to this chapter, vocabulary exhibits closer ties to culture than other language features. This close connection between words and things is one reason linguists have viewed the lexicon as marginal. In order to talk about vocabulary change it is necessary to talk about cultural change, and this necessity does not fit in well with the goals of "autonomous linguistics" (Newmeyer 1986). New objects of material culture require new words. New concepts and lifestyle choices also require new words, or new uses for old ones. As knowledge of certain domains of life fades, or objects and tools no longer are relevant, words for them disappear. In contrast, the need to express certain grammatical relations will remain, though the means of expressing them may change. This distinguishing aspect of vocabulary can either be viewed as a reason for its dismissal from linguistic inquiry or as an opportunity to build bridges between linguistics and other disciplines such as anthropology, sociology, and history. These fields all study aspects of human behavior that find expression in the lexicon. It is not easy to step outside of a particular area of specialization to bring in insights from other disciplines. It is difficult to judge the reliability of evidence without having a solid foundation of knowledge in the field; misinterpretation is more likely. Yet sociolinguists are beginning to realize that they need to collaborate with social theorists, psychologists, historians, and others in looking for explanatory principles for linguistic behavior. This was a recurrent theme among papers presented at the second conference on Language Variation in the South (1993, cf. Bailey, in press) and it continues to be an issue for feminists (Coates 1993) and creolists

(Mufwene, e.g. 1986). The following sections attempt to incorporate information from demographers and historians in discussing some of the factors contributing to lexical change.

Cultural Change and Lexical Change

The context for language change includes a real-world system of meanings as they are constructed through perceptual experiences and the language used by the community. The term "culture" here will encompass institutions, artifacts, and the body of knowledge about these and other aspects of the world shared by a group of people. Artifacts and customs and the terms associated with them may be borrowed or they may arise as innovations within a society. Semantic change by nomination is simply the coining of a new word when a concept either stands for a new invention or has just gained enough cultural importance to deserve its own place in the lexicon. The rise and decline of institutions such as the family farm, the mass media, and the educational system may also lead to expansion and depletion of vocabulary.

This section will examine four influential areas of cultural change and the types of lexical change associated with each: technology, economy, education, and information changes. Cognitive change occurs together with other types of change. The lexicon of a social or regional dialect both reflects and helps preserve certain ways of thinking about the world which may be cultural in nature. Lakoff 1987 claims that lexical meaning is embodied in experiential networks of "idealized cognitive models". These ICMs structure our concepts of the world and thus are a way of describing what "words" mean by delimiting which objects can appropriately be designated by which terms. A number of other researchers have also explored the concept of cultural models as revealed by language, cf. the seminal work of Sapir (1951) and Whorf (1956), and the collection of papers edited by Holland and Quinn (1987). Cultural or cognitive models for categories and prototypes are encoded in the lexicon, which changes as our understanding of the world changes. The vocabulary offers clues about how speakers conceptualize the world (especially reflected in metaphorical usage as described in Lakoff and Johnson 1980 and G. Miller 1978), how they organize their knowledge (Rosch, Mervis, Gray, Johnson, and Boyes-Braem 1975), and how deep their knowledge goes in specific areas (Berlin 1972). The methodology of the present study does not provide sufficient detailed information on cognitive processes of speakers to do a thorough analysis of cultural models in any detail, but the possiblity does exist for further work in this area with some of the vocabulary items discussed below.

Technology. Urbanization, industrialization, and technological advances have produced changes in occupation and in the implements used in the workplace and the home, which have led to changes in vocabulary. Most of the words used more frequently in the 1930s (e.g., *privy, doubletree* and many others; see Appendix 3) have declined in use due to such change. Questions about items related to farming, in particular, more frequently elicited 'No Response' in the 1990 interviews, as the number of farms in the South declined from 2.1 million in 1950 to 722,000 in 1975 (Daniel:221). Thus, as familiarity with farming declined, the number of speakers who admitted to lexical gaps in that domain increased. Table 28 lists all the linguistic variables that elicited 'No Response' more frequently in 1990. Thirty-two questions yielded 'No Response' more often in Johnson's interviews, as compared to only two questions where Lowman recorded 'No Response' more often (Table 29).

Table 28: Questions with 'No Response' occurring more frequently in 1990

6. window shades	58. (wagon) tongue
12. wardrobe (furniture)	59. (buggy) shafts
13. attic	60. singletree
17. pantry	61. doubletree
18. clabber	68. calve
19. cottage cheese (homemade)	69. ram
23. calls to cows in pasture	71. stallion
24. calls to calves	72. fowls
28. direction to mule (left)	90. mush
29. direction to mule (right)	103. haslet
31. calls to sheep	105. (cherry) stone
40. valley (of roof)	107. clingstone peach
42. corn crib	108. freestone peach
44. cowpen	127. dragonfly
48. rail fence	176. county seat
52. grindstone	177. Civil War

Table 29: Questions with 'No Response' occurring more frequently in the 1930s

    4. lightwood   130. toadstool

'No Response' answers are clearly related to the semantic field to which an item belongs and the amount of knowledge of that field possessed by different groups. The relationships between groups with varying lexical competence within the data sets will be discussed further in the section on culture and variation.

The type of referent may thus have an effect on whether change is more or less likely. Anttila (1972:139) addresses this issue in a discussion of taboo words. He thought that these words would be more susceptible to change due to a tendency toward replacement by euphemisms. Table 30 lists five types of questions along with the percentage of questions in each category with at least one response that exhibited a statistically significant amount of change.

Table 30: Percent of questions by type of referent that show diachronic change

	Old	New
Common (known to all infs., n=81)	74%	53%
Obsolete (in 1990, n=17)	88%	18%
Agricultural/Rural only (in 1990, n=24)	79%	33%
Taboo (in addition to other categories, n=12)	75%	50%
None of the above (n=28)	61%	46%
All referents (n=150)	74%	45%

Examples of "common" referents are *bacon* and *coffin*, i.e., items that all informants in both data sets would have the opportunity to experience. Obsolete items (e.g., calls to sheep [no longer raised in the Southeast], *serenade*) are archaic from the perspective of the 1990 speakers and may have already been in decline by the 1930s. Agricultural/rural terms (e.g., *lines* and *corn crib*) are those that likely would not be known by speakers in urban areas in 1990, though some, like a call to chickens, would have been known in cities as well as rural areas in the

1930s. The taboo items are words for 'bastard', 'boar', 'bull', 'calve', 'pregnant', 'privy', 'ram', 'stallion', 'woodpecker', 'vomit', 'die', and 'devil'. A number of these, especially words for male animals, are no longer taboo, but they may have been years ago (cf. *gentleman cow*). Some questionnaire items do not belong to any of these categories. They would not have been familiar to all informants, but not because of being obsolete or rural. *Gutters*, for example, were not part of all houses. Cherries were rarely grown or sold in the area, so that many informants did not know the term for a cherry stone.

Just 50 percent of the taboo items yielded new words, as compared to 53 percent of the commonly known items. Seventy-five percent of the taboo questions produced terms that were going out of use, compared to the average of 74 percent. Thus the data do not support Anttila's claim, although there are too few taboo items in the questionnaire to make any strong conclusions about them. Table 31, which gives the average number of different words produced for each type of question, does seem to show a difference for taboo terms. Taboo referents show the greatest variety of words due to the cultural need for euphemisms for these concepts.

Table 31: Average number of variants by type of referent

	1930s	1990
All referents (n=150)	6.7	9.4
Common (known to all infs., n=81)	7.0	10.3
Obsolete (in 1990, n=17)	5.2	6.8
Agricultural/Rural only (in 1990, n=24)	7.4	9.0
Taboo (in addition to other categories, n=12)	9.3	14.8
None of the above (n=28)	6.4	8.8

The only type of referent clearly related to the amount of change it displays is the type that refers to things that are obsolete. These questions have high numbers of old variants, and few new ones. The study purposely included such questions because they were likely to exhibit diachronic variation. Items of recent introduction could not be included for comparison, since they would not have been part of the Linguistic Atlas worksheets. While technological change has had a wide-ranging effect on the vocabulary in terms of loss of words, its impact on new vocabulary cannot be fully documented from this study because of the orientation toward the past. Some of the words that have increased in frequency due to change in cultural artifacts and institutions include *den, electrical storm, stroller, bursitis,* five terms for wedding attendants, and *reception. Den* is related to change in housing design, and *stroller* to difference in design of the product. *Bursitis* comes with access to health care and medical terminology, and *electrical storm* is used by the first generations to have electric power in their homes. The wedding terms have come into the lexicon with the spread into the middle class of nuptial ceremonial traditions previously observed only by the wealthy. Innovations of this type are similar to those described in the next section, which looks at the introduction of new terms through commercialization.

Economy. The change from a relatively self-sufficient agricultural economy to one involving enormously increased trade in goods and services has produced changes in the lexicon. Prior to modern grocery stores, customers made a list of things they wanted, which were then brought to them by clerks; they often did not look through the items themselves. Commercialization of products, and familiarity with labels and advertising of items sold nationwide, has brought a loss of regionally marked vocabulary in favor of standardized terms. The following items have decreased in usage due to such influence: *britches; sewee beans; shallots; press peach, plum peach,* and *soft peach; pinders; battercakes, flitters,* and *slapjacks; weatherboarding; dish rag;* and *curds* and *clabber cheese. Dish cloth, siding,* and *peach* are now more common. This type of influence is probably strongest for items that are packaged and labeled at central locations and shipped across the country (though this study includes few of these) and weaker for merchandise that is not packaged with labels (clothing, furniture), or that is packaged or labelled locally (produce, meats).

Education. Adequate funding for a public school system in Georgia was not established until 1951 (Bartley 1990:206). This fact speaks to the amazing amount of change in access to education that took place during the century. The median amount of education for the population in Georgia was 12.2 years in 1980, a figure that represents an increase of 5.1 years over the median for 1940 (Bachtel and Boatright 1992). The influence of education, especially at the college level, on loss of regionally marked variants will be discussed at some length in the next section. Borrowing can also be a result of education, not only due to increased linguistic contact with classmates and teachers from different backgrounds, but because of introduction of vocabulary in textbooks and other teaching materials. The list of terms in Appendix 3 that are currently used more often is mostly made up of words that are used throughout the United States, e.g. *living room, illegitimate child,* and *cornbread.* More detailed etymological work will be required to distinguish borrowings from innovations, but there are many that probably did not originate in the South. Of the 87 newer terms, 20 are discussed in the *Word Geography.* According to Kurath's description of them, twelve seem to be borrowings. *Toilet, outhouse,* and *bellow* are from New England. From Pennsylvania come *kindling* and *chipmunk. School gets out* was previously a local expression confined to New York City. *Bacon* and *burlap bag* were words from the North and North Midland, as were *wishbone, skunk, moo,* and *Merry Christmas,* but Kurath perceptively noted that these latter were spreading into the South and, more specifically, that *moo* and *Merry Christmas* were used by younger speakers in the South. Thus we have information on further changes in apparent time that were confirmed by the comparison between the 1930s and 1990.

Greater access to education may add to an individual's vocabulary while not in itself motivating a loss of dialect terms. As noted in Chapters Two and Three, the total number of words collected in the interviews showed a substantial (40 percent) increase, from 1007 to 1402, while the number of responses per question per informant remained constant for both fieldworkers. Speakers used more different vocabulary items, with an average of 9.4 different responses for each linguistic variable in 1990, compared to the 6.7 average variants per question from the LAMSAS data set. Two major cultural forces may explain this vocabulary increase. The first is exposure to new words from reading, made possible by improved literacy rates, and from exposure to new words from the mass media, discussed below. The second important factor will be discussed in the final section. It involves increased opportunities for language contact between strangers and casual acquaintances, as opposed to lifelong acquaintances and friends within a close-knit community.

Information. People are bombarded today by an unprecedented quantity of information. There were 77 radio stations in the South in 1928 compared to some 3000 in 1948 (Wilson and Ferris 1989:3.173, 175). In 1980, the region had 32 percent of the nation's television stations, 350 of them (ibid., 176), and broadcasts from numerous stations across the country can now be received via cable and satellite. "Multiplex" movie theaters abound in the suburbs, while even the smallest rural hamlets boast a video rental store. Mass communications technology is a powerful cultural agent. Linguists cannot afford to disregard it simply because of misguided statements by popular writers that exaggerate its importance as a linguistic influence. There has been a certain amount of controversy over the influence of the mass media on dialects. Common wisdom says that the more Americans hear the same broadcasters on TV and radio, the more they will begin to sound like these journalists and thus like one another. Linguists have disputed this idea (cf. Kurath 1949: 9 and Chambers 1993), claiming that speech is influenced much more by conversing than by listening. This seems to be true for phonetic differences, since regional differences persist even among the more educated classes, though television has been in common use for over half a century. At the same time, the lexicon may be more susceptible to passive influence than other parts of language, due to the continual, often conscious, learning of new vocabulary that can come from many sources. Little serious research into the effect of mass media on language has been done; rather, students of language variation have used the persistence of difference as an indirect argument against the pervasiveness of media influence.

Like words learned in school, vocabulary learned from movies, television, and radio may be supplemental rather than replacive. (The word in the 1990 set most likely to have come from television is *giddy up*.) It will be difficult to design a research project to assess the impact of mass media on the lexicon, since most new terms that could have been learned from television, for example, could also come from numerous other sources as well. Standard American English terms are constantly available for acquisition all around us, from labels on containers of food and beverages to magazines, newspapers, and billboards, as well as from the speech of teachers, broadcasters, and various people encountered as a part of daily life. If education can be a way of introducing new words into speakers' vocabularies, educational television operates under the assumption that it can serve a similar purpose. A survey of the Algeos' "Among the New Words" columns in *American Speech* reveals a number of words that were first noticed on television or radio, among them *acid jeans, bungee jumping, dramedy, key* and *power* (as adjectives), and *spin* (referring to a public relations ploy). Literature from marketing research might be a fruitful source of information about how new words are presented to the public through advertising.

The mass media may not contribute as much to a loss of regional- and social-based variation patterns as to a general acquisition of new lexical items. These new terms may not display an orderly distribution based on non-linguistic variables to the extent that words learned from interaction with one's peers, neighbors, family, and colleagues do. That is, the model of linguistic innovation, as starting in one social group and then moving to others over a period of time, may be circumvented by words introduced through the media. In this way, education and the media lead indirectly to a decline in the amount of variation that can be linked to particular groups relative to the number of different words in use. This conclusion only fits if all media are equally accessible and influential for all groups, but this is not always the case. To provide some stereotypical examples of differential acceptance of words, younger people may be more influenced by the lyrics of the latest popular musicians and MTV lingo, and rural males may pick up more of the jargon of commentators on stock-car races. Insofar as commercial labels, media, education, and technological changes affect all parts of a society to the same extent, changes in culture, cognition, and language that reflect these changes will not be linked to distinct social groups. In reality, different groups have differential access to technology and education and are affected by different aspects of commercial and other information, so that while group-based lexical differences may have declined during the twentieth century, it is unlikely they will disappear anytime soon. Although fewer regionally-based variants were found in 1990, it does not seem likely that linguistic variation will vanish in favor of a homogenous American English, or even Southern English. The number of lexical choices available seems to be growing; such growth allows room for tremendous diversification.

Society and Language Variation

The amount of variation attributable to various demographic variables may change as the distance (social or geographical) between groups increases or decreases. Diffusion of linguistic change is thus affected by the amount of contact between groups of speakers. This principle is of great importance for dialectological and sociolinguistic research, yet, as noted in Chambers 1992 (673), variationists have not often explicitly studied the particular mechanisms of how language contact effects change (though cf. Payne 1980 and Chambers 1992 for studies of dialect acquisition by residents who have moved into a community from elsewhere). This seems to be changing, led especially by the Milroys' work. J. Milroy's book, *Linguistic Variation and Change* (1992a), attempts to trace the path of language change through an analysis of the speech of individuals and the people they interact with. To explore these contacts, he utilizes the sociological concepts of social networks and the strong and weak ties within and between them.

This approach signals a change in the sociolinguistic tradition of linking change to social prestige. Prestige is problematic as an explanatory mechanism because it subjectively means different things to different people and can lead to contradictory role models. For example, according to Reed 1986 (77), the regional social types with the greatest appeal to the white middle class in the South are the "lady" (of aristocratic origin) and the "good old boy" (from yeoman farmers). Prestige is essentially a psychological construct that cannot be easily applied to increase and decrease of difference between social and regional groups. The discussion of groups of speakers and their changing relationships to one another presented in this chapter is not in terms of prestige but is more in the spirit of Milroy's model of change, though at a macro- rather than his micro-level of analysis. He summarizes the difference between the two approaches as follows (1992a:175):

> The model of the innovator that I shall propose differs in many ways from Labov's characterization. It is not based primarily on the idea of prestige, or on the operation of prestige in the social class dimension, but on the rather different model of *speech community* that I have been explaining in this book. This model is based on the strength of social ties that can exist between individuals, and innovation is conceived of as passing through relatively weak ties. The model is therefore less personalized than Labov's model appears to be: it is not so much about a kind of person as about the kind of links that exist between persons, and between groups of persons.

Weak ties are more numerous than strong ties and are those which obtain between casual acquaintances (people encountered in daily interactions who are not a part of a close-knit group). Close ties inhibit change by maintaining existing speech patterns, while weak ties form bridges between groups that allow borrowing to take place. The opportunities for, and obstacles to, forming strong and weak ties have changed in the southeastern U.S. during the years spanned by this survey.

Table 7, reproduced from Chapter 2, shows the percent of lexical variants that can be linked to each non-linguistic variable. It is shown here as a reference for a discussion on changing patterns of variation. Given the decline in the number of variants that show a link to a social or regional group, there is really very little change. Only the variable "region", denoting the geographic divisions into coastal, piedmont, and mountain areas, showed a robust change in its pronounced decline in importance. Of the words used in the 1930s interviews, 6.35 percent were linked to region, as opposed to only 1.45 percent of the terms used in 1990. The effects of rurality and education also declined, from associations with 4.51 and 4.10 percent of this subset of vocabulary to 2.89 percent each. With the demographic changes that have occurred, especially regarding the roles of women and African Americans in society, it would seem that the variables "sex" and "race" would have changed as well, thus the lack of change bears explaining here.

Table 7: Percentage of variants linked to each non-linguistic variable

	1930s	1990
Number of Variants Tested	488	484
Region	6.35	1.45
Rurality	4.51	2.89
Education	4.10	2.89
Race	2.66	2.89
Age	2.05	2.69
Sex	1.43	1.65

The rest of this chapter is dedicated to a discussion of each of the social and regional categories. For each category, the question of language contact will be explored, i.e., whether contact between groups has increased or decreased. If rurality, for example, has become a less polarizing distinction as revealed by the linguistic data, what cultural factors have contributed to its declining influence? Since the effect of race has remained the same, what does this say about contact between members of different races? What would a knowledge of demographic history lead one to expect in the way of change in linguistic variation? The assumption, then, following a theoretical model of change and variation based on language contact, is that if there is less contact between groups this will show up as an increase in differential language use. Likewise, if the importance of a category within a society diminishes, and social distance along with it, linguistic associations tied to groups of speakers divided on the basis of that category will become fewer. Multiple causality is not ruled out here by the focus on contact as an explanatory principle. Certain groups of people may be associated with particular words due to cultural reasons other than limited contact opportunities. Examples of factors that can influence the use of specific terms will be covered in each subsection. All the terms that were linked to social and regional groups are listed in Appendix 2.

Sex. Though there has been a tremendous change in women's roles and occupations between 1930 and 1990, the gap between men's and women's lexicons has not changed, with seven variants linked to sex in the 1930s and eight in 1990. Common sense would dictate that as females enter occupations, political positions, etc., that were formerly reserved for males only, their speech would more closely approximate that of men. This may eventually be the case, but it is not yet apparent.

Sexually integrated workplaces are still not the norm, and those professions that include both genders have only done so recently. In fact, though women entered the (paid) workforce in large numbers both during World War II and since 1970, they have mostly worked in jobs with other women or children, such as teaching, clerical and sales positions, or in private households (Bartley 1990:183). Even in industrial occupations, women have been consigned to the more menial tasks (Wilson and Ferris 1989:4.428), and some industries employ men almost exclusively (e.g., lumber and pulpwood), while others employ many women (e.g., textiles and poultry). Contact between sexes in the workplace remained limited during most of the twentieth century, with little if any increase due to industrialization and urbanization. It should be noted that even in an agricultural economy, women were participating in the workforce. In 1920, 90 percent of black sharecropper (tenant-farmer) women along with 67 percent of white tenant women and 40 percent of white land-owning women worked in the fields some of the time (Wilson and Ferris

1989:4.427). For the most part, however, women and men remain segregated socially and at work to some extent and thus the differences in lexicon remain.

Of the fourteen terms that are used more frequently by one sex or the other, only a few are relegated to use by a particular sex because of cultural norms. Taboo restrictions that apply more strictly to women are a factor in women's higher use of *woodpecker*, which, besides being the more standard term, is an alternate to *peckerwood*, sometimes used to refer to a man in a derogatory way by an oblique genital reference. The same cultural rules apply to men's greater use of *stud* for a male horse, one of the very few variants to be associated with the same group in both the 1930s and 1990 data. Light (ms.), in her study of expletives in the LAMSAS data, shows that greater adherence to taboo restrictions does cause differences in women's speech, though most of the other taboo items, e.g. 'bull' and 'bastard', did not show such differentiation.

One term, *living room*, was used more frequently by women and relates to "woman's place" in the household (Lakoff 1973), and one term, *doubletree*, was used more often by men and is indicative of men's greater expertise in the technology of horse-drawn transportation. There were many, many more terms that could have been so divided but were not (like *coverlet, cobbler, fishing worms,* or *grindstone*), indicating less of a gap in knowledge than might have been expected. The relationship of the lexicon to culturally determined realms of experience is clearest for the analysis of 'No Response' answers (cf. Table 17, Chapter 2).

Ten variants tied to sex (e.g., *lightwood* and *named for*) have no obvious cultural motivation other than as markers of sexual identity, in the same way other words can serve as regional markers without being tied to referents found only in a particular region. Some lexical variables thus act in a similar way to phonological variables. Females' pronunciation of /e/ at a different articulatory location from males' pronunciation of the same vowel, to give a hypothetical example, is not caused by biological factors, nor can the specific quality of this vowel be attributed to socialization of female children. The connection between a particular phonological feature and a particular group is accidental (Newmeyer 1986). Thus, it is clear for variables without referential meaning that variation is primarily a carrier of social meaning (Lavandera 1978). For vocabulary items, referential meaning and its ties to cultural roles and events can mean that a particular form is connected with a particular group in a non-arbitrary way. This chapter will focus on such connections to try to clarify the effects of cultural factors on lexical variation and change, but it should be noted, as above, that not all lexical variation is directly motivated by such factors.

Race. The effect of contact on linguistic differences by race is like that for sex; the remarkable progress made in integrating society racially since the 1930s would lead one to believe whites and blacks should be speaking more alike. This is not the case, as 13 words were associated with race in the 1930s and 14 in 1990. The cultural changes, like those involving sex, are probably too recent to show an impact on language variation for the mostly older people interviewed for this study. Real change has occurred that should favor convergence, not divergence, at least in the South, though these results confirm that it continues to be slow in coming.

Rather than a gradual change in racial integration throughout the century, segregation actually became more entrenched as a way of life during the first half of the century. *Brown v. the Board of Education* made segregated educational institutions illegal in 1954, but it was ten years after *Brown* when, with increased bitterness between the races, most school systems in the South took even token steps toward integration (McGill 1992 [1963]). Integration of Georgia schools only really began in earnest in the early 1970s (M. Miller 1978). Racially mixed workplaces have been even slower in coming, and some areas of society, like churches, have hardly become integrated at all, though one poll showed that 82 percent of whites and 84 percent of blacks report that they have entertained a person of another race in their homes (*Atlanta Journal and Constitution*, 1992).

A decline in agriculture began with the invasion of the cotton crop by the boll weevil in the teens and early twenties and was hastened by the failure of small farms during the Depression. This, combined with a climate that fostered violence against African Americans, provided the impetus for many African Americans to migrate northward, encouraged by Northern labor agents. This emigration pattern only began to abate in the 1970s (Wilson and Ferris 1989:1.299). On the farms, blacks and whites, men and women, had worked and lived side by side. Though sexual and racial divisions of labor were fairly rigid, linguistic contact was frequent. With the advent of Social Security, minimum wage laws, other New Deal programs, and increasing industrialization in the South, rural farm workers began moving to the towns and taking "public work" that maintained separation of the races (Daniel 1986:123). Though small towns usually had racially segregated residential patterns, older urban areas and rural areas did not. The suburbanization that began following

World War II was essentially a white demographic movement, increasing polarization in housing (Wilson and Ferris 1989:4.298).

Other social forces, such as the growth of the black middle class, have worked to bring blacks and whites closer together, but only recently. The main trend of racial relations during the century has served to maintain and sometimes increase the distance between the races. Still, the situation is far removed from the one that exists in Northern areas, where African Americans have historically been ghettoized in large, depressed neighborhoods of the inner cities. Contact between the races has always been more common in the South (as noted by McDavid in Kretzschmar et al. 1994) despite Jim Crow laws designed as barriers, due to the higher percentage of African American population and its relative dispersion throughout the geographic area. (This does not include the mountain areas, where some counties have never had black residents.) Race does not have a greater effect on lexical choice than most of the other social variables in this part of the United States.

The use of particular lexical items by certain racial groups involves various cultural considerations. Whites used *doubletree* more often and were more likely to own the two mules requiring its use. Economic considerations may also play a part in use of the book word *midwife* by whites, compared to *granny*, the term used more by blacks, since these women more often served blacks, who had less access to doctors and hospitals. African Americans were later in acquiring modern conveniences such as stoves, hence the use of *spider* for 'frying pan', derived from the version with legs used in a fireplace.

White Southerners have been notoriously xenophobic at times, and may have an exacerbated distrust of strangers remaining from the voter registration drives and other civil rights actions involving outsiders to the region, hence their greater use of *foreigner*, a somewhat derogatory term. Whites are more likely to use the term *mush*, an alternative to the African-derived *cush*. Yams are also of African origin and African Americans continue to be more likely to use the unmarked *potato* for 'sweet potato', more common in the diet of poor people than the *Irish potato* because it is cheaper and more nutritious. *Bridemaid* should probably be considered a phonological or morphological rather than a lexical variant, related to either simplification of consonant clusters in Black Vernacular English or its lack of the possessive [s]. BVE use of *daddy* for 'lover' may provide a structural basis for its greater use for 'father' by whites.

African Americans, as well as females, were more likely to be unable to respond to questions involving obsolete, agriculturally related artifacts. The degree to which white rural males retained the use of archaic terms reflects their previous dominance over the entire social structure. As a result of redistricting mandated by the 1990 census, 1993 was the first time suburban and urban representatives outnumbered rural ones in the Georgia state legislature. A reluctance to embrace language change is an understandable facet of the resistance to giving up power. Kroch 1978 discusses the same phenomenon, an inhibition of language change by those who have a larger investment in maintaining the status quo.

Age. In assessing the degree of contact between age groups, the only prominent trends are those that have led to less contact: institutionalization of the elderly and a possible decline in contact with the extended family. Like the variables sex and race, however, the effect of age on variation has not changed significantly. Frequent linguistic contact between adults of all ages seems to argue against age as a differentiating factor. The most reasonable explanation for variation by age groups is the one that underlies assumptions about language change in apparent time: that age differences mirror diachronic change in the language. Ten words in the 1930s and thirteen in 1990 are linked to age. Eleven of the 23 terms linked to age were also involved in change over time. Some words may have cultural correlates. The remaining words distributed by age may be markers of generational identity if lack of language contact does not play a role in age differences.

Among the lexical items associated with older speakers that reflect cultural change in their lifetimes are: the unmarked *pen* for 'hog pen' (hogs are rarely raised in the region now, with the exception of some commercial operations), *bridles* and *lines* for 'reins' (horseback riding has become almost exclusively a hobby of the rich), *pail* (used in this area mostly in the compound *milk pail*), and *vomick* (likely replaced by the standard variant *vomit* by the influence of education). As for items used more frequently by younger speakers, *bakery bread* in the earlier data has a cultural connection. Attics became less common in newer houses, and the younger speakers' use of the standard term replaces the previously socially-stratified terms *garret* and *loft*. The name *casket* became more common with the advent of the modern rectangular shape, as opposed to the older hexagonal one; it may also have arisen as a euphemism or commercial term. *Sooey* and *here chick* seem anomalous as younger usage, since the practice of keeping farm animals has declined, but they actually reflect a lack of knowledge: *sooey* was originally more common as a term to drive hogs away rather than call them, and *here chick* is a new term which may have been built on the *here kitty* model.

Education. The amount of variation attributable to education has declined from twenty words in the 1930s data to fourteen in 1990. This is a smaller decline than that for region, but large enough to be of interest. Differences in speech that are linked to education may be declining not due to increased contact between educational groups, but rather due to a leveling effect brought on by more educational opportunities for everyone. The number of years of schooling has increased drastically for the entire population during the time interval of this study. Support for public education in the South only began in earnest around 1930 (McGill 1992 [1963]). College graduates and illiterates appear in both Lowman's and Johnson's samples, but the 1990 informants are more clustered in the middle. In order to retain equivalent numbers of speakers in each group, educational groupings for low, middle, and high had to be changed from earlier groups that were based on 1) less than elementary school education, 2) elementary (but not high school) graduates, and 3) high school and college graduates combined, to a grouping scheme of 1) elementary graduates, 2) high school graduates, and 3) college graduates. With compulsory education laws now in effect, a general trend toward leveling of educational differences would be expected to continue. Such laws would not yet have had an impact on the older speakers in this study, since, at least in Georgia, strict laws mandating school attendance did not take effect until the 1940s (Bartley 1990:155). Some linguistic variation based on educational differences will continue, however, because differences in access to higher education remain, though years of schooling have increased for everyone.

Diminishing differences in educational attainment are also linked to the increasing size of the Southern middle class, especially after World War II (Wilson and Ferris 1989:4.229). For the LAMSAS informants, information on wealth or income and ownership of goods and property as socioeconomic indicators is not sufficiently available to be used as a classifying mechanism. Occupations are given for each speaker, but the most common, farmer, gives no indication of social class. One variable we can use as an approximation of class is education. The LAMSAS category of "cultivated" informants is directly tied to a high level of social status (usually, though not always, indicative of wealth), and all such speakers fall into the highest educational group in this analysis.

Some terms used more often by the middle and highest education groups were likely a direct result of their schooling. Other words, also more standard or used throughout the United States, are less likely to have been explicitly taught in school, but reflect a less provincial outlook and speak of contacts beyond the boundaries of the South, whether through reading or travel. Examples of these two types include: *student, attic, Happy New Year, cottage cheese, mantel, doughnut, freestone peach, woodpecker, orphan,* and *vomit. Stroller* and (window) *shades* could reflect this group's higher wealth and ability to own such things; the lower educational groups lead in the use of *car*, but consider the now more formal alternative, *automobile*. Certainly the use by the better-educated of *best man* in the earlier data set relates to the fact that formal weddings were uncommon among the poorer classes. Some informants, even in the 1990 survey, had never been to a wedding.

The lower educational groups used more terms that were regionally marked or considered to be nonstandard, such as the morphophonemically altered plural *shavs* for *shafts*. These people were less likely to be able to employ a cook and were more familiar with the process of removing the hull from beans, or *shelling* them. The built-in closet was previously not familiar to the poor, who used nails in the wall or boxes of some kind for storing clothes and who more frequently use the full descriptive term *clothes closet* for this modern convenience.

Rurality and Region. The effect of geographical region (coastal, piedmont, or mountain) on lexical choice declined considerably in the course of the years between 1930 and 1990, from a link with 31 variants in the 1930s to only 7 in 1990. Differences between rural and urban dwellers also declined, but not to the same extent as region. Social changes that bring people into contact with one another from different regions of the South also operate to bring city and country residents together. These forces include transportation and educational advances, industrialization, and the militarization of the nation that began with the first World War and was maintained at high levels, especially from World War II onward. Factors such as these, that contributed to the decreasing differences for the categories of region and rurality, will be the first topic in this section.

The different rates of decline are not easily explainable in terms of contact, but must be seen in light of cultural conditions that enhance or undermine group loyalty. This brings up questions about social identity, a psychological construct similar in some ways to prestige and "covert prestige" (Labov 1972, Trudgill 1974). Social identity leads to the use of language to show solidarity, or identification with one's own group as opposed to another group which might possess more prestige within the larger community. Ryan, Giles, and Sebastian (1982:9) note that "the language or dialect of one's family life, intimate friendships and informal interactions acquires vital social meanings and comes to represent the social group with which one identifies." This study goes even further in assigning such social meaning to the dialect used by the group a person may identify with by reason of shared gender, generation, ethnicity, region of residence, etc. (which may of course be the same as the dialect of one's intimate friendships). The discussion of cultural identity will add to this assessment of how region and rurality are alike and how they differ, at least in the sociohistorical milieu of the southeastern United States in this era. This section will also cover particular terms used by specific groups (rural, urban, and regional) for a variety of cultural and geographical reasons. Finally, this chapter will consider reasons for the overall decrease in the amount of variation linked to demographic variables.

Most roads are paved today, highways link towns together, and Interstates 75, 85, 95, 20, 40, 77, 26, and 16 cross the area that was surveyed. All were nonexistent when Guy Lowman traveled through the region in the 1930s. The availability of cars and roads has certainly made transportation easier, and travel outside of one's village, county, and state more common. McGill (1992 [1963]:12-13) recalls an interview circa 1947 with a centenarian in the mountains about the days when timber had to be floated down the rivers because there were no roads.

> I remember the ox-carts strainin' and creakin' and complainin' along the ridges. I think of men walking a hundred and sixty miles to Augusta—walked it myself a few times—and fetching back things they needed on their backs, or maybe packin' it in on a horse. Some drove oxen there. It took a couple of months to come and go . . . Today, I don't know. What with all the radios a-squallin' and all the useless goin' and comin' on the blacktop roads, I sometimes sit here and say to myself that maybe the oxen were the best after all. A feller sure didn't hitch up and go some place unless he needed to, or wanted to mighty bad.

Industrialists from other parts of the country, who had begun exploiting the mineral and human resources in the South in the 1880s much like in colonial countries elsewhere in the world, took advantage of the cheap labor available from people who could no longer make a living by farming. These new occupations were no longer tied to a specific piece of land in a rural area, and most were in larger towns or cities, which entailed either moving or, more recently, commuting. Textile mills were the most common industry in Georgia, South Carolina, and North Carolina. In South Georgia, pulpwood and naval stores developed as worn-out cotton lands were planted in pine, and many North Carolinians were employed in cigarette factories. Wartime industries brought many people to the cities during World War II, and many returning soldiers were encouraged by the VHA to remain near the cities in the new suburban tract housing that sprang up after the war. In addition, industries often brought in managerial staff from outside the local area. The effects of industrialization and urbanization in the South are discussed at length in McDavid 1979 [1970].

Southern politicians have been especially adept at bringing federal dollars into the economy by securing the location of military bases in their home districts. While these are usually located outside of major cities, they have been instrumental in changing rural areas into urban ones, including some in this study (e.g., Liberty County, Georgia, the location of the Army's Fort Stewart). Such bases have brought many nonnatives into the local communities and provided loci for increasing linguistic contact. McDavid notes that "the presence in local military posts of many . . . servicemen with [constriction of /-r/ and] a more sophisticated line of conversation, has led many Southern girls to the conclusion that a person with constriction can be acceptable as a date" (1979 [1948]). Of the 12 million Americans who entered the armed services during World War II, at least half spent time at a Southern base (Jubera 1990).

Not only are there disproportionately many military installations in the South, but there are more Southerners in the military. According to Jubera (1990), more than half of the nation's military payroll, including retirement, goes to Southerners. Armies have always looked to the poorer classes and regions to provide recruits, and the South was for many years the poorest region of the United States, with few opportunities for secure employment outside of military service in some areas. *The Encyclopedia of Southern Culture* (Wilson and Ferris 1989, e.g., 3.461) also blames the infamous Southern propensity toward violence for the overrepresentation of the region in the armed forces. The men, and now women, who join up are immediately relocated with hundreds of other recruits from all over the country, speaking a variety of dialects. They invariably have a story to tell about an experience of linguistic awareness of peculiarities (as perceived by others) in their own speech.

Education has led to increasing contact by providing the opportunity for a college education to larger numbers of young adults. Recently, junior colleges and technical schools have sprung up near even the smallest cities, offering the possibility of schooling beyond high school that may not involve contact with speakers from other regions. Before such schools were widely available, however, college students in the South mostly attended either the large land-grant universities in their own states or the more elite Southern schools in their own or a neighboring state, with relatively few going outside the Southeast. Many contacts were made from outside the students' home counties, certainly leading to changes in speech patterns.

We have seen how changes in transportation, industry, urbanization, the military, and higher education can contribute to increasing contact between rural and urban dwellers and between people from different areas of the South, thus causing a decrease in the effect of both region and rurality on language variation. Since region has become far less important than it previously was, but rurality is only somewhat less influential, the following paragraphs attempt to sketch some reasons for the difference in magnitude of this decline. Cultural reasons for the different behavior of these non-linguistic variables include the multifaceted nature of the categories, especially region, and past and present conflicts that have served to enhance the differences between groups.

There is a multiplicity of differences embodied in each of the non-linguistic variables. Besides the major categorizing feature, most of them encode other differences between groups as well, e.g., African Americans in the survey (and the population) have lower educational levels, urban residents are younger and better educated, etc. The above combinations all involve elements that are analyzed in this study. The variable region has another variable hidden within it that is not separately analyzed in detail. This is a difference in ethnic/religious origin, which includes the racial groups in the analysis but is broader in scope. The three regional categories of mountain, piedmont, and coastal can be construed as two distinct settlement areas and a transition zone.

The coastal areas were settled first, with the dominant social group being Anglicans from the south of England. Since the climate and soil were suitable for growing labor-intensive crops like cotton and rice, a plantation culture, sustained by the importation of slaves from Africa, developed in this area. While lacking any political or economic power to influence society, these forced laborers did constitute the majority of the population in some areas, and their speech was thus a strong influence on the southern British dialects it was originally modeled after (Schneider 1989).

The mountain areas were settled much later, chiefly by Presbyterians and other evangelical groups that came from the north of England or from Scotland (some via Ireland). Some of these settlers went directly to the piedmont area upon arrival, taking the less fertile lands on the frontier not already claimed by the planters to the east. Some arrived after following the Shenandoah Valley through the Appalachians down from original settlement areas on the Pennsylvania frontier. Cultural and linguistic differences attributable to these varying origins continue to this day according to Fischer (1989) and Montgomery (ms.), though they are diminishing over time, as evidenced by the results of this study.

One area that especially requires further research on the influence of settlement patterns is the regionally marked vocabulary. Historical work like that undertaken by Montgomery on the Scotch-Irish origins of Appalachian speech might offer more clues as to the source of different words in the different dialects of the early settlers (Montgomery 1990, 1991). Crozier 1984 shows that the words *fireboard, hull, poke,* and *sook* all come from Ulster. *Fireboard, hull, paper poke, soo-calf,* and *soo-cow* were all used most frequently in the mountain region in this study.

Altogether, 14 variants are used more along the coast, with 24 more common in the mountains; a larger number of terms are associated with the mountains, as compared to the coast. The Appalachian areas have fewer cities, and these were only established in the nineteenth century, while there have been large urban areas near the coast since the beginning of the colonial period. Charleston attracted immigrants and travelers from all over Europe, and was both multicultural and multilingual. The greater number of items linked to the mountain area is probably a reflection of its greater cultural homogeneity and its status as a relic area, both of which are related to its rural character. Although these characteristics lingered on to the earlier part of this century, they no longer are true today. The foothills of the Appalachians are the newest exurbs for cities like Atlanta and Charlotte. Tourists and retirees are moving in while natives either migrate or commute to neighboring urban areas to find work. While some coastal areas, like the one near the submarine base in St. Marys, Georgia, are growing, many small towns in this geographic region have been faced with a drastic drop in population during the twentieth century. As noted above, many of the African Americans who contributed a great deal to ethnic distinctions between regions moved either to the North or to the cities of the piedmont area.

The same forces that are increasing cultural contact between people from different regions are contributing to a mixture and diversity in the population, leading to fewer ethnic and religious differences. Geographical distances between regions are shrinking due to advances in transportation. Meanwhile, the distance in time is growing between the current residents in these regions and the distinct cultures of their original settlers. It may be that the strictly geographic component of region remains comparable to that of rurality. The ethnic/religious component of region continued to be important in the earlier part of this century, but it is less viable today as a basis for linguistic differences.

Historically, there were other distinctions between the regions within the South than the fact that their settlers came from different parts of the British Isles and Africa. For many years, the wealthy planter class from the Low Country dominated the rest of the region economically, politically, and socially. Charleston's hegemony over the rest of South Carolina lasted until the middle of this century, and is described by McDavid (1979 [1955]), who also notes the hostility felt toward Charleston's elite by inland upcountry residents. This interregional rivalry has diminished with the transfer of much of the region's power and wealth to larger cities in the piedmont. With the demise of this conflict, the need for distinguishing linguistic features to mark regional identity has likely diminished as well.

While region encompasses past economic and political divisions, rurality includes some very present ones. Bartley (1990:110) notes that residents of urban/suburban areas (with the exception of depressed inner city neighborhoods) have higher incomes than those of rural areas, and that rural-urban conflict has been a central feature of twentieth-century Georgia politics. He sums up such conflict in the latter part of the century:

> Planters, farmers, and small town dwellers watched the disintegration of their way of life with mounting horror and hostility. Their children moved away to the cities

and many of their . . . communities wilted. Vast and impersonal social and intellectual changes as well as labor union organizers and black civil rights proponents challenged [their customs]. . . . Grantham [1963:88] wrote: "Adverse economic and demographic forces have baffled and frustrated many rural people, exacerbating their fears of social change and their bitter hostility toward the city. Their declining economic and social status has made them more than ever the great conservators of the South's traditions." (Bartley 1990:187)

In terms of group identity then, conflicts between coastal and upcountry regions and between urban and rural dwellers might lead to increased use of linguistic markers of loyalty to one's community. Although rurality has declined in its influence on language (from 21 to 14 associated vocabulary items) due to more contact between urban and rural speakers, it has not declined as much as region (from 31 to 7 terms) because the social divisions between urban and rural groups remain sharply delineated. Rurality retains its social component, while region does not.

Throughout this section on culture and variation, special cases have been noted where vocabulary differs because of cultural differences. If there were a number of words specifically related to occupations only practiced in either rural or urban areas, for example, these lexical differences would remain regardless of the amount of contact between rural and urban residents. Such differences, based on differences in material culture or lifestyles, are reflected in the terms listed in Table 32.

The selection of items for Table 32 takes into account the relative wealth of urban dwellers compared to rural ones. For example, rural informants rarely wore *trousers*, even to church. Many wore their nicest pair of overalls, a term not included in the set for this linguistic variable. The list also follows the principle that familiarity with an item, and more frequent use of the term denoting it, will favor the retention of traditional lexical variants. Weinreich explains that, "other things being equal, the frequent words come easily to mind and are therefore more stable; relatively infrequent words of the vocabulary are, accordingly, less stable, more subject to oblivion and replacement" (1953:57). Borrowing occurs more easily in the less-common areas of the vocabulary, thus the urban use of *toad* or *frog* and *firefly* rather than the common *toad frog* and *lightning bug*, and the rural continuation of *polecat*.

Table 32: Words associated with urban and rural groups due to cultural differences (taken from Appendix 2)

\+ denotes words that were more frequent in the 1930s data

ques. no.	variant	alternatives tested

RURAL
Set 1
56. line(s)+ [driving]   reins
61. doubletree+   double singletree
105. [cherry] seed+   stone
13. loft+   attic, garret

Set 2
48. rail fence(s)+   fence, split rail fence
56. lines+ [driving]   reins, rope
59. shav(s)+
118. pole cat(s)+   skunk

URBAN
Set 1
1. drawing room   si{e}tting room, front room, parlor, big house, living room
35. dish towel   dry(ing) rag, dry(ing) cloth, dish cloth, wip(ing) rag
41. garden house   back house, closet, privy
122. toad   toad-frog
171. trousers   britches, pants, pantaloons

Set 2
57. rein(s)   lines
171. trousers   pants
122. frog(s)   toad, toad-frog
126. firefly(-ies)   lightning bug

Fewer regionally marked variants (as opposed to those linked to rurality) seem to be of this type, i.e. words that refer to something that

Culture and the Lexicon 109

is more familiar to one group than another. Most of the terms that vary by region denote items that are found throughout the entire area. Terms for those referents that are not equally distributed are listed below.

Table 33: Words associated with regional groups due to geographical differences (from Appendix 2)

+ denotes words used more in the 1930s
> denotes words used more in 1990

ques.   variant   *alternatives tested*
no.

COASTAL
Set 1
112. sieva beans   lima beans, sewee beans, butter beans

COASTAL, PIEDMONT, MOUNTAIN continuum
Set 1
106. [peach] kernel+   seed, stone
107. press (peach)+   cling, clingstone (peach), plum peach

MOUNTAIN / MOUNTAIN AND PIEDMONT
Set 1
31. sheepie [to sheep]   co(o)-nannie, sheep, co(o)-sheep
81. gully   washout
106. [peach] seed+   kernel, stone
107. plum peach+   cling, clingstone (peach), press (peach)

MOUNTAIN, PIEDMONT, COASTAL continuum
Set 2
119. chipmunk(s)>   ground squirrel

    Chipmunks, gullies, and sheep are not typically found in the coastal regions. Peaches are not grown in the mountain region, hence the generic *seed* for that part of a peach, rather than *kernel*, and *plum peach* (in comparison to a more familiar fruit) for the type that must be cut away from the seed. *Sieva bean* is a variant of *sewee bean* that is apparently named for the coastal Sewee Indians, who became extinct shortly after colonists began arriving, though the exact relationship of this variety of lima bean to the tribe cannot be determined.

Another possible explanation for the decrease in region-based variation without an equivalent decrease in rurality-based variation has to do with the greater proportion of terms denoting obsolete referents that were linked to the variable region. Table 34 gives the percent of terms linked to each variable that are obsolete or agricultural in reference. Since the words used more frequently in particular regions are preponderantly those that belong to the category having obsolete referents, it follows that variation by region would lessen as these words disappear from the vocabulary. This assumes, of course, that geographical, social, or psychological distance has diminished so that new variants do not follow the same pattern of differences.

Table 34: Percentage of questions exhibiting variation linked to social or regional variables that denote obsolete or agricultural referents

Rurality	Education	Race	Sex	Age	Region	All Questions
n=27	n=29	n=26	n=13	n=21	n=31	n=150
22%	24%	27%	31%	33%	42%	27%

Rurality continues to exert a strong influence on speech. Even though many of the terms used by rural speakers declined in frequency, their continued use in rural areas, along with the use of a number of different words in cities, has kept up a distinction between rural and urban speech. Though this distinction is reduced in magnitude, rurality is now the primary geographical variable with an influence on language variation, with an effect comparable to that of education, race, and age.

Amount of Variation. The last change involving variation that has not been discussed in terms of cultural explanations is the decrease in the amount of variation that is linked to particular groups. The Milroys' research, which finds a connection between the use of socially marked forms and membership in a tight-knit social network, suggests indirectly that if strong network ties were less prevalent in a society, group-based variation might decline. The status of social networks in the modern

South compared to previous years is controversial and beyond the scope of the present research. Some historians feel that as older networks dissolved with urbanization, new ones were formed. A more common observation is that Southern communities in the early twentieth century were self-sufficient entities with homogeneous populations, relatively orderly and fixed in their daily patterns (Wilson and Ferris 1989:3.451), and that the breakup of families, the decline of communities and the small rural churches that bound them together, and the loss of neighborliness in general that were caused by population movements have destroyed this sense of community. Whether new social networks are bound by equally strong ties is questionable. Bartley, a historian little given to romanticizing the old ways, says that, "The traditional Georgia virtues that revolved around family, clan, community, and church found little support in a maturing market society and consumer economy" (1990:187). Fewer strong network ties should cause a decline in the maintenance of linguistic differences, as found in this survey. A larger number of weak ties would favor the introduction of new terms, hence growth of vocabulary, another change that has been documented by this analysis. Certainly there are more opportunities than ever before for casual contact with strangers during the course of a day.

Important changes such as these in the social structure have been brought on mostly by demographic trends, though there are doubtless other contributing factors. Raymond Arsenault, writing in Wilson and Ferris 1989 (1.545) even claims that the technological innovation of air-conditioning has contributed to a decrease in frequent interaction among neighbors and friends. Mrs. Carl Porter (1992), who writes a column for the *Jackson County Herald*, offers the following description: "I passed a country home the other day that attracted my attention. The family had a number of visitors and they were all on the porch talking, visiting, and having a good time. . . . You seldom see a scene like that today. Instead, when you pass a home you never know whether anyone is at home. The family might be inside with the doors shut and the air conditioner on. . . . They would probably have on the television, VCR, or other inside entertainment." Thus, isolation of individuals rather than isolation of communities may become more common, with a concomitant decline in group-based language variation. Fewer people are married today, and more young single adults live alone rather than with parents (McLanahan, Sorensen, and Watson 1989), so that opportunities for linguistic interaction with family may actually have declined as well, though, as noted above, such issues will require further study.

If we look at the speech of an individual as a composite of several speech (and cultural) systems appropriate to that individual's age, sex, occupation, education, race, and geographic location, and check the historical record of how these systems interact, we begin to get a truer picture of the sociohistorical nature of language change. Further research on the participation of individuals in these interrelated dialect systems will be required to fully develop this theory, but it presents an attractive, if highly complex, alternative for those who are interested in the scientific study of language differences. Change does not often occur along simple linear cause-and-effect chains, but rather comes about through interactions among the elements of the system, or community, and between the system and larger systems, including the context in which it is embedded. Although historical and demographic evidence has been chosen here as the preferred explanatory mechanism, this does not mean that psychological factors are irrelevant.

Dialects reflect the way people see themselves and may even be instrumental in creating one's self-image. Mead (1974 [1936]) says that, "the human self arises through its ability to take the attitude of the group to which he [sic] belongs—because he can talk to himself in terms of the community to which he belongs." Whether people identify more with a particular social role or with the region they live in is subconsciously revealed through the way they talk. If individuals within social groups do not identify with that group, either consciously or unconsciously, they cannot be expected to use to the same extent the linguistic elements associated with the group. The relative strengths of social and regional dialects can reveal much about an individual or cultural group's sense of identity (e.g., Eckert 1991). Southerners who are striving to be upwardly mobile, as defined by the larger urban-dominated American culture rather than by the local hierarchies that may have been more important in the earlier part of this century, will reflect this in their language by discarding regionalisms, avoiding even those used by the local elite. Whether the loss of regional distinctions only applies within the South, or entails also a loss of general Southern terms cannot be determined here. The *Atlanta Journal-Constitution* Southern Poll (1992) reports that 61 percent of 1140 respondents disagreed that speaking with a Southern accent is a drawback, but that 76 percent considered themselves to be Southerners (even 30 percent of those who had lived in the South 10 years or less). This indicates that there are conflicting social pressures at work: despite a relatively high degree of regional identification, many Southerners are aware that their dialect carries a stigma in other parts of the country. An optimistic view for the future holds the hope that this stigma will decrease in tandem with a decrease in prejudice against African Americans, who make up a large percentage of the region's population, and an increase in economic prosperity relative to other regions and to previous eras.

* * * * *

This study was designed as an investigation of language change in its social and cultural context. The choice of lexical variables provides us with numerous examples of speech differences that are not incremental, but categorical, and often directly relatable to cultural artifacts. Historical linguistics rarely has such detailed evidence of language in its myriad forms at one point in time. Sociolinguistics rarely has comparable historical evidence available, and must base claims of change on differences in age groups (apparent-time differences). This project has taken advantage of the available records from the Linguistic Atlas files and combined them with a matching sample of current speech to gain insight into both change and variation in a new way by using materials and methods from dialectology, analytical tools from sociolinguistics, and inspiration from historical and anthropological linguistics.

Appendix 1: Biographical Sketches

PGM – Paternal Grandmother   MGM – Maternal Grandmother
PGF – Paternal Grandfather   MGF – Maternal Grandfather

Georgia

Chatham County
GA 1F: Savannah, S. of Broad. F, single homemaker, 78. B. here. Spent only week or so on rice plantation out of city; often spent summers on farm plantation in north GA.—F., PGF both b. here; PGF's F. and M. from Wales; PGM b. here; PGM's F. b. England (British Consul in Savannah); PGM's M. b. NY; M. b. here; MGF b. Charleston, SC; MGF's F. and M. lived Charleston; MGM b. here; MGM's F. lived CT; MGM's M. from VA.—Ed.: governess.—Episcopalian.—Knows own mind; exact and objective in reporting what she would naturally say, although easily horrified at things the "common people" say. Prominent family, yet poor all her life since the War; belongs thoroughly to the old tradition. Broader cultural background than her New England counterparts.—Cultivated informant.

GA 1F2: Savannah, S. of Broad. F, retired homemaker, 90. B. Satilla Bluff (name of estate) at Woodbine in Camden Co.; moved as infant to St. Simons Island in Glynn Co.; age 12 to Savannah. Lived for a few years in country house 14 mi. out of town when first widowed.—F. b. Camden Co., managed mills for post-Civil War lumber empire across S. GA, PGM English, PGF b. Boston; M., MGM b. Camden Co., MGF b. ME.—Ed.: governess on island, public h.s. in Savannah, St. Marys School (Episcopal college) in Raleigh grad.—Episcopalian; early member of Historic Savannah preservationist group, United Daughters of the Confederacy.—Long, interesting, but difficult interview, done in two parts. To avoid being embarrassed by her deafness, she didn't let FW ask questions, but took off into long narrative monologues. Bubbly personality, wonderful range of adjectives. Aux. inf. was friend who has lived with her for many years, F, c. age 80.

Liberty County

GA 3A: Flemington. M, farmer, miller, 80. B. here. Spent winters until 12 yrs. old on plantations in lower part of country. After 1865 never lived there.—F. b. here; PGF b. Sunbury (coastal Liberty Co.); PGF's F. of stock of original settlers; PGM b. here (old stock); M. b. here; MGF b. Eatonton (Putnam Co. GA).—Ed.: private school at 8 yrs., when 10 to public school till 12 or 13.—Presbyterian (the original Congregational Church became Presbyterian in the 1880s); Mason; tax receiver; magistrate.—A splendidly preserved, intellectually able, and rugged figure. Hard of hearing, but has the dignity of the old aristocracy. Was reared with about 70 Negroes, no white companions. His speech is considered notably old-fashioned or Geechee.

GA 3A2: Fleming (c. 10 mi. E. of Flemington). M, tree farmer, 80. B. 3 mi. away. F., PGF, PGM b. in Co., F.'s GF from Germany; M., MGM b. in Co., M.'s GF from Ireland.—Ed.: till 7th grade in Fleming, age 16 or 17.—Methodist, formerly Baptist; served in National Guard 3 yrs., Lions Club.—Very old-fashioned in outlook, somewhat taciturn, supplemented by wife (see below).

GA 3A2*: Fleming. F, housewife, 75. B. here.—F. b. NC, M. b. in Co.—Ed.: Fleming School, then to Hinesville to Bradville Institute (h.s. grad.).—A very beautiful and hospitable woman.

McIntosh County

GA 4N: Crescent. M, farmer, fishing guide, 53. B. Sapelo Island. Lived there till 16, then just across on mainland.—F. b. Sapelo Island, PGF b. Africa, came here as a child; M. b. AL, but died when inf. young.—Ed.: illiterate.—Baptist.—Very intelligent and trustworthy.—Speech in most particulars that of the old Negro.

GA 4N2: Meridian (c. 5 mi. S. of Crescent, at Sapelo ferry landing). M, shrimper, fisherman, 46. B. here, went as a teen to summer camp in NJ, has been in FL, TX, and Mexico on fishing trips.—F. b. Co., PGF b. here; M. b. Co., MGF b. near Jesup in Wayne Co. (next W.), MGM b. here.—Ed.: grad. of Darien HS.—Baptist, Sunday School teacher, active in groups at several churches; "don't join nothing", but in truth is a community leader. Belongs to a couples' social club that meets in homes.—Quite modern in speech and views, although locally oriented.

Loquacious, and affable, even though FW was keeping him from preparing Sunday school lesson.

Evans County

GA 10A: Manassas.—M, farmer, 67. B. here.—F. b. here, illegitimate; M., MGF b. Screven Co., c. 30 mi. away, moved here, MGM b. Bulloch Co., close ancestry with MGF.—Ed.: 2-3 mos. a year till 22 yrs. old.—Primitive Baptist.—Limited intelligence and experience. Unused to visitors or diversions; content to sit down (with wife) and spend entire day with FW. Prob. had little idea of what interview was about, but intro. from Co. Tax Commissioner made situation better.—Slow and deliberate speech. Some nasalization and slurring; weak articulation.

GA 10A2: Claxton (Co. seat, 7 mi. E. of Manassas).—M, carpenter, farmer, 85. B. SC, but moved as child to farm about 3 mi. out of town; at age 34 built subdivision 1 mi. out and lived there 15 yrs., then moved into town.—F. b. SC, Allendale Co. (was Barnwell), came here and ran a store, PGP lived SC, F.'s GGF a Lutheran from Heidelberg; M. b. Jesup in Wayne Co., MGP Wayne Co., of Scotch-Irish descent.—Ed.: through 9th grade here.—Methodist (M. Baptist), church steward.—Claimed to be too busy to do interview, but proved friendly and informative.

Effingham County

GA 13A: Rincon.—M, farmer, 69. B. here.—F., PGF both b. here; PGF's F. and M. both b. Salzburg, Austria; PGM b. here; PGM's F. and M. both b. Salzburg, Austria; M., MGF both b. here; MGF's F. and M. both b. Salzburg, Austria; MGM b. here; MGM's F. and M. both b. Salzburg, Austria.—Ed.: here, about 18 mos.—Lutheran; Woodmen of the World.—Gentle, genial soul. Father always clung tenaciously to the old German customs.

GA 13A2: Near Berryville, Springfield P.O. (c. 10 mi. N. of Rincon). M, farmer, 15 yrs. as mail carrier, 71. B. Savannah, moved here age 7, served 5 1/2 yrs. in Army in the Pacific.—F. b. Savannah, PGF b. Charleston, PGM from Brooklyn, NY, prob. German; M., MGF, MGM b. here, Salzburgers.—Ed.: through 7th grade at Berryville, grad. of h.s. in Springfield.—Lutheran background, no clubs or church membership and never married: considers himself something of an outsider and eccentric. Contact with others through 3 films that have been shot on location at his farm (on the National Register of Historic Places) and the Salzburger Society.—Unusual, old-fashioned speech patterns. Somewhat shy, but enjoyed telling jokes and stories. Hobby is applied mathematics: makes baskets and wooden geometrical figures and toys.

Burke County

GA 15A: Alexander. M, farmer, 83. B. here.—F., PGF b. here, PGF's F. b. SC (English descent), PGM, PGM's F. b. here (Carolina descent); M., MGF both b. here, MGF's F. b. Charleston, MGM b. here, MGM's F. of Carolina descent.—Ed.: 2 mos. only.—Baptist.—Very quick and intelligent. Uneducated and natural.

GA 15A2: Mobley Pond Church, Girard P.O. (c. 10 mi. E. of Alexander).—M, farmer, worked for state Dept. of Revenue, 77. B. here.—F. b. here, PGF, PGM b. in Co.; M. b. Barnwell, SC, just across Savannah R., MGF, MGM b. Barnwell Co., SC.—Ed.: h.s. in Girard, 2 terms at Burke Co. Jr. College.—Methodist; had belonged to Farm Bureau, Masonic Lodge.—Old-fashioned speech, straightforward manner. Wife, former schoolteacher, made several long-winded interruptions.

Baldwin County

GA 24A: Mt. Pleasant Church, Milledgeville P.O.—M, farmer, 64. B. here.—F. b. here, PGF b. AL; M., MGF b. here.—Ed.: illiterate.—Baptist.—Rather quick, bright mind. Friendly and completely subservient in manner, "realizing his duty toward a gentleman".

GA 24A2: Mt. Pleasant, now Gordon (Wilkinson Co.) P.O.—M, farmer, has worked at state hospital and canning plant; once ran a junkyard, 78. B. here, lived in town, Milledgeville, for several years; has been to FL, VA, NY, IN for 2 or 3 days each.—F., PGF, PGM b. in Co., PGF's F. from Ireland; M. b. Wilkinson Co. (just S. of here), MGF, MGM from Toombsboro in Wilkinson Co.—Ed.: through 8th grade at one-room school in Cooperville.—Baptist, considered joining KKK, "they used to do good work".—Soft-spoken, hesitant, slow to respond. Speech sometimes indistinct due to chewing tobacco. Some lack of *it* and *she; he* serves as all-purpose third person pronoun, including for inanimate objects and a female cat.

GA 24A2*: F, housewife, 70, wife of GA 24A2. B. in Co.—F., M. b. Co.—Ed.: through 11th grade at Union Point, an orphan's home in Macon.—Baptist.—Caught husband several times in offering standard forms rather than natural ones (suggested *younguns* rather than *children*). Straightforward and congenial, treated FW to "dinner" (noon meal).

Clarke County
GA 34A: Bogart. F, housewife, 65. B. 8-9 mi. from here in Oconee Co.; moved to Clarke Co. age 3.—F. b. Madison Co., PGM b. Oglethorpe Co.; M. b. here, MGF b. Jackson Co., MGM, MGM's F. b. Co. (MGM's F. owned 10,000 acres here).—Ed.: till 14 (Athens).—Baptist.—Quick, busy, enterprising. Was embarrassed to be "caught" picking cotton by FW, perhaps because family once so prosperous. Although she reads some and feels educated, her speech is genuine. Unconsciously uses the older type of pronunciation.

GA 34A2: Bogart. F, housewife, has worked in a "rug plant" (carpet mill) and once ran a store with husband who later became truck driver, 68. B. here (in Bogart, but on Oconee Co. side), has traveled to other states in the SE US, longest trips 1 mo. in TX and 2 mos. in OK with relatives.—F. b. Walton Co. (next one W.), PGF, PGM lived in Clarke Co., orig. from Carolinas; M. b. Bethebara in Oconee Co., MGF b. Wilkes Co. (to E.), MGM b. Oconee Co. of VA descent (inf. compiling genealogy in order to join DAR).—Ed.: graduate of Bogart HS (11th grade).—Baptist, church choir, women's group; volunteer for Meals on Wheels (delivering meals to invalids), Co. Aging Council, served on City Council 6 yrs., Eastern Star.—Friendly, talkative, good local source. Due to social activities, education, more of a modern than old-fashioned type A informant, but natural in speech.

Union County
GA 43: Lonesome Cove, Blairsville P.O. M, farmer, 85. B. here.—F. b. here, PGF b. Buncombe Co., NC (Irish), PGM b. Buncombe Co., NC ("Black Dutch"); M. b. here, MGF b. White Co., GA (Irish), MGM,

MGM's F. b. White Co. ("Dutch").—Ed.: here (very little).—Baptist; has been circuit judge.—Rather a high type of citizen compared to the average; very primitive; speech genuinely rustic.

GA 432: Gaddistown, Suches P.O. M., ran a store, farmer, 74. B. here.—F., PGF, PGM, M., MGF, MGM all lived in comm., b. either Gaddistown or Canada (next dist.).—Ed.: Pleasant Valley, school was held in church bldg., very little.—Baptist, Masons.—Interview conducted in inf.'s country store, amid frequent interruptions. Flattered to be chosen for interview, at end took a photo of FW with tape-recorder. Natural at beginning, toward end became more self-conscious of language, concerned with not being able to give correct terms, tried to offer some he wasn't sure how to pronounce. Some terms from wife "from S. GA".

South Carolina

Horry County
SC 1A: Burgess P.O. (P.O. abandoned c. 1935), Socastee Twp.—F, housewife, 81. B. other side of Chinners Swamp, further up the Pee Dee River in Horry Co.; moved as an infant, grew up at Pawley's Swamp 5 mi. east of Pee Dee River and 10 mi. from Conway. Came here in 1893, aged 37.—F., M. b. other side of Chinners Swamp in Co.—Ed.: very little.—Baptist.—Old-fashioned; honest and cooperative.

SC 1A2: Good Hope, Conway P.O. (about 20 mi. N. of Socastee). F, farmer, school lunchroom worker 13 yrs., 81. B. Joiner Swamp in Co. (c. 10 mi. E.), has been to adjoining states on vacation trips only.—F., PGF, PGM b. in Co., at Joiner Swamp; M., MGF, MGM b. Dillon Co. (next NW).—Ed.: through 8th grade at Joiner Swamp.—Baptist.—Soft voice almost a whisper at times in noisy environment. This, combined with a very old-fashioned pronunciation, made inf. the most difficult to understand of any FW has interviewed. Lively, amused by interview.

Charleston County
SC 11N: Charleston.—M, carpenter, 58. B. here. Lived age 9–16 in Smithville.—F. b. here: free, part Indian; M. b. Sand Island near Georgetown, came here when young; MGF coachman Sand Island; MGM seamstress Sand Island (both at Flagg Estate).—Ed.: priv. 7 yrs, white

teacher.—Baptist.—A city Negro of the respectable working classes. Likable, quick and imaginative. Not always attentive. Highly superstitious.

SC 11N2: Charleston.—M, retired school principal, 62. B. Adams Run, Toogadoo River in Co., in Yonges Island area, St. Pauls Parish c. 20 mi W. of city, came to Charleston to attend h.s. and stayed ever since except for brief stays in the army and away at school.—F., PGF, PGM, M. all b. Yonges I., MGF, MGM b. White Point, Yonges I. area.—Ed.: h.s. Charleston, B.S. SC State in Orangeburg, M.Ed. Columbia U. in math education, Ed.S. Wayne State.—Baptist, church clerk and trustee; YMCA, Boy Scouts, NAACP, board member Sickle Cell Anemia Foundation and Charleston Civic Ballet, Omega Psi Phi, teaches literacy.—More formal education, civic involvement than prev. inf., but has authentic speech, very fast. Didn't understand interview, thought focus was on his life, consequently spent a lot of time digressing on biographical info. and became bored and irritated by further questioning.

SC 11N2*: Charleston, East Side.—M, blacksmith, 78. B. Daniel Island, came to Charleston age 7.—Ed.: in Charleston until 13.—Has been to DC to participate in Smithsonian Folk Artist programs. Was present to be interviewed by 11N2's son-in-law who was interested in black artists.

SC 11I: Charleston: South of Broad.—F, 51. B. here.—F., PGF, PGF's F. b. here (of early Scots descent), PGM b. here (desc. from early colony); M., MGF (old stock), MGM b. here, MGM's F. b. here (Huguenot stock), MGM's M. English, desc. of signer of Declaration.—Ed.: private finishing school.—Episcopalian.—Highly intelligent and cultivated woman of the old and best families of Charleston. Has never traveled because she has been at home caring for the older members of her own family. Extremely distinguished siblings: schoolmistress, surgeon, history prof., county engineer. Enjoyed interviews.—Extremely quick, rapid speech.—Cultivated.—pp. 7–11, 14–19 are by SC 11I*.

SC 11I*: Charleston: South of Broad. F. Maiden lady of cultivated stock living a block away from SC11I.

SC 11I2: Charleston: on peninsula South of Calhoun, living on James Island for the past year.—F, watercolor artist, taught school 5 yrs., 47.

B. here, lived in S. GA from age 6 wks. to 6 yrs., lived here since except when away at school for 1 yr. in MN, 1 in LA.—F., PGF b. Thomasville, GA, PGM b. NC; M., MGF, MGM all from outside Thomasville; ancestry Scots, Scotch-Irish, English, and Welsh.—Ed.: h.s. in Charleston, B.S. College of Charleston, M.S. Univ. of So. IL, grad. studies at LSU, UNC, Rochester State, and the Citadel.—Episcopal; DAR, Garden Club, active with sorority alumni, various art associations, incl. Charleston Artists Guild, Watercolor Society, etc.—Although inf. has lived here nearly all her life, she lacks in some ways that true Charleston accent that marks the real "blue-bloods," as she calls them.

Dorchester County
SC 12B: Byrd Station, St. George P.O. F, housewife, 70. B. 3 mi. away.—F. b. here, PGF b. St. George, PGF's F. b. Germany, PGM b. St. George; M. b. here, MGF, MGM b. Harleyville.—Ed.: St. George till 16; 1 yr. Meminger HS, Charleston.—Methodist.—Intelligent, interested, natural. Comes of thrifty, respectable ancient German peasant stock in SC.—Speech very dialectal.

SC 12B2: St. George.—F, retired county treasurer (began in treasurer's office as clerk) 71. B. Indian Field nearby in Co., lived in Rosinville comm. 8 yrs., here since age 35.—F., PGF, PFM b. Indian Field, of German descent; M., MGF, MGM b. Rosinville.—Ed.: St. George HS graduate.—Methodist, volunteer with senior citizens, women's circle, Sunshine (travel) Club, card club.—Pleasant interview, some old-fashioned features. Some younger (white) women FW met at courthouse showed speech patterns very similar to blacks of the area.

Colleton County
SC 14A: Hendersonville, Heyward Twp.—M, farmer (clerk when young), 84. B. Hendersonville, lived ages 1–5 in St. Marys, GA (near FL), 5–22 in Walterboro (10 mi. N.), then 3 yrs. in Albany in SW GA, 8 yrs. on Combahee R., SC; in Hendersonville since he was 34.—F. b. Paris, France, died when son was 5 (F. had come to America when 21); M. b. Colleton Co., MGF b. Colleton Co. (Eng. descent), MGM b. Colleton Co. (German descent).—Ed.: Walterboro till 14.—Baptized as Roman Catholic, later Methodist.—Remarkable man: vigorous, active, quick-thinking, quick of speech. Conscious of his planter origin and duty

as a gentleman, but aware that children and grandchildren of his "backwoods" neighbors are educated and often smarter than those of his class, yet he mourns that they are lacking in the character which really separates the two classes.—FW distinguishes between planters such as inf. and "backwoods" people, who are often of German descent.

SC 14A2: Ehrhardt P.O. (Bamberg Co.), Wymer's Crossroads in Colleton Co., c. 25 mi. NW of Hendersonville.—M, farmer, has also worked in sawmill and one day a week for 16 yrs. at the stockyard, 74. B. Bamberg Co., came here when 3 wks. old.—F. b. Calhoun Co., Sandy Run near St. Mathews, PGF, PGM b. Germany; M., MGF, MGM b. Bamberg Co., 3 mi. N. of here.—Ed.: here through 4th grade, then at Lodge through 10th grade.—Baptist, Sunday school director and teacher, deacon; formerly Grange member.—Very locally oriented, old-fashioned type.

Beaufort County
SC N19: Hilton Head. M, farmer, takes clams to Savannah every Saturday on boat, 53. B. Hilton Head.—Parents b. Hilton Head.—Willing inf., but untrustworthy about keeping appointments and giving accurate replies.—Extremely rapid tempo; extremely gesticulatory.

SC N192: Hilton Head. M, gas station owner, 62. B. here (Chaplin community), was in Army 2 yrs., spent 1 yr. NY City, 3 yrs. St. Augustine College in Raleigh.—F., PGF, PGM, M., MGF, MFM, all b. on island.—Ed.: elem. sch. on island, h.s. at St. Helena, St. Augustine College, grad. from Savannah State.—Baptist, deacon, former chairman of deacons; member town council, NAACP, Kappa Alpha Psi, past master Masons.—This inf., despite his educ., had an old-fashioned pronunciation if few old gramm. forms. Somewhat taciturn. Claimed never to have known anyone on island who really spoke Gullah.

Kershaw County
SC N22: Camden. F, domestic at home, has worked out for others, 65.—F., M. b. here.—Not a very satisfactory subject; judgment not clear enough, and too slow.—Has certain speech habits which throw light on African or Indian sounds (is she part Indian?).

SC 22N2: Camden. F, retired farmer, has done domestic work, 74. B. about "6 mi. out in the Sand Hills" near Galloway Hill, lived for 32 yrs. off Old Wire Rd. in Co., has been in Camden 12 yrs., traveled to PA, NJ, NY on visits.—F. b. Kershaw Co., didn't know PGPs; M., MGF, MGM b. Lee Co., next one E.—Ed.: a little at Emanuel.—United Methodist.—Natural, old-fashioned speech, knows no other way of talking. Toward end of interview became tired, couldn't think as quickly, but was lively and talkative at beginning.

SC 22B: Camden. F, housewife, 65. B. 7 mi. below Camden; when age 7 stayed in city and went to school.—F., M. and their parents b. here.—Ed.: till 17.—Presbyterian.—A rather cultivated woman; old-fashioned rural type. Refused to continue record, pleading illness, but prob. felt self-conscious about her speech because of her sister's remarks (FW feels record as made is accurate and honest).—Very delicate speech with a slight drawl.

SC 22B2: Camden. F, retired secretary, is completing a volume of local history, 65. B. here, lived 3 yrs. in Newberry, 1 yr. Greenville, lived 12 mi. out of Camden in Co. on family's land near abandoned plantation for 10 yrs.—F. b. Flat Rock in Co., PGF b. Flat Rock, PGM b. Wake Forest, NC, daughter of a professor; M. b. Camden, lived in FL and on plantation, MGF b. Columbia was newspaper reporter in FL, later lived in DC, MGM b. Longtown.—Ed.: Camden HS, no college.—Episcopal; Kershaw Co. Historical Soc., Fine Arts Ctr., Camden Dist. Heritage Foundation, Friends of Library.—Cultivated background, gracious, but middle-class type in education and residence. Helpful, introspective about usage.

Richland County
SC 25A: Lykesland.—F, housewife, 78. B. 11 mi. out of Columbia on Old Camden Rd.—F., PGF, PGM b. Cooks Mount, SC (Irish Prot. descent); M., MGF, MGM b. here (Scotch descent).—Ed.: limited, local; chiefly in Sunday school.—Baptist.—Sat puffing away at her pipe, enjoying the questionnaire from beginning to end. Composed, companionable; a sparkle of Irish wit.—Not at all guarded about her speech; speech is quaintly antique and vulgar.

SC 25A2: Columbia, Olympia Village (mill village).—F, retired textile mill worker, had also managed root beer/fast food stands, 82. B. Capital City area of Columbia, lived 10 yrs. in Lexington Co. (next one W.), other places in Richland Co., incl. Dentsville, Pontiac, Wateree, Centerville; has been in Olympia Village 40 yrs., has traveled with Sr. Citizens group.—F. b. Centerville, worked as overseer near Blaney, PGF some Scotch-Irish ancestry b. near Longtown, Fairfield Co. (next one N.), PGM from NC, "cousin of R. J. Reynolds"; M., MGF, MGM b. lower Richland, toward Sumter.—Ed.: Olympia HS grad. (only 11 grades then).—Mormon, Relief Society; sec. of the Sr. Citizens Club, We Are Olympia commun. assoc.—Fascinating tales of Mormon persecution, union pickets, and late husband's Klan activity. Energetic, strong and independent-minded woman. 52-year-old retarded daughter also present at interview. Speech perhaps not as old-fashioned as would be expected due to intense community and church involvement.

Edgefield County
SC 30A: Philipps Church, Johnston P.O.—M, farmer, 63. B. neighborhood.—F. b. Orangeburg Co., came here as boy, PGF b. Orangeburg Co., PGF's F. b. Ireland, PGM b. Aiken Co., of "Dutch" descent; M., MGF b. in Co., of Scotch descent, MGM b. Co., of partial "Dutch" descent.—Ed.: 3-4 yrs. school.—Baptist.—Very quick and bright. Speaks absolutely naturally. Takes no interest in modern way of talking.

SC 30A2: Hominy, Johnston P.O.—M, farmer, 65. B. same comm., 2 mi. from here.—F., M., b. in Co.; all GPs b. Saluda Co. (next co. N.), of English and French descent.—Ed.: Johnston HS, 1 yr. Furman Univ.—Methodist; Farm Bureau, Young Farmers.—Speech natural and fairly old-fashioned, no pretension. Chewing tobacco caused some slurring and loss of consonants.

SC 30A2*: Hominy.—F, 66. B. in community.—F., M. born here, some German ancestry.—Ed.: Johnston HS.—Wife of 30A2: born a mile apart, went to school together, married 47 years. Her speech hints of a higher social background.

Anderson County

SC 41A: Eureka Church, Anderson P.O. F, housewife, 79. B. near Keys Lake, 2 mi. west of Anderson.—F. b. here, PGF b. Southern Ireland, PGM prob. b. here, Scotch-Irish stock (had strong brogue); MGF b. Belton, SC (c. 10 mi. E. of Anderson), MGM b. here (prob. all Scotch or Ulster Scots).—Ed.: till 12-13 off and on.—Baptist.—Plain, sensible, serious-minded. Felt she was contributing valuable information and took pains to be thoroughly honest. Intelligent in all she told, but incapable of realizing when she had been tricked into using old-fashioned forms. Belongs to the plantation class, but obviously of common, very respectable stock, with none of the gifts or glamour of the Low Country.

SC 41A2: Williamston (c. 15 mi. NE of Anderson).—F, housewife, worked a few years as store clerk, 84. B. Pendleton in Co., ages 5-23 lived just over Pickens Co. line near Liberty, when married lived for 40 yrs. Little Hydro comm. on the Saluda River in Co. (husband worked at power plant), has been here 20 yrs.—F., M., both b. Co., doesn't know about GPs.—Ed.: through 11th grade (h.s. grad.) in Liberty.—Baptist, Women's Missionary Union.—Didn't understand reasons for questions or interview protocol, but was open and talkative. Somewhat senile, tended to repeat things several times. Noisy air conditioner obscured parts of tape.

North Carolina

New Hanover County

NC 23B: Myrtle Grove Sound, Wilmington P.O., Masonboro Twp.—F, housewife, 46. B. here.—F. b. Duplin Co. (near Wallace) and came here when young, PGF b. Duplin Co. (Scotch-Irish descent), PGM b. Duplin Co.; M. b. Greenville Sound (New Hanover Co.), MGF b. Brunswick Co., MGF's F., MGF's M. both b. near Greensboro, MGM b. Masonboro Sound (New Hanover Co.), MGM's F. b. Onslow Co. (Scotch-Irish descent), MGM's M. b. on Little Sound (New Hanover Co.).—Ed.: till 16.—Presbyterian.—Perhaps somewhat too careful of certain particulars in her speech, though FW believes they are thoroughly natural to her adulthood.

NC 23B*: Wilmington.—F, housewife, 45.—Parents b. here.—Ed.: moderate.—Not very quick or bright, but conscientious. Her husband stopped the interview at p. 30.—Lips immobile; sounds difficult to catch.

NC 23B2: Myrtle Grove Sound.—F, bookkeeper, has worked in factory, dress shop, clerical work, 52. B. Columbus, GA, at 3 mos. moved to Kure Beach, c. 8 mi. S. for 12 yrs., then here to Sound.—F. b. AL, came here from Columbus, GA, PGF, PGM from the AL/Columbus area; M. b. Shallotte, 25 mi. S. in Brunswick Co., MGF, MGM from Holden Beach area in Brunswick Co.—Ed.: New Hanover HS grad., some classes at Cape Fear Tech.—Baptist, was Christian; belongs to American Business Women's Assoc., women's church group.—Somewhat self-conscious, but eager to be of help. Lots of malapropisms.

Brunswick County
NC 24N: Calabash, Shallotte P.O.—M, farmer, 89. B. Columbus Co. on a plantation. At end of war (age 17) came to Little River just over line in SC. After some years, came back here to this part of Brunswick Co. (did not live in Brunswick Co. until grown).—F. b. Columbus Co. (father was sold away so inf. did not know him); M., MGF, MGM all b. in Columbus Co. on same plantation.—Baptist.—Quick; highly intelligent. Cooperative, but tendency not to remember the most old-fashioned forms.

NC 24N2: Longwood.—F, retired, has been farmer, housekeeper, 80. B. here (8 mi. N. of Calabash), has traveled to SC, DC, CT on visits.—F., PGF, PGM all b. here, prev. called Butler Bay, Ash P.O.; M., MGF, MGM b. Supply, c. 15 mi. E. in Co.—Ed.: through 7th grade here.—Baptist, church women's group and other church and senior citizen activities.—Very polite, slow-speaking.

NC 24A: Freeland, Waccamaw Twp. (NW corner of Co.).—F, housewife, 70. B. here.—F. b. on Roanoke River in VA and came here as a small boy (died when inf. was 9 yrs. old), PGF, PGM both b. on Roanoke River in VA; M. b. here, MGF b. Co., MGM b. Columbus Co., near here.—Ed.: a little.—Missionary Baptist.—Intelligent; obliging. Perhaps not as old-fashioned as FW could have found.

NC 24A2: (Old) Brick Landing, prev. Saspan Neck.—M, retired, has worked as farmer, in construction, on dredges and tug boats, 64. B. Mill Branch, Waccamaw Twp., lived in Bladen Co. as child, also out of town for work and during WWII but here for past 51 years.—F. b. Waccamaw, Ash P.O., PGF, PGM b. Mill Branch, Green Swamp; M. b. Waccamaw, MGF, MGM then moved to Seaside, S. of Shallotte.—Ed.:

through 4th grade at Bladenboro, Bladen Co., then through 6th grade at Shallotte.—Pentecostal Holiness, deacon and Sunday school supt.; Moose, American Legion, Disabled American Veterans, VFW, pres. Shallotte Sr. Citizens Club, VP Co. Council of Sr. Citizens.—Very out-going, with a sense of humor, talkative and friendly.

NC 24B: Royal Oak, Supply P.O. M, farmer and sawmill worker, 45. B. here.—F. b. 10 mi. S. near coast, PGF, PGM b. Co. (PGM's name an old one here); M. b. Supply, MGF, MGM b. Co.—Ed.: here till 18.—Baptist.—Progressive middle-aged type. Slightly hesitant about being fully cooperative at all times.

NC 24B2: Shallotte.—M, town building inspector and maintenance supv., has worked for engineering dept. of Co. hospital, as farmer, 36. B. hospital in Columbus Co., but parents lived at Longwood, in Co., now lives in town of Shallotte.—F., PGF b. Longwood, PGM b. Crusoe in Columbus Co.; M. b. Sandy Plains in Columbus Co., MGF b. OH, MGM b. Columbus Co.—Ed.: grad. of Waccamaw HS.—Baptist, church music director.—Somewhat shy, but likes to tell jokes. Embarrassed at some questions.

Sampson County
NC 25A: Clinton, Mints P.O.—M, farmer, sawmill worker, 73. B. here.—F. b. just across river in Cumberland Co., PGF b. near London, Eng., PGM b. Cumberland Co.; M., MGF, MGM b. here (MGF's people came from Tar River near present Rocky Mount). —Baptist.—Talkative, somewhat unconnected, but thoroughly capable of answering questions.—Loud, harsh, coarse voice.

NC 25A2: Hamtown, Clinton P.O.—M, farmer, worked during WWII in shipyard in Onslow Co., VA, 74. B. here.—F., PGF, PFM, M., MGF, MGM all b. in comm.—Ed.: at Ingold 8–10 yrs. through the 7th grade.—Universalist, raised Baptist, once belonged to Woodmen of the World and a farm organization.—Slow, with a gruff voice and mumbling articulation, and taciturn. Stereotypical type A: old-fashioned, only local contacts.

NC 25A2*: Hamtown.—F, wife of NC25A2, c. 70. B. Co.—Parents b. in Co.—Ed.: h.s. grad.—Universalist.—Kept trying to "help" husband with interview; some answers supplement his.

NC 25B: Turkey.—M, farmer (Co. Road Commissioner, 20 yrs. Justice of the Peace, State Legislature 1929), 68. B. here.—F., PGF, PGF's F. b. here, PGF's PGF b. Isle of Wight Co., VA (Scotch-Irish), PGF's M. of German descent, PGM, PGM's F. and M. all b. here (English descent); M., MGF, MGF's F., MGF's M., MGF's MGF b. here (latter of "Irish" descent), MGM, MGM's F., MGM's M., MGM's MGF all b. here (English descent).—Ed.: here till 16.—Methodist.—Both parents were college grads. Interested in worthy, intellectual things as his family would have liked him to be. Gr-gr-grandfather a Revolutionary general, buried here on the old place.—Tempo more rapid than most. Articulation fairly precise.

NC 25B2: Turkey.—M, college teacher (history), was school principal 21 yrs., 74. B. here, lived 1 yr. in Atlanta in college, 1 yr. in NY at Columbia, 4 yrs. on ship in WWII, travel to Europe, Canada, throughout the US.—F., PGF, PFM all b. here, family on same property since 1754 (from land grant); M., MGF, MGM b. Chatham Co., NC, MGM came here in lumber business.—Ed.: B.A. UNC Chapel Hill, M.A. E. Carolina Univ.—Episcopalian, lay reader; Sons of the American Revolution, Sons of Confederate Veterans, Sampson Co. Historical Society (has a museum on property), NC Literary and Historical Society, Shriners, Masons.—Accomplished storyteller, detailed knowledge of local history, informative. Sure of social position, "doesn't depend on what kind of car I drive or clothes I wear", somewhat affected. Young cousin (college student) present at interview. Some responses may have come from reading, not experience.—Cultivated.

Robeson County
NC 29B: Barker Ten Mile, Lumberton P.O.—F, housewife, 43. B. here.—F., PGF b. 5 mi. E. (perhaps of Irish descent); M., MGF b. Robeson Co. (perhaps of Irish descent), MGM b. here.—Ed.: till 18.—Methodist.—Timid; worried about her performance.—Rather slow tempo.

NC 29B2: Long Branch, Lumberton P.O.—F, waitress, has worked in plants, dept. stores, as a lab technician, keeps books for husband's upholstery shop, 38. B. Lumberton, lived in Tampa, FL 2 mos., has traveled some on vacation.—F., PGF, PGM, b. Infield (?) near VA; M. b. Bladenboro (15 mi. E.), MGF, MGM also b. Bladen Co.—Ed.: elem. at Allenton, some h.s. at Littlefield, left and went back to earn h.s. equiv. from program at Robeson Comm. College.—Church of God.—Interested, intelligent, and understood purpose of interview: tried to keep M. (see below) from giving answers.

NC 29B2*: F, retired housewife and cab driver, mother of NC29B2, 68. B. Bladenboro in Bladen Co. (next one E.). Old-fashioned speech.

Guilford County
NC 46B: Guilford College.—M, farmer, 44. B. here.—F., PGF, PGF's F. b. Guilford Co. (of Nantucket, MA, Quaker ancestry); M. b. Deep River (8 mi. W.).—Ed.: till 23 at Guilford College School (1 1/2 yrs. at "College").—Methodist.—Slow; shy, cautious, and fearful.

NC 46B2: Lawndale Homes, Greensboro.—M, salesman with textile company, 43. B. Greensboro, spent 2 years Ft. Bragg, NC (Hoke Co., about 70 mi. SSE.) and some time in the Caribbean while in the army, travels for his job.—F. b. Ansonville (Anson Co., c. 70 mi. S.), was sheriff of Guilford Co., PGF, PGM from near Ansonville; M. b. Co., MGF b. Yanceyville (Caswell Co., next one to NE), MGM b. Graham (Alamance Co., next one E.).—Ed.: Brooks Elem., Greensboro Sr. HS, B.S. in Political Science from Guilford College, all Greensboro.—Presbyterian; was a Co. commissioner for 4 yrs.; Kiwanis, Bd. of Health, Mental Health Bd., coaches children's soccer.—Interested in project and in how the region is changing. Sense of humor, enjoyable interview. Honest about what he didn't know.

NC 46C: Greensboro.—F, executive sec. of Girl Scouts, 48. B. here.—F. b. near Greensboro, PGF b. Greensboro, PGF's F. of German descent, PGM, PGM's F. b. near Greensboro, PGM's M. b. Co.; M. b. near Alamance Co., MGF, MGF's F. b. E. Guilford Co., MGF's PGF b. PA (parents from Paisley in Scotland), MGF's PGM (rescued from Indians), MGM b. Co.—Ed.: Womans College (Greensboro) 1 yr., Queens College, Charlotte (Mecklenburg Co.), 1 yr., then back here 2 yrs.—Presbyterian (now Methodist).—Father typical merchant. Inf. perhaps somewhat affected.—Cultivated.

NC 46C2: New Irving Park, Greensboro.—F, "crime consultant" (gives safety talks to civic groups), former elem. school teacher ("as all good Southern ladies"), has worked for airline, in real estate, and giving presentations for local college, 43. B. in Greensboro, grew up in Kirkwood neighborhood, spent a total of 15 yrs. in Atlanta, NYC, and LA, returned to Co. c. 5 yrs. ago.—F., PGF, PGM all b. Summerfield in Co. (10 mi. N.), some French ancestors on F.'s side; M., MGF, MGM b. Greensboro.—Ed.: Page HS, Greensboro, UNC Chapel Hill B.A. in Ed.—Presbyterian, church circle; belonged to many groups in h.s. and since, now only Eastern Music Festival Auxiliary, Garden Club.—Hectic schedule, worked on materials for upcoming presentation during interview. Disdainful of regional attitudes and rural ways.—Insisted she was not the right person to interview, having little knowledge of farm life, but FW chose to continue, since time in other cities seemed not to have affected her pronunciation, although she may have lost certain regionalisms from lexicon. Found some questions ridiculous.—Cultivated.

Anson County

NC 52N: East Rocky Ford, Wadesboro P.O. F, housewidow, 90. B. 13 mi. W. on plantation. At age 21, began moving closer to town.—F. b. Richmond, VA, and sold here as a young man; M. b. Richmond Co., NC; MGF lived Richmond Co.—Ed.: none.—Baptist.—Very quick, intelligent; cooperative; extensive contact with white people keeps inf. from having a very old-fashioned type of speech.

NC 52N2: Morven.—F, retired farm field worker, 90. B. a few miles away at Sneedsborough, Galilee area, lived in Baltimore 8 yrs., visits relatives there.—F., PGF, PGM, M., MGF, MGM, all b. Co.—Ed.: illiterate.—Methodist; Eastern Star.—No teeth, not very clear enunciation, difficult to understand and she had difficulty understanding FW; sister-in-law (see below) acted as interpreter and added many responses of her own.

NC 52N2*: Morven.—F, retired housekeeper, sister-in-law of NC52N2, 78. B. Darlington, SC, c. 45 mi. S., moved here age 11, lived 6 yrs.

OH, some time in Winston-Salem.—F., M. b. Cairo in Co.—Ed.: Morven HS grad.—Baptist, community activist.—Outspoken, intelligent woman, a leader in the community, has met with many local politicians, etc., but maintains natural old-fashioned speech.

NC 52N2**: Morven.—M, retired sharecropper, some construction work, 89. B. here, farmed at Cason Old Field, 5 mi. E. in Co. only out of Twp. 32 mos. of his entire life.—F. b. GA into slavery, owner moved to Co., M. b. here.—Some communication difficulty due to a few missing teeth. Very old-fashioned speech, helpful and interested.

NC 52B: Jones Creek, Morven P.O. M, farmer, 48. B. here.—F., PGF b. Lilesville Twp., PGF's F. b. VA, of a MD family (Irish descent), PGM b. Scotland Co.; M., MGF, MGF's F. all b. Lilesville, MGF's PGF b. VA, MGM b. Morgan Twp., MGF's F. b. Co.—Ed.: here till 15.—Presbyterian.—Well-to-do gentleman of successful family; only local contacts.—Some vowels seem to point to contacts with SC (boats came up the Pee Dee River from Georgetown) as well as to VA. Co. seems different from any of the surrounding cos. Extreme NW corner of Co. is like Stanly Co. (PA German).

NC 52B2: Morven.—M, farmer, has done some construction work, 57. B. here, only traveled on vacations.—F., M. both b. Cason Old Field in Co., c. 5 mi. E., all GP b. in Co.—Ed.: Morven HS grad.—Methodist; mayor for 7 yrs.—Locally oriented, somewhat timid about being interviewed in open area of City Hall (at least until employees went home). Aux. infs. are city clerk (**), middle-aged white woman, and engineer (*), white male about 30.

Mecklenburg County
NC 56A: Hopewell, Huntersville P.O.—F, housewife, 60. B. locally.—F. b. Sugar Creek (near Charlotte), PGF b. Co. (Scotch-Irish descent), PGM, PGM's F. b. Co., PGM's PGF b. No. Ireland, PGM's PGM b. here, PGM's M. b. Sugar Creek; M. b. Hopewell, MGF b. Co., MGF's F. b. in Holland and came to PA, MGM, MGM's F. b. here, MGM's PGF b. 1726 in PA, MGM's PGM b. MD, MGM's M. b. south Mecklenburg Co. (Scotch-Irish descent).—Ed.: here till teenager, attended White Hall, a grammar school taught by northerners in Cabarrus Co., and Asheville Normal School (less than 1 yr.).—Presbyterian.—Co-

operative; middle-aged type.—Articulation mumbling and indistinct as in Scottish speech.

NC 56A2: Long Creek, Huntersville P.O.—F, housewife, worked in school cafeteria for 13 yrs., 55. B. here, lived in Mobile, AL for 6 yrs., Charlotte 18 yrs.—F., PGF, PGM, M., MGF, MGM all born Huntersville.—Ed.: elem. at Huntersville, grad. N. Mecklenburg HS.—Presbyterian; does volunteer work for Red Cross.—Closer to type B than type A informant, at least in lang. used for interview. Fairly self-conscious, stressed that people around there were never really "backwoods" types. Noted that some words she'd heard only from movies.

Stokes County
NC 57B: Piedmont Springs, Danbury P.O. M, farmer, 36. B. here.—F., PGF, PGM all b. here; M. b. S. of Patrick Co., VA.—Ed.: Danbury till 17.—Baptist.—Obliging "typical citizen".

NC 57B2: Walnut Cove (10 mi. S. of Danbury).—M, draftsman in Co. tax dept., has been land surveyor, worked for hwy. dept, 31. B. in hosp. in Forsyth Co., but has always lived in Co. near Walnut Cove; brief trips to VA, TN, SC, GA, FL.—F., PGF, PGM, M., MGF, MGM all b. Northview section of Co.—Ed.: grad. of S. Stokes HS, some technical courses at UNC Chapel Hill.—Christian.—Interview conducted at Co. admin. bldg. Inf. quick, honest, straightforward; grew up on farm with older parents, knew more farm terms than some elderly infs.

Ashe County
NC 62B: Nathans Creek, West Jefferson P.O.—F, housewife (wife of former postmaster), 52. B. Nathans Creek, has lived last 18 yrs. at West Jefferson.—F. b. near Jefferson, PGF b. on Reddies River (Wilkes Co.), PGF's F. b. Wilkes Co., PGF's PGF b. Rowan Co. (now Davidson Co.), PGF's PGF's F. b. Staten Island or NJ, PGF's PGF's PGF b. Staten Island or in England, PGF's PGF's M. b. NJ, PGF's PGM b. Ashe Co. (Scotch-Irish descent), PGF's M. b. Wilkes Co., PGM, PGM's F., PGM's M. all b. Ashe Co. (PGM's M. of German descent); M. b. Nathans Creek, MGF b. Iredell Co., MGM b. Jefferson.—Ed.: Nathans Creek and Plummer Seminary at Crumpler (Ashe Co.) 2 summers.—Baptist.—Old French Huguenot family (son of man who fought

under Cromwell came to Staten Island in 17th cent.; his son stayed on to be the tax collector there). Inf. complacent, obliging, cooperative; not particularly intelligent.—Tempo deliberate; vowels and diphthongs tend to remain short. Good, clear enunciation on the whole.

NC 62B2: Beaver Creek, W. Jefferson P.O.—F, postmaster, former secretary, 59. B. Warrensville, c. 5 mi. N., lived 2 yrs. in Winston-Salem NC, 1 and a half yrs. Wash., DC.—F. b. Warrensville, PGF, PGM b. Co. of German descent; M. b. Benge in Co., MGF, MGM b. Co. of Scotch-Irish descent.—Ed.: West Jefferson HS, 2 yrs. Draughons Business College in Winston-Salem.—Baptist, Sunday school teacher and trustee; director Chamber of Commerce, bank director, vice-pres. Womans Club.—Delightfully candid and down-to-earth in a town where many women refused to admit they were even in this age bracket. Enlisted the help of 2 postal clerks on some questions, both were locally born white males, approximately ages 25 and 35 (interview conducted in post office while inf. sorted the mail).

Polk County
NC 69A: Mill Springs.—M, farmer, 77. B. locally.—F., PGF both lived here; M. b. here, MGF lived here, MGM b. Co., MGM's F. of "Dutch" descent.—Ed.: illiterate.—Baptist.—Very slow; talkative.

NC 69A2: Mill Springs.—M, farmer, has been rural mail carrier, bookkeeper ("county manager"), worked in a textile mill, and served in the military, 67. B. 1 1/2 mi. away.—F., PGM b. here; M. b. here, MGM b. Green Creek in Co., most ancestors "from Ireland".—Ed.: locally through 7th grade, then Sterns HS.—Baptist, deacon; American Legion, Boy Scouts.—Somewhat of a shady character. Enjoyed playing the role of expert, but not always clear on what usage was his own. Has apparently done a lot of reading, closer to type B than A informant.

Buncombe County
NC 71B: Lower Hominy, Candler P.O.—M, farmer, 54. B. Newfound (on the Haywood Co. line, northwest of Asheville).—F., PGF both b. on Hominy in Co., PGF's F. b. here, PGF's PGF b. PA 1755 (of Welsh

descent), died Buncombe Co. 1824.—Ed.: Newfound; then 3 years at the Haywood Institute at Clyde (Haywood Co.)—Presbyterian.—Intelligent, sensible. Rather inclined not to give himself away in speech at times; his wife made him admit some things he had not planned to. Perfect calm; he can't be hurried.

NC 71B2: North Turkey Creek, Leicester P.O. (c. 5 mi. from Newfound, 10 mi. N. of Candler, all in western part of Co.).—M, farmer, assistant Co. Agent, "field man" for a dairy, 62. B. here, lived short time in Waynesville, Haywood Co. (c. 25 mi. W.).—F., PGF b. here, English, PGM b. Bethel in Haywood Co; M., MGF b. Old Turkey Creek, Scotch-Irish, MGM b. Madison Co. (next Co. N.).—Ed.: Leicester HS, BS in animal industry from NC State in Raleigh.—Methodist; Farm Bureau.—Friendly and intelligent. Natural speech and demeanor; mumbling.

NC 71B2*: North Turkey Creek.—F, 55-60. B. Mars Hill in Madison Co.—Ed.: probably h.s.—Wife of 71B2. Offered commentary on differences between this and her natal community.

NC 71C: Asheville.—F, housewife, 49. B. here.—F. b. Gudgers Mill (14 mi. W.), PGF b. Co., PGF's F. b. Madison Co. (Scottish descent), PGM, PGM's F. both b. Co. (English descent); M. b. Leicester in Co., MGF b. Co. (Irish descent), MGM b. Henderson Co.—Ed.: city schools until 16; Converse College, Spartanburg, SC, 4 yrs.—Methodist.—Wife of a lawyer; delightful; thoroughly natural; full cooperation.—Cultivated.

NC 71C2: Black Mountain (c. 10 mi. E. of Asheville).—F, owner of gallery and boutique, has been Spanish teacher, mental health counselor, and artisan (jewelry), 46. B. in hospital at Asheville, parents lived in Black Mountain; lived 2 yrs Raleigh-Durham area, 4 yrs. in Laurinburg NC, travels to Europe and Mexico.—F. b. Blk. Mtn., PGF b. Bakersville (N. of here in Mitchell Co.), PGM b. either Blk. Mtn. or Blowing Rock; M., MGF, MGM b. Durham.—Ed.: h.s. in Blk. Mtn., BA in Spanish from St. Andrews Presbyterian College.—Presbyterian; Sierra Club, once in Jr. Women's Club.—Fairly self-conscious and easily flustered when unable to recall a common term, but observant of local usage and introspective about her own. Of a philosophical bent, feels a great difference between herself and her friends versus less educated natives of the community, but without a superior attitude.—Cultivated.

Cherokee County

NC 75A: Head of Beaverdam, Grandview P.O.—M, farmer and cattleman, 83. B. here.—F. b. Buncombe Co., came here c. 20 yrs. old, PGF b. Buncombe Co. ("Dutch" descent), PGM of "Dutch" descent; M. b. Yancey Co.—Ed.: illiterate.—Humble origin, but has made money raising cattle (has taken cattle to Richmond, but has always come straight back again, uncontaminated). Quick, alert; quick answers, although sometimes forgetful.

NC 75A2: Murphy.—M, retired "service station" manager and worker, worked some in cotton mill, 83. B. Ranger in Co., c. 10 mi. SW of Murphy, 20 mi. S. of Beaverdam, lived 5 yrs. in Gastonia, in Murphy last 60 yrs., has traveled to several other states on vacation trips.—F. b. Swannanoa, Buncombe Co. near Asheville, PGF, PGM from Haywood Co., descendants of first whites to settle this area; M. b. Ranger, of SC stock.—Ed.: Walker schoolhouse at Ranger through 7th grade, 6 mos. a yr.—Methodist; Mason, Eastern Star, Civitan.—Hesitant, poor memory. Kept trying to refer FW to local museum, didn't feel qualified to answer.

NC 75B: Peachtree, Murphy P.O.—F, housewife (wife of retired Methodist missionary), 52. B. here.—F. b. Marble in Co., PGF b. Lincoln Co. (partly Dutch descent), PGM b. just over line in Tennessee; M. b. here, MGF b. Morgantown (Burke Co.), MGM b. Lenoir (Caldwell Co.).—Ed.: here till 16.—Methodist.—Quick, intelligent, cooperative. This the quickest record FW made in South (3 1/2 hours instead of the usual 5 or 6).

NC 75B2: Martin's Creek, Murphy P.O.—F, asst. director at senior citizens center, has been dept. store mgr., worked in textile and sewing plants, 50. B. Peachtree, lived total of 12 yrs. in Athens, Cleveland, and Chattanooga, TN, 1 yr. in FL, 2 yrs. in OH, 6 mos. in GA.—F. b. Clay Co. (next one E.), PGF, PGM from Clay and Cherokee Cos.; M. b. Macon Co. (E. of Clay Co.), MGF from Macon Co., of Lubbock TX descent, MGM b. Franklin in Macon Co.—Ed.: through 8th grade at Murphy, 9th in Charleston, TN, h.s. equiv. degree by attending night school in Murphy, 1 1/2 yrs. Tri-County Comm. College.—Methodist; involved with 4H Club, served as president of the Community Dev. Club and of the Homemakers Ext. Club (Woman of the Year), volunteer with senior citizens and church youth group.—Excellent informant, intelligent, open and willing to talk, certain of local usage and not self-conscious.

Appendix 2: Variants Associated with Regional or Social Groups

* significant in more than one category   > new   + old

ques.   *variant*   *alternatives tested*
no.

COASTAL
Set 1
3. mantelpiece   mantel, mantel board, fireboard
78. threatening+   changing, (v.) bad weather, making up for
                                 a storm, clouding up, (v.) falling
                                 weather
112. sieva beans   lima beans, sewee beans, butter beans
121. spring frog(s)+   frog, greenfrog
139. relative(s)   relations, kin, kindred, kinfolks

Set 2
127. mosquito hawk   dragonfly, snake doctor

COASTAL AND PIEDMONT
Set 1
44. cowpen+   milkgap

Set 2
18. clabber   clabbered milk

COASTAL, PIEDMONT, MOUNTAIN continuum
Set 1
32. chick [to chickens]   chickie, biddie, biddie$_2$ [to little ones]
103. haslet(s)*+   liver and lights
106. [peach] kernel+   seed, stone
107. press (peach)+   cling, clingstone (peach), plum peach
123. earthworm   baitworm, bait, fishing worm, mud worm,
                                 red worm
154. scholar+   student

MOUNTAIN, PIEDMONT, COASTAL continuum
Set 1
76. bawl	hum, low, moo
36. paper poke	sack, paper sack, paper bag, bag
103. liver and lights	haslet
109. family pie+	tart, deep dish pie, pot pie, cobbler

Set 2
33. skillet	fry pan, frying pan, spider
119. chipmunk(s)>	ground squirrel

MOUNTAIN
Set 1
86. corn dodger	corn pone, cornbread, pone of cornbread, pone of bread, pone, pone bread
114. hull [beans]	shell
3. fireboard+	mantel, mantelpiece, mantel board
30. piggie [to pigs]	pig, (sucking), goop, pigoo(p)
31. sheepie [to sheep]	co(o)-nannie, sheep, co(o)-sheep
37. tow sack+	bag, crocus sack, croker sack, tow bag, sack, crocus bag, burlap bag
44. milkgap+	cowpen
68. bring a calf	freshen, come in, come in fresh, calve, drop a calf, find a calf, have a calf, be fresh
107. plum peach+	cling, clingstone (peach), press (peach)
123. red worm(s)	baitworm, bait, earthworm, fishing worm, mud worm
127. snake feeder	mosquito hawk, dragonfly, skeeter hawk, snake doctor

Set 2
75. bawl+	bellow, cry, blate, maa
45. lot	hog pen, pen, pig lot, pig pen

MOUNTAIN AND PIEDMONT
Set 1
81. gully	washout
23. soo(k)-cow [to cows]	co-eh, co-(w){e,a}nch, sook
24. soo-calf+ [to calves]	sook, sookie
106. [peach] seed+	kernel, stone

Set 2
140. carriage(s)>	baby carriage, buggy, stroller(s), wagon

Appendix 2

RURAL
Set 1
7. bedspread	spread, coverlet, counterpin
25. k{o,ᴜ,u}p+ [to horses]	kw{o,ᴜ}p
56. line(s)+ [driving]	reins
61. doubletree*+	double singletree
105. [cherry] seed+	stone
13. loft*+	attic, garret
38. weatherboarding+	weatherboards
148. turn(s) out+	lets out

Set 2
48. rail fence(s)*+	fence, split rail fence
56. lines+ [driving]	reins, rope
59. shav(s)*+	
118. pole cat(s)*+	skunk

URBAN
Set 1
2. andirons	firedogs, dog irons
38. weatherboard(s)	weatherboarding
94. cruller	doughnut, fritter, marvelle
122. toad	toad-frog
148. let(s) out	turns out
1. living room*>	s{e,i}tting room, front room, parlor, big house, drawing room
1. drawing room	s{e,i}tting room, front room, parlor, big house, living room
7. spread	bedspread, coverlet, counterpin
35. dish towel	dry(ing) rag, dry(ing) cloth, dish cloth, wipe(-ing) rag
41. garden house	back house, closet, privy
108. freestone*	clearstone, clearseed (peach), open (peach), openstone, soft (peach)
143. (is) the image of	favors, takes after, resembles, looks like
151. telltale	tattletale, taleteller, tattle box, tattler
171. trousers	britches, pants, pantaloons

Appendix 2

URBAN, continued
Set 2
57. rein(s)	lines
110. spring onion(s)	green onions, multiplying onion, nest onion, onion, onion sets, scallion
171. trousers	pants
38. clapboard(s)	weatherboard, weatherboarding, board, lap siding board, siding
66. mutt	dog, cur dog, feist, heinz, sooner, yard dog, mongrel, mixed breed
77. changing	breaking, clearing up, clearing off, fairing up, fairing off
115. Idaho potatoes*	Irish potatoes, new potatoes, potatoes
115. new potatoes >	Idaho potatoes, Irish potatoes, potatoes
122. frog(s)	toad, toad-frog
126. firefly(-ies)	lightning bug

HIGH EDUCATION
Set 1
130. toadstool	frogstool
32. biddie [to chickens]	chick, chickie, biddie₂ [to little ones]

Set 2
2. andirons	dog irons, dogs, firedogs
72. fowl	poultry
150. truant >	laid out, skipped school, played hookey
12. armoire	chifforobe, wardrobe
125. turtle(s) >	cooter, gopher, snapping turtle, terrapin

HIGH AND MIDDLE EDUCATION
Set 1
3. mantel >	mantelpiece, mantel board, fireboard
19. cottage cheese	clabber cheese, homemade cheese, curd
154. student*	scholar
179. Happy New Year(s)* >	New Year's Gift
94. doughnut(s)	cruller, fritter, marvelle
108. freestone*	clearstone, clearseed (peach), open (peach), soft (peach), openstone

Appendix 2

HIGH, MIDDLE, LOW EDUCATION continuum
Set 1
13. attic*   loft, garret
164. best man   bridesmaid, groomsman, waiter
Set 2
169. graveyard+   family plot, cemetery

MIDDLE AND HIGH EDUCATION
Set 1
  6. shade(s)   curtains, blinds, window curtains, window shades
117. woodpecker*>   peckerwood, sapsucker
146. orphan   orphan child, mother(less) and fatherless child
157. vomit   puke, spew, vomick, throw up

MIDDLE, HIGH, LOW EDUCATION continuum
Set 1
13. garret+   loft, attic
Set 2
140. stroller(s)>   baby carriage, buggy, carriage, wagon

MIDDLE, LOW, HIGH EDUCATION continuum
Set 1
41. back house+   garden house, closet, privy
Set 2
173. foreigner(s)*   outsider, stranger, visitor, damn Yankee, flatlander

MIDDLE AND LOW EDUCATION
Set 1
45. hogpen(s)+   pen(s)

LOW EDUCATION
Set 1
13. loft*+   attic, garret
146. orphan child   mother(less) and fatherless child, orphan
Set 2
11. clothes closet   closet
59. shav(s)*+
45. pen(s)*   hog pen, lot, pig lot, pig pen

LOW AND MIDDLE EDUCATION
Set 1
62. car   automobile
Set 2
114. shell [beans]

LOW, MIDDLE, AND HIGH EDUCATION continuum
Set 2
2. firedogs   andirons, dog irons, dogs
107. press (peach(es))+   cling peaches, clingstone, peaches

YOUNG
Set 1
13. attic*   loft, garret
168. casket   coffin
179. Happy New Year(s)*>   New Year's Gift
92. bakery bread+   bought bread, light bread, loaf bread, store bread, baker's bread
110. spring onion(s)   sallet ingan, shallot, scallion
Set 2
99. fatback>   middlings, side meat, streak o' lean
30. sooey [to pig]   pig, piggie
32. here chick [to chicken]   chick, chick chickie, chickie
105. [cherry] pit>   kernel, seed, stone

OLD
Set 1
57. bridle(s) [riding]   bridle reins, reins, lines
157. vomick   vomit, puke, spew, throw up
Set 2
57. line(s) [riding]   reins
76. low(ing)+   bellow, moo
99. middling(s)+   fatback, side meat, streak o' lean
80. electric storm   electrical storm, thunderstorm

OLD AND MIDDLE
Set 1
21. pail   piggin, bucket
147. younguns+   children
Set 2
59. shav(s)*+

OLD, MIDDLE, YOUNG continuum
Set 1
101. breakfast strip(s)+   breakfast bacon, bacon

Set 2
118. pole cat(s)*+   skunk
45. pen(s)*   hog pen, lot, pig lot, pig pen

MIDDLE (age group)
Set 2
10. bureau(s)+   chest, chest of drawers, dresser, wash stand

MIDDLE AND OLD
Set 2
100. skin   bacon rind, meat skin, rind

Appendix 2

BLACKS
Set 1
146. mother(less) and fatherless (child)	orphan, orphan child
6. window curtain(s)	curtains, shades, blinds, window shades
33. spider	skillet
79. big rain	heavy rain, hard rain, cloudburst, downpour, gully washer, pourdown
80. thunder squall	thunder cloud, thunderstorm, thunder shower
108. clearstone	clearseed (peach), open (peach), openstone, soft (peach), freestone

Set 2
38. weatherboard(s)	weatherboarding, board, clapboard, lap siding board, siding
91. bread	sourdough bread, yeast bread, homemade bread, light bread, loaf bread
116. potatoes	sweet potatoes, yams
121. greenfrog(s)	spring frog, frog, rain frog, treefrog
142. granny	granny woman, midwife
159. passed	gone on, passed on, passed away, died, expired, deceased, kicked the bucket
28. gee or haw>	haw
29. gee or haw>	gee
123. worm(s)	night crawler, wiggler, red wiggler, red worm, blood worm, earthworm, fishing worm
155. neuritis	rheumatism, arthritis, bursitis, gout
164. bridemaid(s)	groomsman, maid of honor, attendant, best man, bridesmaid, matron of honor

WHITES
Set 1
61. doubletree*+	double singletree
90. mush+	cush
142. midwife	granny-woman, granny
154. student*	scholar
176. county seat	county site
52. grindstone+	grindrock
137. grandfather+	granddaddy, grandpap, pa, grandpa(w), grandpae

Appendix 2

WHITES, continued
Set 2
81. gully(-ies)   ditch, washout
135. daddy>   dad, papa
173. foreigner(s)*   outsider, stranger, visitor, damn Yankee, flatlander

FEMALE
Set 1
144. [named] for   after
  1. living room*>   s{e,i}tting room, front room, parlor, big house, drawing room

76. moo>   hum, low, bawl
117. woodpecker*>   peckerwood, sapsucker
Set 2
161. spirit(s)   ghosts, haints
115. Idaho potatoes*   Irish potatoes, new potatoes, potatoes

MALE
Set 1
103. haslet(s)*+   liver and lights
71. stud   male horse, stallion, stud horse
153. school mistress   school marm, school teacher, teacher
Set 2
  4. lightwood   lighterd, lighterd splinters, fat lighterd, fatwood, kindling, lighter wood
48. rail fence(s)*+   fence, split rail fence
61. doubletree+
71. stud(s)   horse, stallion, stud horse
115. Irish potatoes   Idaho potatoes, new potatoes, potatoes
155. rheumatis(m)+   arthritis, bursitis, gout, neuritis

Appendix 3: Variants Exhibiting Diachronic Change

Variants Used More Frequently in the 1930s (p<.05)

question	variant
1. living room	s{i,e}tting room
2. andirons	dog irons
3. mantel	fireboard
5. sofa	sofa
7. bedspread	counterp{in,ane}
10. chest of drawers	bureau(s)
12. wardrobe (movable)	wardrobe(s)
13. attic	loft
13. attic	garret
14. junk	plunder
14. junk	rubbish
14. junk	trash
17. pantry	pantry(-ies)
19. cottage cheese	curd(s)
19. cottage cheese	clabber cheese
22. calls to cows (milking)	so
23. calls to cows (pasture)	co-(w){e,a}nch
24. calls to calves	soo(k)-calf
25. calls to horses	k{o,ᴜ,u}p
26. get up	(cluck)
26. get up	get up
26. get up	go on
28. calls to mules—left	haw
29. calls to mules—right	gee
30. calls to pigs	pigoo(p)
30. calls to pigs	goop
31. calls to sheep	co(o)-nannie
32. calls to chickens	chickie
33. frying pan	frying pan(s)

Appendix 3

Variants Used More Frequently in the 1930s (p<.05)

question	variant
34. dish cloth	dish rag(s)
36. bag (paper)	paper sack(s)
37. sack (burlap)	tow sack(s)
38. siding	weatherboarding
41. privy	privy
41. privy	back house
42. corn crib	crib(s)
42. corn crib	corn house
44. cowpen	milkgap
44. cowpen	cowpen
45. hog pen	hogpen(s)
46. barnyard	lot
48. rail fence	rail fence(s)
52. grindstone	grindstone
56. lines (driving)	line(s)
57. reins (riding)	bridle reins
58. tongue	tongue
59. shafts	shav(s)
60. singletree	swingletree
61. doubletree	doubletree
62. car	automobile(s)
65. driveway	avenue
65. driveway	lane
66. mongrel	cur dog
66. mongrel	feist
66. mongrel	cur
68. calve (verb)	find a calf
69. ram	ram
71. stallion	stud horse
71. stallion	stallion(s)
72. fowls	fowls
73. setting hen	s{e,i}tting (hen)
75. bawl	blate
76. low	low(ing)
76. low	hum

Appendix 3

Variants Used More Frequently in the 1930s (p<.05)

question	variant
76. low	bawl
77. clearing up	clearing(-s) up
77. clearing up	fairing off
78. clouding up	(x) falling weather
78. clouding up	threatening
79. heavy rain	heavy rain
80. thunder storm	thunder cloud
83. sweet corn	roasting ear(s)
85. silk	silk(s)
90. mush	mush
91. wheat bread	light bread
92. store-bought bread	bakery bread
92. store-bought bread	baker's bread
95. pancakes	battercakes
95. pancakes	flitters
95. pancakes	slapjacks
96. snack	lunch
98. peanuts	pinder(s)
99. salt pork	middling(s)
99. salt pork	smoke meat
99. salt pork	bacon
101. bacon	breakfast bacon
101. bacon	breakfast strip(s)
102. wishbone	pull bone
103. haslet	haslet(s)
105. stone (cherry)	seed
106. pit (peach)	kernel
106. pit (peach)	seed
107. clingstone peach	press (peach(es))
107. clingstone peach	plum peach
108. freestone peach	soft (peach)
109. cobbler	family pie
110. spring onions	shallot(s)
112. lima beans	sewee (beans)
118. skunk	pole cat(s)

Appendix 3

Variants Used More Frequently in the 1930s (p<.05)

question	variant
120. bullfrog	bloody noun
121. treefrog	spring frog(s)
122. toad	toad frog(s)
125. terrapin	terrapin(s)
128. grasshopper	locust(s)
129. spiderweb	cobweb(s)
130. toadstool	frogstool(s)
135. father	pae
135. father	pap
135. father	pa
136. mother	ma
136. mother	mae
136. mother	mammy
137. grandfather	grandfather
137. grandfather	grandpa(w)
138. grandmother	grandmae
140. baby carriage	baby carriage
141. pregnant	(in {the, a}) family way
142. midwife	(old) granny-wom{e,a}n
143. resembles	favor(s)
143. resembles	look(s) (just) like
145. bastard	woods colt(s)
147. children	youngun(s)
148. lets out	turn(s) out
149. starts	begin
150. played hookey	lay(-id) out of school
151. tattle-tale	tattler
152. horseshoes	quoits
153. teacher	school teacher(s)
154. student	scholar
155. rheumatism	rheumatis(m)
157. vomit	puke(d,-ing)
157. vomit	spew(ed)
159. died	passed out
161. ghosts	h{a,ai}nt(s)

Variants Used More Frequently in the 1930s (p<.05)

question	variant
162. devil	devil
164. best man	waiter(s)
166. serenade	serenade
166. serenade	serenading
168. coffin	coffin
169. cemetery	graveyard
171. pants	britches
173. stranger	stranger(s)
177. Civil War	Confederate War
178. Merry Christmas	Christmas Gift
179. Happy New Year	New Year's Gift

Variants Used More Frequently in 1990 (p<.05)

question	variant
1. living room	living room
1. living room	den
3. mantel	mantel
4. lightwood	fat lighter(d)
4. lightwood	kindling
5. sofa	couch
10. chest of drawers	chest of drawer(s)
12. wardrobe (movable)	chifforobe
14. junk	junk
21. pail (tin, water or milk)	milk bucket
22. calls to cows (milking)	be still
25. calls to horses	(by name)
25. calls to horses	(whistling)
26. get up	giddy up
28. calls to mules---left	gee or haw
29. calls to mules---right	gee or haw
34. dish cloth	dish cloth(s)

Appendix 3

Variants Used More Frequently in 1990 (p<.05)

question	variant
37. sack (burlap)	burlap bag(s)
38. siding	siding
41. privy	toilet
41. privy	outhouse
41. privy	outdoor toilet
45. hog pen	pigpen
48. rail fence	split rail fence
65. driveway	driveway
66. mongrel	mixed breed
73. setting hen	hen
76. low	moo(s)
76. low	bellow(s)
79. heavy rain	flood(s)
80. thunder storm	electrical storm
83. sweet corn	sweet corn
86. cornbread (large cake)	cornbread
91. wheat bread	homemade bread
92. store-bought bread	light bread
99. salt pork	fatback
101. bacon	bacon
102. wishbone	wishbone
105. stone (cherry)	pit
106. pit (peach)	pit
108. freestone peach	peach(es)
109. cobbler	cobbler(s)
109. cobbler	pie(s)
115. potatoes	potato(es)
115. potatoes	new potatoes
116. sweet potatoes	sweet potato(es)
117. woodpecker	(x) woodpecker
118. skunk	skunk
119. chipmunk	chipmunk(s)
121. treefrog	rain frog(s)
121. treefrog	tree frog(s)
123. earthworm	night crawler(s)

Appendix 3

Variants Used More Frequently in 1990 (p<.05)

question	variant
125. terrapin	turtle(s)
129. spiderweb	web(s)
135. father	daddy
136. mother	mama
139. relatives	family
139. relatives	people
140. baby carriage	carriage(s)
140. baby carriage	stroller(s)
141. pregnant	pregnant
143. resembles	((is the) spitting image (of)
143. resembles	(is) (exactly, a lot, just) like
145. bastard	illegitimate (child, kid)
147. children	kid(s)
148. lets out	{get(s), got} out
150. played hookey	truant
151. tattle-tale	tattletale
153. teacher	teacher(s)
154. student	pupil(s)
155. rheumatism	bursitis
155. rheumatism	arth(u)ritis
159. died	kicked the bucket
159. died	passed on (*x*)
162. devil	Satan
162. devil	boogey(-r) man
164. best man	bridesmaid(s)
164. best man	attendant(s)
164. best man	maid of honor
164. best man	matron of honor
164. best man	ushers
166. serenade	reception
170. vest	vest(s)
173. stranger	outsider(s)
173. stranger	(damn, goddamn) Yankee(s)
178. Merry Christmas	Merry Christmas
179. Happy New Year	Happy New Year(s)

Appendix 4: Tallies and Selected Commentary

The tables below are arranged by question number according to the order asked in the interview. The tallies give the number of non-dubious occurrences of each variant. There may be responses with commentary that are doubtful for some reason and thus are not listed in the tally. Due to limitations of space, only select commentary could be included. Comments have been edited and not all are included here. Condensed comments like "also SC1A" denote the same comment given for the same variant. An open or closing parenthesis alone denotes that the preceding or following material forms part of the sentence in which the informant used the word; for example, the phrase "two-seater)" with the variant *privy* means that the speaker said "two-seater privy". None of the standard comments coded in the database (OLD, SUG, AUX, etc.) is noted below. Cultivated informants were previously marked with "!". An index follows in Appendix 5, listing each variant with its question number. Appendices 2 and 3 may also be cross-referenced by question number.

NA = Not Answered
NR = No Response

1. Living Room

1930s		*1990*	
big house	3	back parlor	1
drawing room	3	company room	2
front parlor	1	den	7
front room	8	family room	1
living room	14	front parlor	1
parlor	18	front room	3
parlor room	1	living room	29
quarter	1	NA	1
setting room	10	parlor	11
sitting room	20	sitting room	6

Appendix 4

GA13A	parlor	old name as a boy
SC11N	sitting room	most used
SC11I!	living room	modern combined room
NC71C!	parlor	a little-used room
SC11N	parlor	best room
SC11I!	sitting room	different from living room
SC11I!	drawing room	f.'s house
SC11I!	parlor	only in common people's house
SC19N	front room	fireplace
SC22B	sitting room	plainer
SC22B	drawing room	finer
NC52B	parlor	best
NC52N	big house	white people
NC52N	quarter	for colored
NC75B	parlor	best room
GA1F2	sitting room	in 3-story house, on 2nd floor
GA1F2	front parlor	first floor (of 3) called *parlor floor*
GA10A2	living room	used now
SC12B2	parlor	nobody says *parlor* anymore
SC14A2	sitting room	known today as the)
SC22B2	front room	frowned upon
SC22B2	sitting room	didn't use *parlor*
SC30A2	living room	for "real big company"
NC24A2	parlor	now
NC46C2	parlor	gm. said
NC62B2	parlor	only used for weddings and funerals; gf. used term

2. Andirons

1930s   *1990*
andirons   5   andirons   8
dog irons   12   dog irons   3
dogs   1   dogs   4
fire irons   1   fire irons   1
firedogs   15   firedogs   17
NR   8   NA   3
                              NR   1

SC14A   firedogs   = andirons
SC25A   firedogs   also

GA4N2   firedogs   not the proper name but that's what we call
                       them
GA432   firedogs   we call them
GA432   antlers   you might know them as)
SC30A2   andirons   [-ɪ-], 3 syllables

3. Mantel

1930s   *1990*
fire jamb   1   fireboard   1
fireboard   10   mantel   22
mantel   13   mantel board   2
mantel board   4   mantelpiece   13
mantelpiece   21   NA   3
mantelshelf   1
shelf   2

NC62B   mantel   modern only
NC62B2   fireboard   mgm. said
NC69A2   fireboard   as a child

4. Lightwood

1930s

fat pine	1
light pine	1
lighterd	9
lighterd knot	1
lightwood	14
NR	9
pine	1
rich pine	5

1990

fat kindling splinters	1
fat lighter	2
fat lighterd	5
fat lighterd splinters	2
fat lightwood	2
fat pine wood	1
fat splinters	1
fatty wood	1
fatwood	5
firewood	1
heart of longleaf pine	1
kindling	12
lighter wood	3
lighterd	8
lighterd knots	2
lighterd splinters	3
lightwood	7
NA	3
NR	1
pine	2
pine knots	1
pine resin knots	1
rich pine	2
splinter pine	1
splinter wood	1
splinters	2

GA3A	lighterd	uneducated
GA4N2	lighterd	main term used
GA10A2	lightwood	in the *Market Bulletin*
GA13A2	lightwood	since it made a bright light one could read by
GA15A2	fatwood	not split
GA432	rich pine	rare here
SC11N2	lightning	corrected to *lightwood*
SC11I2	fat lighter	heavy stress on first word
SC22B2	lighterd	servant said
NC24B2	lighterd	common term

5. Sofa

1930s			*1990*	
bench		5	bench	1
couch		2	benches	1
lounge		10	couch	14
sofa		35	davenport	1
			daybed	1
			lounge	3
			loveseat	2
			NA	6
			settee	5
			sofa	13
			sofa bed	1

GA1F!	sofa	two arms and sloping back
GA1F!	lounge	= davenport
GA3A	couch	generally with back; headrest
GA3A	lounge	no side or back or headrest
GA10A	sofa	two arms and back
GA13A	sofa	two arms
GA13A	lounge	back and headrest
SC12B	lounge	same as sofa
SC12B	sofa	same as lounge; natural
SC14A	lounge	no arms and back
SC19N	sofa	sit on
SC19N	couch	lie on; natural, common
SC19N	lounge	lie on
SC25A	sofa	narrow—can't lie on; two arms and back
NC24B	lounge	no back, head—one end
NC25B	lounge	one arm and back
NC25B	sofa	two arms and back
NC56A	sofa	[drawing shows high at one end]
NC71B	sofa	rare
GA3A2	sofa	wouldn't call it that in past
GA34A2	davenport	leather, opened into a bed
GA432	benches	not upholstered
SC12B2	lounge	one arm

SC14A2	lounge	no arms, just back
NC24A2	daybed	had a shuck (-stuffed) cushion
NC75B2	loveseat	short
NC75B2	couch	long
NC75B2	lounge	leather; high back, one arm; back reclined

6. Window Shades (on rollers)

1930s			*1990*	
blinds	3		blind	1
curtain	1		curtains	1
curtains	6		NA	3
shade	2		NR	8
shades	24		shade	2
window blinds	2		shades	19
window curtain	2		window shades	7
window curtains	3			
window shades	8			

GA43	window shades	none used here
NC71B	blinds	rare
NC75A	window blinds	also
GA10A2	curtains	= old-fashioned kind of shades

7. Bedspread

1930s			*1990*	
bedspread	15		a white sheet	1
counterpane	2		bedspread	16
counterpin	37		counterpin	6
coverlet	2		coverlet	3
coverlid	7		coverlets	1
spread	12		NA	2
			NR	1
			spread	14
			spreads	1

Appendix 4

GA4N	counterpin	[ɛ] not [ɪ] [also SC19N, NC24N, NC29B]
GA10A	counterpin	wove in a piece
GA34A	coverlid	woven wool
GA43	coverlet	wool woven
SC11N	counterpin	finer quality
SC11I!	counterpin	as children
SC22N	counterpin	old kind
SC22B	counterpin	thin
NC25B	coverlid	heavy wool
NC62B	coverlid	woven
NC69A	coverlet	wool woven
NC71B	coverlid	woven
NC71C!	coverlid	woven
GA1F2	spread	from mountains, of woven cotton
GA3A2	comfort	(main) inf.'s m. called it; on top
NC23B2	coverlets	sometimes use quilts for)
NC56A2	bedspread	chenille
NC71C2	bedspread	mass-produced, sometimes lighter than coverlet
NC71C2	coverlet	hand-loomed
NC75B2	spread	chenille

9. Pallet

1930s			1990	
lodging	4		bed on the floor	1
palace on the floor	1		mat	1
pallet	37		NA	2
shakedown	1		NR	5
			pad	1
			pallet	27
			pallet on the floor	1
			pallets	1

SC12B	pallet	for children
GA10A2	pallet	"I've laid on many a pallet myself"
SC11I2	NR	"I have no idea"
SC12B2	pallet	out of style now
SC14A2	NR	has no name for it, but familiar

10. Chest of Drawers

1930s
bureau	39
bureaus	1
chest of drawers	7
chifforobe	1
dresser	12
safe	1
set of drawers	1
sideboard	1

1990
bachelors chest	1
bureau	5
chest	3
chest of drawer	1
chest of drawers	16
chest on chest	1
chests	2
dresser	18
dresser drawer	1
dresser drawers	1
dressing table	1
highboy	2
linen press	1
NA	5
press	1
vanity dresser	1
wash stand	3

GA1F	chest of drawers	no glass
GA10A	dresser	"bought ones"
GA10A	bureau	"bought ones"
GA24A	sideboard	older
SC11N	chifforobe	fancy one
SC11I!	bureau	glass
SC11I!	chest of drawers	tall
SC14A	dresser	low
SC14A	chest of drawers	= bureau
SC25A	chest of drawers	high one, with door at top for hats
SC25A	set of drawers	natural
NC23B	chest of drawers	tall; plain
NC24B	dresser	last 20 years
NC25B	chest of drawers	old; no glass
NC46B	chest of drawers	no glass
NC62B	bureau	no glass
NC62B	safe	drawers and doors

Appendix 4 161

GA13A2	NA	*trunk*: kept rats out
GA24A2	dresser	tall: 4 or 5 drawers; with mirror
GA34A2	chest of drawers	heavy stress on first word
GA34A2	dresser	one had marble top
GA432	NA	*trunk*: aux. inf., *apple boxes*: main inf.
SC11I2	chest on chest	separates
SC11I2	linen press	drawers on bottom, chest on top; to store linens
SC11I2	bachelors chest	goes to floor; doors, space for hats, shallow drawers
SC22B2	bureau	with mirror
SC22B2	highboy	tall
SC22B2	chest of drawers	tall
SC25A2	dresser	long, with mirror
NC25A2	dresser	same as bureau
NC25A2	bureau	same as dresser
NC29B2	chest of drawers	pron. "chesser" drawers
NC46B2	dresser	low
NC46C2	chest of drawers	pron. "chester" drawers
NC57B2	chest of drawers	with mirror; pron. "chester" drawers
NC69A2	chest of drawers	no mirror
NC69A2	dresser	with mirror
NC75B2	chest	taller than dresser
NC75B2	highboy	type of chest
NC75B2	dresser	mirror

11. Closet

1930s			*1990*	
closet	33		closet	27
clothes closet	3		closets	5
clothes press	1		clothes closet	4
NR	2		NA	4
			walk-in closets	1
			wardrobe	1

SC12B	clothes press	shelves
SC12B2	closet	nails in the wall as a child

12. Wardrobe

1930s		*1990*	
clothes press	1	armoire	3
NR	4	chifforobe	9
wardrobe	32	chipporobe	1
wardroom	2	closet	1
		highboys	1
		NA	3
		NR	7
		wardrobe	8
		wardrobes	1
		wardroom	1

SC25A	clothes press	= elaborate piece of furniture
GA3A2	wardrobe	drawers on one side
GA10A2	chifforobe	no [-b]
SC1A2	wardrobes	homemade; drawers on one side
SC30A2	chifforobe	not used
NC62B2	chifforobe	gm. said
NC75B2	chifforobe	drawers on bottom

13. Attic

1930s		*1990*	
attic	18	attic	25
cock loft	1	loft	7
cuddyhole	1	NA	1
garret	13	NR	3
loft	19	overhead	1
upstairs	1	up loft	1
		upstairs	3

GA1F!	attic	rare
SC22B	attic	if a room
GA3A	loft	heard from Negroes
GA34A	loft	when no stairs
SC12B	garret	heard in Charleston
SC14A	garret	inhabitable

SC19N	cock loft	small projection up from flat roof
SC22B	garret	unfinished
NC25B	cuddyhole	when not used for sleeping
GA4N2	up loft	the average person would say
GA4N2	overhead	the average person would say
NC62B2	loft	older than attic

14. Junk

1930s			*1990*	
junk	19		junk	19
plunder	15		NA	16
plunderments	1		NR	1
rags	1		odds and ends	2
rubbish	12		rubbish	1
rummage	2			
trash	21			
truck	1			
trumpery	1			

GA4N	junk	also plural *junks*
SC11N	trash	worst
NC25B	trumpery	f. said

16. Kitchen

1930s			*1990*	
cook room	3		cook room	1
kitchen	39		kitchen	34
kitchen room	1		kitchenette	1
shed room	1			
stove room	5			

GA34A	kitchen	esp. old-fashioned kind
NC25B	cook room	attached
GA3A2	kitchen	could be separate, connected by porch
NC52B2	kitchen	best part of the house: spend 75% of time there
NC75A2	kitchen	could be separate

17. Pantry

1930s			*1990*	
buttry	1		butlers pantry	2
closet	2		closet	6
NR	1		larder	2
pantry	37		leanto	1
storeroom	1		NA	4
			NR	5
			pantries	1
			pantry	23
			pantry room	1
			storage closet	1
			storage room	1
			storeroom	1

SC22N	buttry	butter, dishes
GA10A2	NA	used smokehouse for canned goods, etc.
GA24A2	pantry	also *safe* and *cupboard*
GA432	NR	none; used cellar dug into bank outside house
SC11I2	pantry	"I'd call it"
SC11I2	larder	term not often used
SC22N2	NA	*grocer box*
NC29B2	NA	*cabinets*
NC62B2	leanto	gp.'s had one adjacent to kitchen

18. Clabber

1930s			*1990*	
clabber	32		buttermilk	1
clabber milk	3		clabber	26
clabbered milk	1		clabbered	2
clobber	3		clabbered milk	4
NR	1		NA	2
			NR	3

Appendix 4

GA3A2	clabber	eaten with bread; "haven't et none in 50 years"
GA4N2	clabber	sour milk
GA34A2	NA	verb is *clabber*
SC11N2	clabber	ate on rice
SC14A2	clabber	fed to chickens
SC19N2	buttermilk	fancy name
SC22B2	clabber	ate with sugar and nutmeg
NC24A2	clabber	also to cook *sour milk cake*
NC62B2	clabbered milk	not thick

19. Cottage Cheese (homemade)

1930s		*1990*	
clabber cheese	14	cheese	2
clabber curds	1	clotted cream	1
cottage cheese	15	cottage cheese	8
cream cheese	1	cotted cheese	1
curd	15	cream cheese	1
homemade cheese	3	curd	3
milk cheese	2	curds	1
NR	5	goat cheese	1
smearcase	1	NA	2
		NR	23

GA1F!	curd	put in a press with holes
GA1F!	cottage cheese	tied in cloth, left to hang till absolutely dry
GA3A	cream cheese	in wooden press
GA3A	curd	in wooden press
GA3A	cottage cheese	hung up in thin cloth
GA3A	Dutch cheese	in wooden press
SC11I!	curd	pressed, eaten with sugar, cream, seasoned with salt
SC12B	cottage cheese	old name, also something in it, with it
SC12B	clabber cheese	pressed out more [than clabber curds]
SC22B	clabber cheese	pressed more
SC25A	curd	fresh
SC25A	clabber cheese	matured

SC41A	homemade cheese	older way
GA1F2	clotted cream	curd mixed with cream, eaten with sugar and cinnamon
GA1F2	curd	left after liquid *whey* pressed out
GA24A2	NR	don't know; neighbor made from clabber
SC11N2	cheese	homemade
SC14A2	cottage cheese	made of clabber
SC22B2	curds	(and whey
SC22B2	cottage cheese	curds were like)
NC25B2	cottage cheese	not cooked; drained, from clabber
NC62B2	cotted cheese	with curds; homemade
NC62B2	cottage cheese	in store [this is also a pron. of *cotted cheese* with assimilation]
NC69A2	cheese	just); homemade, like cream cheese

21. Bucket

1930s			*1990*	
bucket	38		bucket	35
milk bucket	1		flower bucket	1
pail	21		milk bucket	10
piggin	4		milk pail	5
water bucket	1		milking pail	1
water pail	1		pail	10
			pails	3
			water bucket	5
			well buckets	1

GA1F!	pail	metal; milk only
GA3A	pail	wood; no handle; set on head
GA4N	pail	wood with wire bail; as a boy always
GA10A	bucket	metal or wooden with bail
GA10A	pail	wood; stave up for handle
GA13A	piggin	wood; one stave up for handle
GA13A	pail	large; for milk
GA15A	pail	wood; stave up for handle
SC1A	pail	wood; stave up for handle
SC11N	pail	wood; one stave up

Appendix 4

SC12B	piggin	wood; stave handle
SC12B	pail	not used now
SC14A	pail	wood; stave at side for handle
SC19N	pail	wood; no handle; like tub
SC19N	piggin	wood; handle at each side; no bail
SC19N	water bucket	metal
SC22N	pail	wood; one stave up at side
SC22B	pail	wood; 2 staves; larger; set in kitchen
SC22B	piggin	wood; stave up; for milk
SC25A	pail	one stave sticking up; wood
SC30A	pail	wood; staves up for handle
SC41A	pail	no bail; stave up for handle; wood
NC24N	pail	wood; stave up for handle
NC24A	water pail	wood; stave up
NC25A	bucket	wood; natural
NC25B	bucket	wood
NC25B	pail	metal
NC25B	milk bucket	metal; small at bottom, large at the top
GA4N2	bucket	wooden ones seen only as part of ice cream churn
GA15A2	bucket	no wooden ones
GA24A2	water bucket	wooden)
GA34A2	water bucket	also wooden)
GA432	bucket	seamless aluminum for milking; *bucket* wooden also
GA432	water bucket	tin
SC11N2	pail	also wooden)
SC11I2	bucket	wooden one used in a well
SC12B2	bucket	didn't call it a *pail*
SC14A2	bucket	also wood): same pattern as barrel, for well water
SC22N2	bucket	aluminum for milking
SC22N2	water bucket	wooden)
SC22B2	bucket	galvanized tin or enamel; *bucket* also wooden
SC25A2	milk pail	strictly for milk
SC25A2	bucket	for water
SC30A2	bucket	three-gallon metal); for milk
SC41A2	water bucket	cedar)
NC24A2	pail	for milk; also wooden *pail*

NC24B2	bucket	also wooden)
NC25A2	pail	wooden)
NC25B2	bucket	for water or milk; of cedar
NC52B2	pail	10-quart)
NC52B2	bucket	never had one of wood
NC57B2	bucket	10-quart)
NC69A2	spriggin	wooden one
NC75A2	bucket	bought lard in; also wooden

22. Calls to Cow (when milking)

1930s			*1990*	
NR	6		(holler at it)	1
saw	9		(push with hand)	1
saw-cow	1		back	1
saw-wench	1		back up	1
so	22		back up your leg	1
sook	1		back your foot	1
			be still	6
			easy now	1
			hike your leg	1
			hold	1
			hold it Nellie	1
			NA	5
			NR	10
			sah	4
			sah sook	1
			saw	1
			so	5
			so cow	1
			so cow so	1
			stand still	1
			suh	1
			wo	1

GA3A2	so	"where he'd be still"
GA4N2	NR	no cows
SC11N2	NA	say something nice to them

SC19N2	NR	"fixed" their foot
SC25A2	NR	just talked to them
NC52N2	stand still	"I'd whup 'em; they'd stand just as nice"
NC56A2	be still	"just sort of talk to them", call by name
NC57B2	(holler at it)	just basically)
NC71B2	hold	sometimes call it cussing
NC75A2	NR	"I never did do no milking much": don't know

23. Calls to Cow (in pasture)

1930s		*1990*	
co-ah	1	(by name)	2
co-anch	1	co-ach (x2)	1
co-anch (x2)	1	co-an	1
co-anchie	1	co-ee	2
co-eh	3	co-eh	1
co-eh (x2)	1	co-eh (x3)	2
co-eh (x3)	1	come (x3)	2
co-eh (x5)	1	come here cow	1
co-en	1	come in	1
co-en (x2)	1	come on (x2)	1
co-ench	3	coo-an	1
co-wanch	1	coo-wit (x4)	1
co-wen	1	core (x3)	1
co-wench	6	here	1
co-wench (x2)	1	here cow	1
come	1	NA	1
dook	1	NR	13
here pooh	1	soo (x3)	1
koli come	1	soo-calf	1
NR	5	soo-cow	1
soo-cow	6	soo-cow (x2)	2
sook	1	sook (x5)	1
sook (x2)	1	sookie (x3)	1
sook (x5)	1	woo [pause] woo kee woo	1
sook-cow	2	woop woop cow	1
sookie	1		

GA13A	koli come	*koli* = obviously little *kuh*
GA1F2	soo-ee (x3)	yard man called then
GA3A2	co-ach (x2)	sent dogs after stock in the woods
SC11N2	come (x3)	(+ name)
SC12B2	NR	didn't call them, but rang "cow bells"
SC19N2	NR	didn't call, came at feeding time
SC22B2	NR	cow kept on a tether
SC25A2	NR	came up at a
NC57B2	NA	"just a little old hollering sound"
NC62B2	here	(+ name)
NC75B2	NR	used a dog

24. Calls to Calves

1930s			*1990*	
calfie	1		co-eh	1
co-bee	1		co-see (x4)	1
co-calf	1		NA	12
come calfie	1		NR	20
NR	10		soo-calf	1
soo-calf	16		soo-cow	1
soo-calf (x2)	2		sook-calf	2
soo-calfie	1		sookie (x4)	1
sook	2			
sook (x2)	2			
sook (x3)	1			
sookie	2			
sookie (x3)	1			

GA3A	sook	to drive them [also GA4N, GA10A, GA13A, SC12B]
GA3A2	NR	didn't call, penned up
GA13A2	NR	come with cows [also GA432, SC12B2, SC14A2, NC24A2, NC24B2, NC25A2, NC62B2]

25. Calls to Horse or Mule (in pasture)

1930s
(whistling)	2
kobe (x2)	1
koop (x3)	1
kope	13
kope (x2)	1
kope (x3)	7
kope (x4)	2
kope (x5)	1
kope-kovee (x5)	1
kup	1
kwope	2
kwup	1
NR	7

1990
(by name)	10
(clucking)	1
(whistling)	9
kope (x3)	1
NA	4
NR	15

SC1A2	NR	weren't let out to graze
SC12B2	NR	stayed in lot or shed
SC14A2	NR	no special call: didn't go out
SC22N2	NR	mules would come at feeding time
SC25A2	NR	stayed close to barn (horse thieves)
SC30A2	NA	"just holler"
NC24A2	NR	"didn't never have to call them"
NC25A2	NR	come up at night
NC57B2	(whistling)	horse; called for mule by name
NC75B2	NR	used a dog

26. Get Up!

1930s		*1990*	
(clucking)	31	(clucking)	10
alright	1	come up	3
come	1	get up	20
come here	1	giddy up	8
come up	4	go	1
come up there	1	let's go	1
get up	32	NR	3
go along	3		
go on	9		
go up	1		
NA	1		

GA1F2	NR	pull on reins
GA4N2	NR	whip them
GA10A2	(clucking)	"suck your lips"
SC11I2	(clucking)	to dumb mule or horse; *give it leg*: for nice horse
NC23B2	let's go	and hit them
NC46C2	NR	kick it
NC57B2	(clucking)	"clicking sound"

28. Calls to Horse or Mule (to turn left)

1930s		1990	
haw	35	gee	1
NR	1	gee or haw	7
waw-comee	1	haw	22
wo-haw	2	NA	1
		NR	6

GA3A2	haw	also pulled on lines
GA34A2	haw	not asked which direction
SC12B2	NR	pulled on lines
SC25A2	NR	pull reins [also NC23B2, NC29B2]
NC71B2	haw	for horses, not mules

29. Calls to Horse or Mule (to turn right)

1930s		1990	
gee	38	gee	22
NR	1	gee or haw	7
		haw	1
		NA	1
		NR	6

GA34A2	gee	not asked which direction
SC12B2	NR	pulled on lines
SC25A2	NR	pull reins [also NC23B2, NC29B2]
NC71B2	gee	for horses, not mules

30. Calls to Pigs

1930s		*1990*	
(blowing)	1	goosh (x3)	1
(sucking sound)	3	gorp (x2)	1
goop	7	here piggie piggie piggie	1
gope	1	NA	1
gwoop	1	NR	6
hoop	1	pi hog	1
hoopee	1	pig (x2)	2
NA	1	pig (x3)	2
NR	4	pig (x5)	1
oo	1	pig woo (x2)	1
oop	1	piggie	1
pee	1	piggie (x2)	1
peeoop	1	piggie (x3)	3
pig	5	piggie (x4)	2
pig (x3)	1	piggie [x4] wooee piggie	
pig (x4)	3	piggie piggeeee	1
piggie	11	sooey	1
piggie (x3)	1	sooey (x2)	4
piggie (x5)	1	sooey (x3)	2
pigoo	5	sookie pig	1
pigooey	1	whoop whoop	1
pigoop	2	woo pig (x2)	1
sooey	2	woo pig pig woo woo	1
wo-ee	1	woo piggie (x2)	1
woo	1	woo piggie (x2) pig	
woop	2	piggie woo piggie	1
		woop woop	1

GA13A	gope	falsetto
GA24A	(blowing)	[f]; if close to pigs
GA43	piggie	when closer to pigs
GA43	pigooey	falsetto
SC1A	pigoop	at a distance
SC11N	oo	falsetto
SC14A	goop	falsetto
SC30A	(sucking sound)	close by
NC24A	pigoop	falsetto
NC24B	peeoop	falsetto

NC46B	piggie	little ones
NC46B	woo	at distance
NC52B	hoop	hogs
GA1F2	sooey	gf. said
GA4N2	whoop whoop	or hit stick on bucket, everybody has different way
GA10A2	woo piggie (x2) pig piggie woo piggie	since I got these homemade teeth I can't call 'em
GA24A2	sookie pig	to big ones
GA24A2	piggie (x3)	to young ones
SC1A2	NR	didn't have to call them
SC11I2	woo pig (x2)	in Georgia; *sooey* to make them go away
SC19N2	NR	didn't call, came up to eat
NC24N2	pi hog	and hit slop bucket; [i]
NC24A2	goosh (x3)	could also be used to drive away
NC24B2	pig (x2)	beat on bucket
NC25B2	pig (x2)	high pitch

31. Calls to Sheep

1930s

co-naa	1
co-nan	1
co-nannie	5
co-sheep	2
co-sheepie	1
come nannie (x2)	1
coo-nannie	1
coo-sheep	2
coo-sheepie	1
cushie	1
lamb (x3)	1
NA	1
naa (x3)	1
NR	15
sheep	2
sheep (x3)	1
sheepie	5
tack (x3)	1

1990

NA	5
NR	33
sheepie (x3)	1

GA13A	co-nannie	esp. used for goats
GA43	co-sheepie	falsetto
GA3A2	NR	don't know; f. had them
SC11N2	NR	don't call them but round them up (they're dumb)
NC71B2	NR	round up with dogs

32. Calls to Chickens

1930s		*1990*	
(clicking)	1	(clicking)	1
bid bid biddie	1	biddie (x3)	1
biddie	3	biddie (x4)	1
biddie (x3)	2	chick (x2)	2
biddie (x4)	2	chick (x3)	6
biddie (x5)	1	chick (x3) chickie	1
chick (x3)	5	chick (x4)	4
chick (x3-5)	1	chick (x5)	1
chick (x4)	4	chick (x6)	1
chick (x5)	5	chick (x6) chickie	1
chick (x6)	3	chick (x7)	1
chick chick chick		chick (x8) chickie	1
chick chickie	1	chicken	1
chick chick chick chickoo	1	chickie (x3)	6
chickie	10	chickie (x4)	1
chickie (x2)	2	chickie (x5)	1
chickie (x2-3)	1	chickie chickie chick woo	
chickie (x3)	5	chickie chickie	1
chickie (x5)	1	come chick	1
chickie chick	1	here chick	1
chickoo (x3)	1	here chick chick	1
NA	1	here chick chick chick	3
pee (x5)	1	NA	2
peep (x4)	1	NR	5

GA10A	chickie (x2)	falsetto [also SC14A]
GA13A	chick (x4)	falsetto [also SC14A, SC19N]
GA13A	pee (x5)	falsetto

SC1A	biddie	little ones [also SC30A, SC41A, NC52B, NC56A, NC57B]
NC52N	widdie	little ones

GA10A2	biddie (x4)	little ones [also NC24A2]
GA24A2	chicken	just holler) (3 or 4 times
SC25A2	chick (x5)	rise in pitch on last repetition
SC41A2	chickie (x3)	high-pitched
NC25B2	chick (x6)	high pitch

33. Frying Pan

1930s			*1990*	
fryer		1	fry pan	3
frying pan		37	frying pan	24
skillet		8	frying pans	2
spider		8	pan	2
			pot	1
			skillet	13
			spider	7
			spiders	1

GA1F!	skillet	same as frying pan
GA1F!	spider	flat bottom; fireplace
GA1F!	Scotch kettle	round bottom for deep frying; wire enclosure keeps foods from touching bottom
GA3A	bake oven	no handle; otherwise same as spider
GA3A	skillet	Negroes call it
GA3A	spider	handle; deep; to bake in; curving top so fire could be made on top and bottom both
GA4N	skillet	"for boil things in"; round bottom
GA4N	spider	bake or fry; flat bottom
GA10A	spider	deep, heavy, flat bottom; legs
GA10A	skillet	light; handle, 3 legs
GA13A	spider	flat bottom; legs
GA13A	skillet	round bottom and spout
GA15A	skillet	3 legs; deep round bottom
GA15A	spider	3 legs; flat bottom
GA24A	skillet	flat bottom
GA24A	spider	iron, 2" or 3"; legs on it for fireplace

GA34A	skillet	flat bottom; fry meat; also for type with 3 legs
GA34A	oven	bake bread; 3 legs
GA34A	frying pan	natural
GA43	skillet	baked in; 3 legs; flat bottom
SC11N	spider	same as skillet
SC11N	skillet	cover on it for baking bread
SC12B	skillet	long handle, 3 legs; deep
SC12B	spider	same as skillet
SC14A	saucepan	more like a pot
SC14A	spider	long handle, 6 legs; deep
SC19N	spider	bake; top; deep, flat bottom
SC19N	skillet	same as saucepan
SC22N	spider	handle; deep, flat bottom; also for type with legs used in fireplace
SC22N	skillet	long handle, legs; very deep round bottom
SC22B	skillet	deep; fireplace; flat
SC22B	spider	open; fireplace
SC25A	spider	handle, on legs; deep; to bake
SC25A	griddle	flat; on legs
SC25A	skillet	3 legs, handle; to boil; deep round bottom
SC30A	skillet	small, wider at top, round bottom; 3 legs
SC30A	spider	flat bottom; 3 legs
SC41A	skillet	3 legs; fireplace; round bottom
SC41A	spider	3 legs; fireplace; flat bottom
NC23B	skillet	heavy
NC25A	skillet	round bottom, small; 3 legs; to heat water
NC25A	spider	deep, flat bottom; legs; for bake or fry
NC25B	spider	deep, heavy iron; short handle
NC25B	skillet	round bottom and 3 legs
NC29B	spider	heavy; 3 legs; fireplace
NC52B	spider	flat bottom; 3 legs
NC52B	skillet	deep, round bottom; 3 legs
NC56A	skillet	3 legs; in fire
NC57B	skillet	3 legs; to fry
NC62B	skillet	3 legs, long handle; flat bottom
NC71B	skillet	3 legs
NC71C!	skillet	heavier iron
NC75A	skillet	3 legs; fireplace
NC75B	skillet	also for type with 3 legs

Appendix 4

GA3A2	skillet	w/legs, to cook over fire; "darkies" used them
GA4N2	spider	gf. said; can be flat or with 3 legs
GA4N2	frying pan	"all I ever called it"
GA15A2	frying pan	may be lighter metal than skillet
GA15A2	skillet	heavy, of iron
GA24A2	frying pan	of iron
GA24A2	skillet	had lid; hung over fire or on legs
SC1A2	spiders	flat on bottom
SC1A2	skillet	with legs
SC14A2	frying pan	that's all they ever called them
SC19N2	skillet	don't know what that means
SC22B2	spider	with legs, to use in fireplace
SC25A2	frying pans	iron)
NC24N2	skillet	6" diameter, 6" deep, with legs and handle
NC24A2	skillet	with legs
NC24A2	spider	same as fry pan
NC25A2	skillet	some say
NC29B2	spider	only for one of cast iron
NC52N2	spider	iron
NC62B2	skillet	with or without legs
NC75A2	skillet	iron)
NC75A2	frying pan	electric)
NC75B2	skillet	iron)
NC75B2	spider	3 legs, m. said

34. Dish Cloth

1930s			*1990*	
dish cloth	6		cloth	1
dish mop	1		dish cloth	14
dish rag	35		dish cloths	1
mop	1		dish rag	16
wash rag	1		dish rags	1
			dish towel	1
			NA	5
			store-bought dish cloth	1
			wash cloth	3
			wash cloths	1
			wash rag	2

GA34A2 dish rag   made of flour sack
SC1A2   dish cloths   of flour sacks
SC25A2 dish towel   tails from worn out shirt
NC24B2 dish rag   most people call it
NC46C2 wash rag   doesn't use one
NC62B2 dish rag   m. says
NC69A2 dish rag   never a *cloth*
NC69A2 store-bought dish cloth   didn't have no)

35. Dish Towel

1930s		*1990*	
cloth	1	dish cloth	5
cup towel	1	dish rag	3
dish cloth	5	dish towel	9
dish towel	14	dry cloth	3
dry cloth	2	dry rag	2
dry rag	4	dry towel	1
drying cloth	4	drying cloth	7
drying rag	5	drying rag	2
drying towel	2	drying towel	1
towel	1	NA	8
wipe rag	2	NR	3
wiping rag	1	towel	2

GA432   NR   piece of towelling
SC12B2 dish cloth   "all have to match"
SC14A2 NR   don't know name, larger than dishrag
NC46C2 NR   none, uses dishwasher
NC62B2 dish rag   m. says
NC69A2 dish rag   dry)

36. Paper Bag

1930s		*1990*	
bag	7	bag	5
paper bag	20	bags	2
paper poke	8	brown sack	1
paper sack	15	grocery bag	3
poke	1	NA	3
sack	7	paper bag	20
		paper bags	2
		paper poke	3
		paper sack	4
		paper sacks	1
		poke	5
		sack	1
		sacks	1

GA3A	sack	small
GA4N	bag	as a boy
GA15A	bag	rarer
GA24A	sack	less
GA43	sack	at least two gallons
SC12B	bag	as a girl
SC19N	sack	later
SC25A	bag	as a girl
SC41A	bag	heard often but not used in family
SC41A	poke	heard often but not used in family
NC52B2	paper bag	used now
NC62B2	poke	m. always said

37. Burlap Sack

1930s

bag	8
bagging sack	1
bark sack	1
burlap bag	3
burlap sack	1
cloth bag	2
crocus bag	10
crocus sack	8
croker sack	5
hemp sack	2
sack	10
tow bag	4
tow sack	14

1990

bag	3
bags	4
burlap bag	11
burlap bags	1
burlap sack	5
burlaps	1
corn sack	1
cotton picking sack	2
cotton sack	1
crocus bag	4
crocus sack	3
croker bag	2
croker sack	9
feed sack	1
fertilize sack	1
fertilizer bag	2
fertilizer sack	1
guano sack	2
hemp sack	1
orange bud sack	1
pea sack	1
sack	6
sacks	3
tow bag	1
tow bags	2
tow sack	5
tow sacks	2

GA1F!	crocus bag	heavy, for potatoes
GA3A	sack	small
GA3A	crocus bag	large, coarse
GA4N	bag	heavy, for potatoes
GA4N	crocus bag	heavy, for potatoes
GA10A	crocus sack	coarse
GA10A	sack	small
GA13A	crocus bag	heavy, coarse

Appendix 4

SC11I!	crocus bag	heavy, coarse
SC11I!	sack	only if very large
SC12B	crocus sack	heavy, for potatoes
SC14A	crocus bag	natural
SC14A	burlap bag	rare
SC22N	bag	natural
SC25A	bag	as a girl
GA3A2	croker sack	= 200-lb. fertilizer bags; "don't see 'em no more"
GA4N2	croker bag	used to hold conchs collected in fishing boat
GA10A2	sack	200-lb.)
GA13A2	croker bag	= 100-lb. bag; used for Irish potatoes
GA15A2	bag	200-lb.)
SC1A2	sack	made *sack sheets* of them to cover crops
SC12B2	burlap bag	used to pick cotton
SC22B2	croker sack	"c-r-o-a-k-e-r"; possibly used to fish for *croakers*
SC22B2	burlap bag	*crocus sack* rejected: "we don't grow crocuses"
NC24N2	croker sack	natural
NC25A2	bags	200-lb.)
NC46C2	sack	as a child

38. Siding

1930s

clapboards	1
siding	1
weatherboard	4
weatherboarding	33
weatherboards	2

1990

board	1
boards	2
clapboard	1
clapboards	3
lap siding	2
lap siding board	1
lapboards	1
lumber	1
NA	1
NR	3
planks	1
shingles	1
shiplap	2
sideboards	1
siding	10
tongue-in-groove	1
weatherboard	2
weatherboarding	12
weatherboards	1

GA13A	clapboards	split, for fence (= palings)
GA13A	siding	rare
SC19N	clapboard	on the roof
GA34A2	siding	not wood
SC25A2	siding	aluminum)
SC30A2	lap siding board	stress on last word
SC41A2	siding	vinyl)
NC75B2	fir strips	narrow, over place where wide boards came together
NC75B2	siding	brick): tar paper printed in brick pattern

39. Gutters

1930s		*1990*	
eave troughs	1	drain	2
eaves trough	1	drain board	1
eaves troughs	1	flange	1
gutter	2	gutter	9
guttering	2	guttering	2
gutters	28	gutters	16
NR	2	NA	3
trough	1	NR	7
troughs	1		
water drainer	1		

| SC25A | troughs | [v] not [f] in *troughs* [also SC30A] |
| NC25B | gutters | not used |

| GA15A2 | gutters | had none |
| NC23B2 | flange | had none |

40. Valley (of roof)

1930s		*1990*	
alley	2	alley	1
alleys	2	eave	1
gutter	6	ell	1
NR	4	gables	1
valley	14	gutter	6
valleys	10	hip	1
		NA	6
		NR	9
		valley	9

SC25A2	NR	don't know; rejected *valley*
NC29B2	joyces	f. said
NC46B2	valley	natural

41. Privy

1930s		*1990*	
back house	24	back house	1
closet	4	closet	2
garden house	3	garden house	2
johnny	1	half-moon house	1
little house	1	house behind the house	1
NA	2	john	3
NR	1	johnny	1
outhouse	1	johnny house	3
privy	21	ladies restroom	1
		out west	1
		outdoor house	1
		outdoor privy	1
		outdoor toilet	6
		outer house	1
		outhouse	22
		outside toilet	3
		privet	1
		privy	10
		toilet	12

GA1F2	privy	of tabby, with 2 or 3 divisions
GA4N2	outhouse	different families had different names for it
GA4N2	out west	brother's term, only used in family
SC12B2	privy	two-seater)
SC22N2	outside toilet	previously in the bushes
SC22B2	outhouse	"colored people called it"
SC25A2	outdoor privy	nicer name than outdoor toilet
NC62B2	outhouse	"we had a 2-holer"

42. Corn Crib

1930s
barn	2
corn barn	3
corn crib	7
corn house	10
crib	23
crib house	1

1990
barn	1
bin	2
bins	2
corn barn	5
corn barns	1
corn bin	5
corn crib	7
corn cribs	1
corn house	1
corn room	1
corn shack	1
corn shed	1
crib	6
cribs	1
house	1
NA	1
NR	9
packhouse	1
silo	1

GA13A	crib	inside the corn house
SC12B	crib	inside part of barn for corn
SC25A	crib	small

GA4N2	NR	kept in barn in sacks
GA10A2	corn cribs	in barn [also NC24A2, NC52B2]
GA10A2	crib	in barn [also SC11I2, NC24A2, NC75A2]
GA10A2	corn house	separate from barn
GA13A2	corn crib	none here, used the barn
GA15A2	NR	stored in barn [also GA24A2, SC12B2, SC14A2, SC19N2, SC25A2, NC24N2]

SC1A2	corn barn	inside barn, not separate
SC22B2	corn bin	in the barn; also *feed bin*
SC30A2	bins	metal
SC41A2	bin	in feed room in barn
NC23B2	bin	inside barn

Appendix 4

NC24A2 bins	in barn	
NC25B2 corn barn	pea barn also, for dry peas	
NC52N2 corn bin	inside barn [also NC57B2]	
NC56A2 corn room	separate building	
NC69A2 crib	separate or it's not a *crib*	
NC75B2 corn bin	large separate bldg.; also stored baled hay there	

43. Loft

1930s		*1990*	
barn loft	2	attic	1
cock loft	1	barn loft	2
hay loft	2	fodder loft	1
loft	33	granary	1
loft of the barn	1	hay loft	7
mow	2	loft	26
up loft	1	NA	1
		NR	1
		overhead	1
		platform	1
		upstairs	2

GA1F!	loft	steps ascent
GA1F!	cock loft	ladder ascent, a higher loft
GA4N2	overhead	stress on second syllable

44. Cowpen

1930s		*1990*	
break	1	corner	1
cow lot	2	cowpen	2
cowpen	32	NA	5
cuppin	1	NR	26
milk gap	6	pasture	1
NR	1	pen	3

Appendix 4

GA24A	cowpen	*milkgap* = sliding pole in cowpen fence
NC25A	break	for 1 cow to keep from kicking
NC25B	cowpen	place for pasturing cows in a field
NC62B	cowpen	*milkgap* is part of cowpen
GA4N2	cowpen	at night; roamed freely in day
SC19N2	pasture	smaller); to keep a calf out
SC22N2	corner	(of pasture

45. Hog Pen

1930s			*1990*	
hog house	1		floored fattening pen	1
hog lot	2		floored pen	1
hog pen	32		flooring pen	1
hog pens	1		hog house	1
hog shelter	1		hog lot	2
pen	3		hog parlors	1
pens	1		hog pen	11
pig pen	1		lot	5
pig sty	1		NA	2
			pen	9
			pens	2
			pig lot	3
			pig parlor	1
			pig pen	10
			pig sty	1

GA34A	hog lot	for running
GA34A	hog house	for sleeping
GA34A	hog pen	for killing
SC25A	hog pen	to fatten
GA3A2	pen	for fattening; also ranged in woods
GA10A2	flooring pen	to fatten them
SC12B2	hog pen	or in woods on a *stob*
SC12B2	pig parlor	indoor
SC25A2	pen	with piglets; otherwise in pasture

NC52B2 floored fattening pen 2-3 months before slaughter;
                              otherwise in pasture
NC69A2 hog house   if many hogs (i.e., 20-40)

46. Barnyard

1930s		*1990*	
barn lot	3	barn lot	2
barnyard	4	barnyard	5
cow lot	2	calf lot	1
horse lot	2	corral	1
lot	32	cow lot	1
		exercising lot	1
		grazing lot	1
		horse lot	2
		lot	21
		mule lot	1
		NA	3
		NR	5
		pen	1
		stable	1

SC41A2 NR   none; pasture began next to barn

48. Rail Fence

1930s		*1990*	
crooked fence	1	fence	2
crooked rail fence	1	fences	1
fence	1	log fence	1
galloping fence	1	NA	3
rail fence	36	NR	5
worm fence	4	rail fence	13
		rail fences	2
		rail fencing	1
		rails	1
		split fence	1
		split rail fence	6
		wooden fence	1

GA10A	rail fence	zigzag
GA10A	fence	any rail fence; *laying the worm* = the first rail
GA24A	rail fence	*lay the worm* [also GA43, SC12B, SC25A, SC30A, NC25B]

GA1F2	fences	of little trees, crossed
GA15A2	rail fence	"before my time", only as a boy
GA432	rail fence	8–10 ft. [-long] rails, 8 rails high
SC25A2	split rail fence	of cedar

52. Grindstone

1930s			*1990*	
grinding rock	2		emery wheel	1
grinding stone	2		emery wheels	1
grindrock	9		grinder	2
grindseed	1		grinding rock	1
grindstone	30		grinding rocks	1
grinstone	1		grinding stone	6
			grinding wheel	2
			grindrock	4
			grindrocks	1
			grindstone	10
			grindwheel	1
			mill stone	1
			NA	2
			NR	6
			stone	1
			stones	1
			whetrock	1

GA10A	grindrock	"more properer"
SC14A	grinstone	Negroes
NC25B	grinstone	natural

GA3A2	grindrocks	turned by hand; 2 people operated it
GA15A2	grindstone	turned by hand
GA24A2	grindrock	two people to hold and one to turn
GA34A2	grindstone	turned by hand [also GA432]

SC11I2	grinding wheel	turned by hand
SC19N2	grinding stone	stress on second word
SC22N2	whetrock	for axe
NC25B2	grindstone	with a treadle
NC25B2	emery wheels	same material as grindstone; turned with a crank
NC46B2	grinding wheel	by foot
NC52N2	NR	tools sharpened by blacksmith with *bellows and anvil*
NC52B2	grindrock	hand- or pedal-turned
NC57B2	grinder	electric)
NC71B2	emery wheel	electric

56. Lines (driving)

1930s			*1990*	
line	1		lines	29
lines	34		NA	1
NA	1		NR	2
reins	11		range	1
			rein	1
			reins	8
			rope	3
			strops	1

GA1F!	lines	cord or rope
GA1F!	reins	leather [also GA13A, SC11N, SC14A]
SC11N	line	rope [also SC14A]
SC19N	line	natural
GA3A2	lines	set of)
GA15A2	lines	plow) [also SC12B2, SC14A2, SC30A2]
GA24A2	strops	of leather on buggy or wagon
GA24A2	lines	plow); of rope
GA432	lines	check)
SC22B2	reins	even if plowing
NC23B2	lines	guide)
NC25B2	lines	remembers leather before rope
NC69A2	reins	if of leather
NC69A2	rope	plow); if of rope

57. Reins (riding)

1930s		*1990*	
bridle	3	bridle	1
bridle reins	11	bridle reins	2
bridles	1	line	1
lines	7	lines	6
NA	1	NA	6
rein	2	NR	1
reins	21	range	1
		rein	2
		reins	19
		ropes	1

SC11N	reins	leather
SC11N	lines	rope
GA3A2	lines	shorter than on plow
GA13A2	reins	[ɪ], not [e]
GA15A2	lines	or held to mane
SC30A2	NR	held to mane
NC24N2	lines	leather)

58. Tongue (of a wagon)

1930s		*1990*	
coupling pole	1	beam	1
pole	2	center piece	1
tongue	36	NA	4
wagon hung	1	NR	8
wagon tongue	1	pole	1
		tongue	21
		wagon tongue	3

59. Shafts (of a buggy)

1930s		*1990*	
cart shavs	1	beam	1
fills	3	NA	2
shaft	1	NR	14
shafts	1	shaft	1
shav	2	shafts	1
shavs	35	shavs	21

GA10A	fills	for a cart
SC11N	shaft	plural
SC25A	cart shavs	on a cart
NC25B	fills	my cart

NC46B2	NR	never saw buggies
NC69A2	shavs	most people say
NC69A2	shaft	proper word

60. Singletree

1930s		*1990*	
cross bar	1	NA	1
singletree	24	NR	8
swingletree	17	singletree	20
		swingletree	7

NC25B	swingletree	often
GA4N2	train	some kind of a)
NC24N2	singletree	[æɪ]
NC69A2	singletree	"real" term
NC69A2	swingletree	local term
NC75B2	swingletree	[æ]

61. Doubletree

1930s		*1990*	
double singletree	6	double	1
double swingletree	1	double singletree	1
doubletree	30	doubletree	14
NR	3	NA	9
		NR	10
		singletree	1
		singletrees	1
		two singletrees	1
		two swingletrees	1

SC11N2 doubletree   also *triple tree*
NC57B2 doubletree   different from two singletrees

62. Car

1930s		*1990*	
auto	2	automobile	4
automobile	37	automobiles	3
car	36	car	18
machine	2	cars	2
mobile	1	NA	13
motor	2		

SC22B   car   common
SC22B   motor   rare

65. Driveway

1930s
alley	1
avenue	18
driveway	2
lane	35
private road	1
road	1
turn in	1

1990
avenue	3
dirt road	2
drive	4
driveway	14
farm road	2
field road	1
lane	4
NA	6
NR	2
private road	1
road	1
roads	1
wagon trail	1
yard road	1

GA4N	lane	fenced
SC22N	avenue	long
SC25A	avenue	straight
SC41A	avenue	rare
SC41A	lane	fenced, esp. now for cows
NC71C!	lane	a road not used much; or house to barn

GA3A2	lane	longer than driveway
GA15A2	avenue	on big plantations
SC11N2	road	little); also (to the road
SC11I2	driveway	in city
SC11I2	avenue	more elegant, with trees; not paved is better
SC11I2	drive	in country
SC25A2	NR	*walkway*
NC24N2	NR	*footpath*
NC25A2	avenue	at wife's home, about 1/2 mile long
NC29B2	NR	*path*
NC52B2	lane	a few people had them
NC75B2	lane	m. said

66. Mongrel

1930s		*1990*	
cur	18	black and tan	1
cur dog	19	catch dog	1
curl dog	1	cur	1
feist	20	cur dog	3
feist dog	1	dog	2
mix-blooded dog	1	dogs	2
mongrel	10	feist	3
mongrel breed	1	heinz	2
NR	1	heinz 57	1
		hound	2
		mix dog	1
		mixed	1
		mixed breed	8
		mixed-up cur dog	1
		mixture	1
		mongrel	6
		mutt	3
		mutt dog	1
		NA	4
		slut	1
		some o' dog	1
		sooner	5
		sorry slut	1
		stray	1
		yard dog	3

GA1F!	feist	small [also GA3A, GA4N, GA10A, GA15A, GA43, SC30A, SC41A, NC25B, NC75A, NC75B]
GA4N	curl dog	natural; will not admit *curl*
GA10A	cur dog	small, short-eared
GA13A	feist	tiny kind [also SC11N, SC12B]
GA13A	mongrel	not used
GA13A	cur dog	= short-eared dog; common
SC11I!	feist	skinny, small variety
SC14A	feist	poodle mix
SC19N	cur	ordinary

SC19N	feist dog	small
SC30A	cur dog	a variety
NC25A	cur dog	old kind; extinct
NC25B	cur	"plain dog"
NC25B	mongrel	recognizable mixture
NC69A	cur	special [also NC75B]
GA10A2	catch dog	mixed shepherd and collie; to catch hogs and cows: hogs by the ear, cows by the nose
GA13A2	dogs	just) [also GA15A2, NC52N2]
SC11I2	some o' dog	"some o' this, some o' that"
SC12B2	slut	female
SC22N2	mutt dog	"ain't too much good for nothing"
SC22B2	mixture	say what we mean
SC22B2	mongrel	speaking on an intellectual
NC24N2	dog	just a common)
NC29B2	dogs	little cute)
NC69A2	heinz	57 varieties
NC75B2	hound	probably a mixture; for hunting

67. Bull

1930s			*1990*	
beast	2		beasts	1
bull	36		boy cow	1
cow beast	1		brute	1
gentleman cow	4		bull	31
he cow	1		bulls	2
male	6		he-cow	1
male beast	4		male	1
male brute	1		NA	1
male cow	2		oxen	1
NR	1		stock animal	1
ox	1			
sire	1			
stock	1			
stock beast	2			
stock brute	1			
top cow	1			
yearling	1			

Appendix 4

GA13A	bull	humorous
SC30A	bull	in hushed voice
NC24N	male beast	polite
NC24B	male beast	used around women
NC25B	yearling	used around women
NC62B	ox	used around women
GA1F2	oxen	for pulling wagons
GA10A2	bulls	the old word is)
SC11N2	he-cow	"said it just like it was"; also *she-cow*
SC22B2	stock animal	"Mammy" didn't approve of *bull*

68. Calve

1930s			*1990*	
be fresh	5		be fresh	2
birth a calf	1		become fresh	1
bring a calf	6		bring a calf	1
calve	5		calve	3
come fresh	3		come in	2
come in	4		coming fresh	1
come in fresh	3		coming in	3
drop a calf	6		drop a calf	4
find a calf	13		fold	1
freshen	6		freshen	2
get a calf	1		freshen in	1
have a calf	7		freshening	1
NR	1		give birth to a calf	1
			have a baby	1
			have a calf	3
			NA	3
			NR	5
			spring	1

NC25B	drop a calf	among men
NC25B	freshen	rare
GA3A2	freshen	refers to quality of milk after birth
GA432	freshen	also *heavy with a calf*

SC25A2	foal	"I think the term they use now is); "we didn't foal nothing, we just birthed it"
NC25B2	NR	don't remember, didn't talk about
NC52B2	spring	she's going to)
NC71B2	coming in	she's)

69. Ram

1930s			*1990*	
boy sheep	1		buck	1
buck	4		male sheep	1
NA	1		NA	10
ram	37		NR	19
			ram	6

70. Boar

1930s			*1990*	
boar	31		boar	26
boar hog	9		boar hog	5
male hog	5		hog	1
NR	2		male	1
stock hog	1		male hog	5
			NA	1
			NR	2
			sow	1
			stock	1

GA3A2	boar	*barrow* if "tended to"
GA4N2	boar hog	*barrow* if castrated: rankness goes out, fit to eat
GA4N2	boar	"spelled b-o, I guess"
SC11N2	boar	men had different term
NC46B2	boar	didn't use term

71. Stallion

1930s
male horse	3
NA	1
stallion	22
stallion horse	2
stock horse	1
stud	14
stud horse	14

1990
filly	1
he horse	2
horse	4
horses	1
mare	1
NA	4
NR	7
stallion	8
stallions	1
stud	8
stud horse	3
studs	3

GA13A	stone horse	from old woman here
SC19N	stud horse	natural
GA3A2	stud	*gelding* if "tended to"
GA10A2	stud	= young colt; we called them)
SC1A2	NR	none, only mules
SC11N2	he horse	can't think of proper name; some "rough" names
SC25A2	horse	just called them all horses
SC41A2	horse	vs. mare
NC29B2	NR	no horses; *mule* for male mule
NC62B2	stallion	used today
NC62B2	stud	main inf. didn't know a term, asked aux. inf. for help
NC71B2	stud	most common term
NC75B2	stud horse	the one they "bred by"

72. Fowls

1930s

chickens	1
flock	2
fowl	1
fowls	23
NR	5
poultry	8

1990

birds	1
farm fowls	1
flock	1
fowl	3
fowls	2
NA	11
NR	13
poultry	3

GA1F!	fowl	= a hen chicken
NC29B	fowls	rare
NC71B	fowls	not used
GA3A2	NR	only chickens [also GA432, SC1A2]
GA15A2	NR	no comprehensive term
SC22B2	fowl	knew term, didn't use it
SC25A2	NR	no comprehensive term, they stay separate
NC62B2	fowl	didn't use term
NC69A2	poultry	"the one you use" [term]

73. Setting Hen

1930s

brood hen	1
NR	1
setting hen	38

1990

brood hens	1
brooder	1
brooding hen	1
hen	6
laying hen	1
mama hen	3
mother hen	1
NA	1
NR	1
setting	1
setting hen	21
sitting hen	2

SC19N2	setting hen	"could be"
NC52N2	setting hen	don't set a hen in May
NC52B2	setting hen	old)
NC57B2	sitting hen	[ŋg]
NC71B2	hen	(a-setting

75. Bawl (calf)

1930s			1990	
bawl	8		baa	2
bellow	1		bawl	4
blake	1		bellow	2
blate	26		bellows	1
holler	2		blate	10
maw	1		bleat	1
NR	3		cries	1
			cry	3
			hollering	1
			hollers	1
			low	1
			maa	3
			moo	2
			NA	2
			NR	4
			whine	2

SC22B2	holler	"Mammy"
SC30A2	blate	loud noise
NC23B2	NR	don't know: an unusual sound
NC46C2	baby moo	sarcastic
NC69A2	blate	"b-l-e-a-t"
NC75A2	blate	"make a racket"

76. Moo

1930s		1990	
bawl	10	bawl	1
hum	9	bellow	7
low	24	bellows	1
moo	12	brawl	1
mow	2	holler	1
NR	2	low	5
		lowing	1
		moo	26
		moos	1
		mowing	1
		NA	1

GA3A	low	once more common
GA10A	low	loud, also for calf
GA15A	hum	gentle [also GA24A, SC1A, NC24N, NC24A, NC24B, NC25A, NC29B, NC52N]
GA34A	low	softer
GA43	bawl	loud [also SC1A, SC41A, NC56A, NC69A]
SC1A	low	loud [also SC25A, NC24A, NC25A, NC29B, NC52N]
SC25A	moo	gentle [also NC46C]
NC23B	moo	soft [also NC75B]
NC62B	moo	rare
GA24A2	bellow	louder than lowing
GA34A2	bellow	[-r] [also SC14A2, NC24A2, NC24B2, NC46B2]
GA432	bawl	occasionally
SC22B2	low	in poetry, don't believe we'd use the term
SC25A2	moo	"it's a sad call"
NC24N2	moos	they)
NC29B2	bellow	[-r] corrected to [-o]
NC75A2	bellows	[-rz]; bull
NC75B2	low	rare

Appendix 4

77. Clearing Up

1930s

breaking	1
breaking off	1
clearing	3
clearing away	2
clearing off	10
clearing up	17
fairing	2
fairing off	11
fairing up	5
NA	3

1990

a beautiful day in downtown Bogart	1
blow over	1
break in the weather	1
break off	1
breaking	3
breaking off	1
breaking up	2
brightening up	2
change of weather	1
changing	5
clearing off	5
clearing up	4
clears up	1
clouds have gone away	1
fair up	1
fairing off	4
fairing up	1
fairs up	1
going to be a pretty day	1
going to be pretty	1
moderated	1
NA	6
partly cloudy	1
scattering	1
sun's finally come out	1
sun's going to come out	1
turned out to be a beautiful day	1
unsettled	1

GA34A2 a beautiful day in downtown Bogart I'd say it's)
NC24N2 clearing off   [ae]
NC62B2 moderated   the weather's)

78. Clouding Up

1930s

changing	12
clouding up	13
fixing to be bad weather	1
fixing to be falling weather	2
fixing to have falling weather	1
fixing to have some falling weather	1
fixing to weather	1
getting cloudy	1
going to be bad weather	1
have falling weather	1
have some falling weather	6
looks like bad weather	1
looks like it's going to be weather	1
making up for a storm	6
NA	3
threatening	10

1990

bad weather	1
blustery	1
changing	4
cloud up	2
clouding up	5
clouds up	1
cloudy	2
dreary, dark day	1
fixing to change	1
fixing to have a storm	1
foul day	1
front moving through	1
getting cloudy	3
getting dark	1
going to be a rain	1
going to have a change in the weather	1
going to rain	1
gotten bad	1
look like wind clouds	1
looks like it's going to rain today	1
NA	6
overcast	1
scuds a-building	1
sort of gloomy	1
storm coming	1
storm coming in	1
stormy	2
threatening	1
thunderhead	1
turning bad	1
turning off cloudy	1

SC11I2	clouding up	"c-l-o-u-d-i-n"
NC69A2	clouding up	(to rain
NC75B2	clouding up	(to storm

79. Heavy Rain

1930s

a pouring down rain	1
awful rain	2
big rain	4
cloudburst	10
downpour	11
flop down	1
gully washer	4
hard rain	4
heavy rain	8
heavy shower	1
large rain	1
lighterd knot lifter	1
NA	3
pourdown	4
trash mover	1

1990

bad weather	1
bottom fell out	1
cloudburst	5
downpour	6
equinoxial storms	1
flash flood	2
flood	5
floods	1
frog choker	1
frog strangler	2
gale	1
gale rain	1
Georgetown lighterd knot floater	1
gully washer	5
gully washers	1
heavy storm	1
high water flood	1
hurricane	3
lighterd knot floater	1
monsoon	1
NA	7
northeaster	1
rain like the devil	1
raining buckets of water	1
raining bullfrogs	2
raining dogs and cats	1
rainstorm	1
rainy period	1
rainy weather	1
someone left the valve open	1
spring shower	1
toad strangler	2
torrent	1
washing rain	2
water spout	1
wet spell	1

SC11N	cloudburst	severe [also SC25A]
SC11I!	cloudburst	very severe
GA10A2	torrent	don't have as many today
GA10A2	washing rain	the)
GA432	gully washer	fairly common
SC19N2	bad weather	"let it go at that"
NC24A2	cloudburst	sheets of water
NC52N2	cloudburst	when frogs come
NC52N2	gale rain	in fall; mess up crops
NC69A2	cloudburst	different from downpour: like water spout
NC69A2	water spout	cloudburst on ocean

80. Thunderstorm

1930s

NA	3
shower	1
storm	1
tempest	1
thunder cloud	11
thunder gust	1
thunder shower	5
thunder squall	3
thunderstorm	23

1990

bad weather	1
electric storm	3
electrical cloud	1
electrical storm	9
Lord's speaking	1
Lord's talking	1
NA	5
rainstorm	1
storm	2
thunder and lightning	1
thunder cloud	1
thunder shower	2
thundering and lightning	1
thunderstorm	14
thunderstorms	1

GA3A	tempest	a little worse than thunderstorm but not anything unusual
GA13A	thunder squall	with wind
GA13A	thunderstorm	with wind [also SC30A]
GA43	thunder shower	light
SC11I!	squall	wind, sudden

Appendix 4

SC25A	thunder gust			dry wind
SC11N2	Lord's speaking			the): "anybody with sense will be quiet"
SC22B2	storm			only kind except ice storm
SC41A2	electrical cloud			initial [l-]
NC71C2	thundering and lightning			it's)

81. Gully

1930s			*1990*	
ditch	1		ditch	3
gully	27		erosion	1
NR	6		gullet	1
wash	2		gullies	2
washout	5		gully	19
washup	1		gully wash	1
			gutter	1
			gutters	1
			holes	1
			NA	8
			NR	1
			small valley	1
			trench	2
			valley	1
			wash	1
			washout	3

GA3A	gully	rare here; of an ocean entering creek
GA4N	gully	low place running through
GA43	gully	deeper than branch, often dry
SC41A	gully	dry
NC52N2	NA	*tass rows* dug for drainage
NC57B2	gullies	little old)
NC57B2	washout	*water furrows* dug along lay of the land

82. (Corn) Shucks

1930s		*1990*	
husk	1	blades	1
NA	2	corn shucks	1
shuck	18	husk	2
shucks	18	husks	2
		NA	2
		shuck	16
		shucks	15

GA432	NA	*shucking* = verb	
NC46B2	NA	*shuck* = verb	
NC69A2	husk	rarely heard	

83. Sweet Corn

1930s		*1990*	
garden corn	2	corn	2
green corn	4	corn on the cob	3
mutton	1	early corn	2
mutton corn	8	eating corn	1
mutton ears	1	garden corn	1
NA	2	mutton corn	3
roasting ear	5	NA	4
roasting ear corn	2	roasting corn	1
roasting ears	27	roasting ear corn	3
sweet corn	1	roasting ears	9
		sweet corn	15
		tender corn	1

GA15A	mutton corn	rare
GA43	roasting ears	even when cut off and creamed
SC30A	roasting ears	even cut off
NC24B	mutton corn	gf. and other old people said
GA4N2	roasting ears	heard of it, but never roasted any

GA13A2	mutton corn	an early corn
GA15A2	sweet corn	earlier than regular field corn
GA24A2	sweet corn	"it make earlier than field corn"
GA34A2	sweet corn	yellow)
GA432	roasting ears	different from sweet corn
SC11I2	sweet corn	also *yellow corn* and *white corn*
SC19N2	corn	corn was just)
SC22B2	corn	vs. field or feed corn
SC25A2	NA	*white corn*: Silver Queen
SC30A2	eating corn	vs. mule corn
SC41A2	roasting ears	ate yellow corn, white was for animals
NC23B2	sweet corn	vs. field corn [also NC57B2]
NC24B2	roasting ears	different from sweet corn
NC46B2	NA	*yellow corn* and *silver corn*
NC46C2	sweet corn	also *white corn*
NC56A2	NA	*Trucker's Favorite*
NC69A2	sweet corn	rarely grown, thought it was "sissy"
NC71C2	NA	*white corn, mixed corn*: yellow and white, new variety
NC75B2	roasting ears	"we didn't put the 't' in there"

85. (Corn) Silk

1930s			*1990*	
corn beard	2		beard	1
NA	2		corn silk	3
silk	27		fuzz	1
silks	10		mane	1
			NA	3
			silk	16
			silks	14
			string	1
			tassel	1

GA10A2	silk	when green

86. Cornbread (large cake)

1930s		1990	
corn dodger	3	bake cornbread	1
corn loaf	1	baked bread	2
corn pone	9	baked cornbread	1
cornbread	25	bread	1
corncake	2	cake of cornbread	1
dodger	1	corn pone	5
gopher loaf	1	corn pones	1
light bread	1	cornbread	33
loaf bread	1	corncake	1
NA	1	egg bread	1
pone	5	hoecake	2
pone bread	3	hoecake of bread	1
pone of bread	3	hoecake of cornbread	2
pone of cornbread	5	muffin bread	1
		muffin cornbread	1
		NA	2
		pone	5
		pone bread	2
		pone of bread	1
		pone of cornbread	1
		pones	2
		turned-over cornbread	1

GA1F!	corn pone	water and salt, baked in a covered oven (spider)
GA3A	corn pone	= a small loaf
GA3A	gopher loaf	larger than pone
GA13A	pone of cornbread	flat and thin
GA34A	corn dodger	same as pone, rare
GA43	light bread	corn and yeast
SC11N	cornbread	in pan
SC11I!	corn pone	hrd. from darkies
SC14A	pone of cornbread	oven
SC22B	pone bread	shape of pone
SC41A	corn pone	plain old way
NC25A	pone bread	2 in spider

Appendix 4

NC46B	corn pone	2 or 3 in pan
NC46C!	corn pone	in oven
NC56A	corn pone	rises
NC62B	corn pone	in skillet, always 2 in it
NC71B	corn dodger	2 together in oven [also NC71C]
NC75A	dodger	2 in a baker; hand-shaped
NC75B	corn dodger	2 hand-shaped
GA4N2	cornbread	1" thick, flat pan; uses mix now
GA10A2	muffin cornbread	1" thick
GA10A2	muffin	m. called it
GA10A2	muffin bread	1" thick
GA13A2	cornbread	didn't eat it; rare, for sharecroppers
GA13A2	hoecake	never had; reckon it's the word you're looking for
GA15A2	cornbread	in skillet
GA24A2	pone	long; two per skillet; more common than hoecake
GA432	pone of bread	also half-pone, quarter-pone
SC1A2	pone of cornbread	thicker than cake; inside oven; shape depended on pan
SC11N2	cornbread	rectangular shape
SC11I2	cornbread	1" thick [also SC12B2]
SC22N2	pone	in big pan, not usual
SC22B2	egg bread	cooked in oven in square pan
SC22B2	corn pone	in skillet in grease on top of stove, 1" thick
SC22B2	bread	from cook
SC22B2	cornbread	cooked in oven in square pan
SC25A2	pone	long: 12 x 6 x 2"
SC30A2	hoecake	in frying pan, 2" thick
NC23B2	cornbread	2" thick
NC24N2	pones	in fireplace; loaf shape
NC24N2	turned-over cornbread	on top of stove
NC24A2	corn pone	= baked bread; size and shape depends on pan
NC25A2	cornbread	in oven
NC25B2	pones	had cracklins in it
NC29B2	cornbread	thin patties, fried
NC46B2	cornbread	fried in skillet

214 *Appendix 4*

NC52B2	hoecake of cornbread	1/2-1" thick, fried in skillet
NC62B2	hoecake of cornbread	2" thick; both syllables of cb. stressed
NC69A2	corncake	round, with lots of baking soda
NC71C2	cornbread	made in round or square pan
NC75B2	cake of cornbread	in oven
NC75B2	pone	on stove, use more grease, same shape as cake of cornbread

90. Mush

1930s
cush	3
mush	36
NA	2
turn mush	1

1990
corn mush	3
cornmeal mush	2
druel	1
mush	14
NA	3
NR	9

GA1F!	mush	fed only to cattle
GA3A	hushpup	from Negroes, i.e. to hush the pups from crying
GA3A	turn mush	of meal
GA3A	turn flour	of flour
GA24A	cush	of bread crumbs
SC14A	turn flour	also
SC22B	Indian pudding	sweetened
SC25A	cush	= cooked over cornbread
GA4N2	corn mush	hrd. from f.; never eaten it
GA10A2	gruel	liquid; boiled milk and meal; eaten when sick [also SC25A2, NC25A2]
GA34A2	mush	for breakfast [also NC56A2]
GA432	mush	supper
SC11N2	mush	something like cream of wheat
SC14A2	corn mush	never eaten [also NC71C2]
SC22B2	mush	never had any [also NC24B2]
SC25A2	mush	as a snack
NC25B2	mush	slaves and old people with no teeth ate it
NC29B2	druel	m.-in-law makes
NC57B2	NR	never heard of it
NC75A2	mush	pron. "mursh"

91. Bread (homemade)

1930s

bread	7
flour cakes	1
light bread	32
light loaf	1
loaf	1
loaf bread	6
NA	1
rise bread	1
rising bread	1
riz bread	2
self-rising bread	1
yeast bread	2

1990

baked bread	1
bread	11
flour bread	1
homemade bread	6
homemade loaf	1
homemade loaf bread	1
light bread	4
loaf bread	7
NA	6
NR	1
rye bread	1
sourdough bread	3
wheat bread	1
white bread	1
whole wheat bread	1
yeast bread	5

GA1F!	bread	yeast
GA10A	wasp nest bread	nickname
GA10A	flour cakes	"sody"
GA13A	light bread	special
SC11I!	light bread	used by darkies and in VA, not in city here
SC12B	riz bread	as a child
SC19N	self-rising bread	baking powder
SC22B	wasp nest bread	nickname; very porous
SC41A	loaf bread	older, as girl
NC25B	light bread	rare; yeast
SC22N2	flour bread	in *pones*
NC23B2	homemade bread	as a novelty
NC25A2	bread	not common
NC52B2	yeast bread	made up once a year for church sale
NC75A2	wheat bread	in *pones*
NC75B2	loaf bread	m. said

92. Bread (from store)

1930s		*1990*	
baker's bread	18	baker's bread	1
bakery bread	6	bought bread	3
bought bread	4	bread	14
light bread	3	brown bread	1
light loaf	1	Jewish rye	1
loaf bread	5	light bread	10
NA	1	loaf bread	12
store bread	4	NA	4
store-bought bread	2	pumpernickel	1
town bread	1	rye bread	1
wasp nest bread	1	sandwich bread	1
wasp nest breads	1	sliced bread	1
		store bread	1
		store-bought bread	3
		store-bought homemade bread	1
		wasp nest	1
		white bread	1
		whole wheat bread	1

SC12B	wasp nest bread	nickname for oven bread; store rare
SC19N	town bread	
NC25B	wasp nest bread	nickname for baker's bread
GA3A2	light bread	sister-in-law from Bryant Co. says
GA4N2	light bread	gf. said
SC22B2	light bread	not used often
NC29B2	store-bought homemade bread	not sliced
NC69A2	light bread	seldom used now
NC69A2	loaf bread	fairly frequent

94. Doughnuts

1930s

cruller	3
doughnut	12
doughnuts	13
fingerbread	2
flat bread	1
fried bread	1
fried cookies	1
fried marvels	1
fritter	3
fritters	2
jumbles	1
kneecakes	1
loaf cake	1
marvelle	3
marvelles	1
NA	1
NR	11
puff pancake	1
puffs	2
sweet marvel	1

1990

doughnut	2
doughnut holes	1
doughnuts	4
flitters	2
fried bread	1
fritters	3
knee cakes	1
marvels	1
marvelles	1
NA	10
NR	7

GA1F!	doughnuts	with hole [also GA10A, SC11N, SC11I, SC12B, SC14A]
GA1F!	cruller	with hole; crisper
GA1F!	fritter	made with baking powder; small, round; dessert
GA3A	fritters	round, spoon-dipped
GA3A	marvelle	square; strips
GA10A	fried bread	dough; deep fat
GA10A	puffs	rolled; deep fat
GA10A	fritters	batter; deep fat
GA13A	kneecakes	hole didn't go clear through; German
GA13A	fritter	spoon-dipped; less yeast than puffs
GA13A	puffs	small; made with yeast
GA13A	marvelle	flat square; slit
GA15A	marvelles	fried in deep fat; hole in center

GA15A	doughnut	baked; squares of rich dough
GA43	doughnuts	modern only [also SC41A]
SC11N	puff pancake	yeast
SC11I!	cruller	hole
SC12B	fried marvels	"spoon-dipped lump"
SC12B	fingerbread	long piece, slit in 3
SC14A	fritter	round lump, plain dough
SC14A	marvelle	round, flat; strips on them
SC19N	flat bread	thin, flat, round; no hole; deep fat
SC25A	fingerbread	not in deep fat
SC25A	sweet marvel	thin; made in shallow grease
SC25A	doughnut	none as a girl
SC30A	fried cookies	small, round; no hole
NC62B	loaf cake	= doughnut
GA1F2	fritters	cooked in frying pan, flat like battercakes
GA3A2	fried bread	cooked in a skillet
GA10A2	marvels	puffy; eaten with syrup
GA13A2	knee cakes	had a dimple
GA15A2	fritters	thicker than pancake, deep fried
GA34A2	fritters	flat; cornmeal (modern) or flour
SC1A2	flitters	like pancake but fried in grease
SC22B2	doughnuts	not made locally at home
NC24N2	flitters	cooked in fat
NC25B2	doughnuts	*fritters* have salmon, squash, or eggplant in them
NC69A2	NR	none; had fried pies
NC75B2	fried bread	similar to pancakes, more grease

95. Pancakes

1930s

batter bread	1
battercake	5
battercakes	16
dabs	1
flannel cake	2
flannel cakes	1
flapjack	1
flapjacks	2
flitter cakes	1
flitters	15
flitters bread	1
fritters	9
griddle cakes	2
NA	1
pancake	5
pancakes	21
slapjack	4
slapjacks	3
waffles	2

1990

battercakes	3
flapjacks	10
flitters	3
fritters	4
hotcakes	2
johnnycake	1
pancake	1
pancake flitters	1
pancake fritters	1
pancakes	22
waffle	2
waffles	7

GA1F!	griddle cakes	rarer, = battercakes
GA1F!	flannel cakes	milk and egg
GA1F!	pancakes	very greasy, sweet kind
GA4N	slapjack	large ones [also SC14A]
GA4N	flitters	small [also SC30A, NC75A]
GA15A	flitter cakes	larger than fritters
GA15A	battercakes	with fruit in it
GA24A	pancakes	large [also GA43, SC12B, SC41A, NC75A]
SC11I!	fritters	sweetened, eaten as dessert
SC12B	battercake	large or small
SC12B	slapjacks	small
SC14A	flannel cake	very light
SC14A	battercake	large
SC19N	flitters bread	smaller
SC19N	pancake	later
SC22B	flannel cake	very thin

Appendix 4

SC22B	griddle cakes	greasy
SC22B	fritters	greasy
SC22B	waffles	in different iron
SC25A	fritters	dough, rolled thin, various shapes
SC25A	slapjack	very little grease, big, of dough rolled
SC25A	waffles	even as a girl
NC24B	pancakes	modern only
NC25A	pancakes	less
NC25B	battercakes	small
NC25B	dabs	large, same as flapjacks, common
NC25B	flapjack	large [also NC75A]
NC25B	fritters	small
NC62B	pancakes	buckwheat [also NC71B]
NC71C!	fritters	batter with fruit, etc., filling
NC75B	flitters	less used
GA4N2	hotcakes	some call them
GA34A2	pancakes	less grease than fritters
SC14A2	pancakes	fritters: "connected somehow with your potatoes"
SC14A2	waffles	made over coals
SC22B2	battercakes	rejected *pancakes*
NC23B2	pancakes	cake-like
NC23B2	fritters	bread-like
NC23B2	flitters	bread-like
NC24B2	fritters	thicker than pancakes
NC25A2	flitters	same as pancakes
NC46B2	flapjacks	gp. said
NC56A2	waffles	Sunday night supper
NC62B2	hotcakes	m. calls them

96. Snack

1930s		1990	
bite	5	between-meal snack	1
bite to eat	1	evening snack	1
lunch	23	leftovers	1
NA	2	NA	13
piece	1	nicknacks	1
piecemeal	3	repast	1
snack	28	snack	20
		snacks	1

GA13A	snack	rare
SC11N	snack	small
SC14A	snack	a bite or two
NC25B	snack	short

GA4N2	repast	light meal, party buffet
GA4N2	nicknacks	= refreshments
NC69A2	grazing	from old man, school superintendant

97. Make (coffee)

1930s		1990	
boil	5	boil	4
draw	9	boiled	1
fix	1	draw	1
make	32	made	1
NA	2	make	9
steep	1	NA	21
		percolate	2
		perk	3

GA15A	make	(a drawing of coffee
SC11I!	make	*draw* for tea
NC25B	draw	boiled
NC46B	make	natural

GA4N2	draw	in pot	
GA4N2	make	instant [also GA10A2, GA15A2]	
GA34A2	perk	on stove	

98. Peanuts

1930s		*1990*	
goober peas	5	goober	1
goobers	12	goobers	4
ground pea	1	ground peas	5
ground peas	12	groundnuts	1
groundnut	1	NA	5
groundnuts	4	peanut	1
NA	2	peanuts	20
peanut	1	peas	1
peanuts	30	pinders	6
pinders	17	Spanish peanuts	1
stewfers	1		

GA3A	goobers	rare
GA4N	grassnut	wild variety (round black nuts for animals) only 1 nut
GA4N	choofers	wild variety (round black nuts for animals)
GA10A	goobers	round, only 1 nut
GA10A	pinders	long hull: 2 or 3 nuts
GA13A	peanuts	modern only [also SC12B, SC22B]
GA13A	ground peas	single nut in a round shell
GA24A	ground peas	most natural response
GA34A	goobers	mostly
GA43	goobers	natural
SC1A	pinders	mostly [also SC14A]
SC11N	peanut	after being parched
SC12B	pinders	rare
SC12B	groobers	as a girl
SC14A	groundnuts	rare
SC14A	peanuts	not used much here
SC25A	pinders	4 or less in shell
SC25A	stewfers	stewed up when dry; in clusters

SC41A	goobers	original name here
NC24A	pinders	as a child
NC24B	pinders	a small "Spanish" kind
NC25B	pinders	only one nut to shell, usually
NC52N	pinders	modern only
NC62B	goobers	as a child
NC71C!	pinders	probably SC influence
GA13A2	groundnuts	/d/ omitted
GA432	peanut	few here
SC11I2	goobers	from song "Eating Goober Peas" [also NC69A2]
SC12B2	pinders	a lot of people still use the term
SC14A2	pinders	as a boy
SC22B2	pinder	common, "old-time people"
SC30A2	goober peanuts	big ones
SC30A2	Spanish peanuts	small ones
SC41A2	goobers	a lot of people call them
NC23B2	goobers	larger ones
NC24N2	pinders	some call it
NC24B2	ground peas	gf. said
NC25B2	peanuts	types: Spanish, Virginia half-bunch
NC52N2	ground peas	they call them 'round here (but not in Darlington, SC)
NC56A2	goobers	nickname
NC69A2	goober	of African origin; common

99. Fatback

1930s		*1990*	
bacon	28	backbone	2
butts meat	4	bacon	2
canned pork	1	boiling meat	1
dried meat	1	cured meat	1
fat meat	3	dry salt	1
fat pork	1	fat meat	2
fatback	3	fatback	20
flat back	1	middling	5
meat	2	middling meat	1
middling	17	middlings	1
middling meat	4	NR	1
middlings	5	pickled pork	1
NA	1	salt pork	2
salt bacon	1	side	1
side meat	6	side meat	9
sides	1	smoked bacon	1
smoke bacon	2	sow belly	1
smoke meat	11	streak o' lean	3
smoke middling	2	streak o' lean streak of fat	1
smoke sides	2	streak of fat	1
sow belly	1	streaked meat	2
white meat	5	white bacon	2
white pork meat	1	white meat	1
white sides	2	white side meat	1

GA1F!	bacon	smoked [also GA3A, SC11N, SC12B, SC14A, SC19N, SC41A, NC23B]
GA3A	white meat	= side
GA10A	bacon	= all kinds
GA10A	middlings	= side meat, never unsmoked
GA13A	smoke bacon	= middlings
GA15A	bacon	smoked; more used
GA24A	bacon	smoked; esp. when bought
GA34A	middling meat	home
GA34A	smoke meat	not made now
GA34A	bacon	cured, not smoked [also SC22B, SC30A]
GA34A	fatback	store

Appendix 4

SC14A	butts meat	jowls
SC14A	canned pork	locally
SC14A	white pork meat	when you buy it
SC14A	white sides	factory word
SC22B	flat back	pure fat
SC22B	smoke meat	if smoked
SC25A	middlings	sides
NC23B	smoke meat	as a child
NC25B	sow belly	not when eating
NC25B	side meat	lean streaks
NC57B	fatback	as a child
NC57B	bacon	rare
GA3A2	bacon	seasoned differently from other bacon
SC14A2	middling	from sides
SC14A2	fatback	used now; used to be used for lard
SC19N2	butt meat	some people call it
SC22B2	streak o' lean	in the market now it's called
NC24A2	pickled pork	in brine
NC29B2	side meat	has a streak of lean in it
NC52B2	side meat	from middling
NC69A2	sow belly	"it's inferior bacon is what it boils down to"
NC75A2	streaked meat	3 syllables
NC75A2	side meat	same as streaked meat
NC75B2	streaked meat	3 syllables; m. said

100. Bacon Rind

1930s

hide	1
meat skin	1
NA	1
rind	4
skin	35

1990

bacon rind	2
bacon rinds	1
meat skin	2
meat skins	1
NA	4
NR	2
pork rind	1
pork skin	1
rind	5
skin	25

GA1F!	rind		rare	
GA34A2	skin		best part of it	
SC1A2	meat skins		used to oil saws	
SC25A2	bacon rinds		bought fried	
SC30A2	skin		fry and eat it	

101. Bacon

1930s			*1990*	
bacon	4		bacon	29
breakfast bacon	21		breakfast bacon	2
breakfast meat	1		breakfast meat	1
breakfast strip	13		dry salt	1
breakfast strips	2		fatback meat	1
NA	1		middling	2
strip	2		NA	5
			streak o' lean	1

GA4N2	bacon	from sides
GA432	bacon	made from middling
SC22B2	breakfast bacon	when young
NC25B2	bacon	from side meat
NC52N2	bacon	of middling [also NC52B2]
NC57B2	fatback meat	sliced and fried

102. Wishbone

1930s			*1990*	
breaky bone	1		breastbone	3
breastbone	2		NA	4
forked bone	1		pulley bone	14
goodie bone	1		wishbone	20
lucky bone	2			
NR	1			
pull bone	7			
pulley bone	25			
pulling bone	1			
wishbone	9			

SC11I!	meriwether	f. said
NC46B	pulley bone	more
NC46C!	pulley bone	usually
GA10A2	wishbone	some people call it
GA13A2	wishbone	*fifth quarter* = back; *preacher's nose* = tail
SC19N2	wishbone	didn't wish on it, would just eat it
NC46C2	pulley bone	as a child

103. Haslet (hog organs)

1930s			*1990*	
hashlet		1	entrails	3
haslet		25	guts	1
haslets		1	haslet	2
liver		1	lights	2
liver and lights		7	liver and lights	2
NR		4	liver and the lights	1
offal		1	NA	20
			NR	8

GA4N	haslet	= lungs (eaten here)
GA10A	haslet	= liver and lights
SC19N	haslet	= liver, lights, heart
NC71B	liver	includes lights
GA3A2	hassle	connected to the liver, cooked small piece with liver
GA4N2	NA	everything but the squeak
GA13A2	haslet	*innards* connected to it; *melt* = spleen
GA15A2	NR	don't know: used to cure meat in
GA432	NA	"call it what it was" (*lungs*)
SC19N2	NA	used "everything except the hoof"
SC22B2	NA	"a hog liver's a dreadful thing"
NC23B2	lights	not sure what it was
NC23B2	entrails	3 syllables
NC24N2	haslet	"liver and lights and heart"
NC52N2	hash	cooked
NC75A2	lights	can mean just lungs or be comprehensive

105. Stone (cherry)

1930s		*1990*	
kernel	2	kernel	3
NA	2	NA	2
seed	32	NR	8
stone	6	pit	12
		seed	13
		stone	3

GA24A2	seed	mostly wild, but had one "tame" one (tree)
SC22B2	stone	cherries were exotic; unfamiliar term
SC22B2	seed	more likely than stone
SC25A2	NR	"just a little old hard knot"
NC71C2	pit	more common than stone

106. Pit (peach)

1930s		*1990*	
kernel	25	core	1
NA	2	kernel	16
seed	21	peach kernel	2
stone	6	peach seed	1
		pit	7
		pith	2
		seed	13
		stone	3

GA4N	kernel	modern only
SC14A	stone	rare
SC25A	seed	outside

GA1F2	pith	outside
GA4N2	throne	(or thorn
GA34A2	peach seed	*pit* found in plum, not peach
SC1A2	seed	some call it

107. Clingstone Peach

1930s

cling	7
clingstone	6
clingstone peach	1
NA	2
peach	1
plum peach	8
press	3
press peach	16

1990

cling	5
cling peaches	1
clingstone	6
Indian peach	1
Indian press	1
may peaches	1
NA	2
NR	7
peach	2
peaches	1
pickle peach	1
press	4
press peach	8
press peaches	1
white peach	1

GA3A	cling	rare
SC41A	clingstone	proper
GA1F2	clingstone	for making brandy or pickled peaches
GA10A2	press	also yellow press, red press
GA13A2	press peach	pressed against the seed; white, yellow
GA13A2	clingstone	peachy peaches: not grafted
GA13A2	Indian press	red
GA15A2	cling	meat clings to seed
SC11I2	peach	"a peach is a peach is a peach"
SC14A2	press peach	for making sweet pickles [also NC52N2]
SC30A2	cling	used for pickles
SC41A2	clingstone	white meat
SC41A2	white peach	has white meat
NC24N2	press peaches	kind that cling
NC24A2	press peach	would cling
NC25B2	NR	don't know term; used for pickles
NC57B2	Indian peach	small, red, sweet
NC62B2	clingstone	m. says

108. Freestone Peach

1930s		1990	
clearseed	3	clearseed	4
clearseed peach	2	clearseed peach	3
clearstone	8	clearstone	1
freestone	10	cling-free	1
loose-seed peach	1	freestone	8
NA	2	freestone peach	3
open	1	NA	2
open peach	4	NR	5
openstone	7	open	1
slipseed peach	1	openstone	2
slipstone	1	peach	2
slipstone peach	1	peaches	4
soft	2	slipseed	1
soft peach	7	softstone	1
softstone	1	whitestone	1

SC41A	freestone	proper
NC75A	openstone	natural
GA3A2	peaches	I call them)
GA24A2	clearseed peach	"will bust open purty"
NC62B2	peaches	just)

109. Cobbler

1930s		*1990*	
apple cobbler	4	cobbler	14
apple dumpling	1	cobbler pie	1
apple jack	1	cobbler pies	1
apple pie	1	cobblers	1
apple pot pie	2	crisp	1
apple pudding	1	deep dish apple pie	2
apple sonker	1	deep dish cobbler	1
apple tart	3	deep dish pie	3
berry dumpling	1	deep pan pie	1
cobbler pie	1	dumpling	1
deep dish apple pie	1	NA	2
deep dish berry pie	1	NR	1
deep dish pie	1	peach pie	1
dinner pie	1	pie	10
dish pie	1	pies	1
family pie	10	pot pie	2
grunter	1	sonker	1
NA	1		
NR	5		
pan pie	1		
pot pie	6		
slice pie	1		
two-story Dutch tart	1		

GA3A	apple tart	small, round, deepish
GA4N	berry dumpling	no apples here
GA13A	two-story Dutch tart	3 crusts, berries, fried in deep fat
GA13A	Krapfen	= turnover, fried in deep fat
GA13A	pot pie	baked in pot on hearth
GA15A	pot pie	layers of dough in it
GA24A	apple pie	layers of dough, several inches deep
GA34A	apple cobbler	= hoecake with apples poured over (like shortcake)
SC12B	deep dish berry pie	no apples here
SC22B	deep dish apple pie	rare

SC25A	pan pie	thin, dumplings through it, only top crust
SC25A	apple pudding	only top crust
SC41A	apple cobbler	the original old name here
NC25A	apple jack	in layers
NC62B	gundy pie	an aunt said
NC62B	apple sonker	as a child
NC69A	dinner pie	in pot, with dumplings
NC69A	pot pie	small
GA4N2	cobbler	peach) [also GA10A2, SC12B2, SC30A2, NC52N2]
GA10A2	pie	peach) [also GA13A2, SC30A2]
GA15A2	deep dish apple pie	or peach
GA24A2	peach pie	always deep (*apple pie* always shallow)
GA24A2	pie	just a) [also GA432]
GA34A2	cobbler	peach, apple, blackberry, sweet potato
SC1A2	cobbler	if blueberry
SC1A2	crisp	if peach [also SC30A2]
SC11I2	cobbler	deep, with strips on the top
NC25B2	dumpling	apple); also huckleberry dumpling
NC52B2	cobbler	2" deep
NC69A2	boiled pie	not common
NC69A2	rangjanglin pie	several types of fruit, whatever she (neighbor) had

110. Spring Onions

1930s

crapped onions	1
green onions	1
NA	2
NR	1
sallet ingan	3
sallet onion	1
sallet onions	1
scallion	9
scallions	2
shallot	12
shallots	6
spring onion	4
spring onions	1

1990

garlic onions	1
green onion	1
green onions	3
multiplier	1
multiplying onion	2
multiplying onions	2
NA	2
nest egg onion	2
nest onion	2
nest onions	2
NR	1
onion	1
onion sets	1
onions	3
salad onion	1
salad onions	1
scallion	3
scallions	4
sets	2
shallots	2
spring onion	2
spring onions	7
white onion	1

GA10A	scallions	up to tops; multiplies on top
GA13A	scallion	longer, less root; always here
GA13A	shallot	not variety
SC11N	scallion	bunch onions grow on top
SC12B	scallions	little green onions
SC12B	shallots	small bulb; open leaves; strong
SC14A	scallion	grows to stalk, young ones on top
SC14A	shallot	green
SC22B	shallot	early
SC25A	shallot	multiply in bunches on ground
SC25A	scallion	long tops; no seed on tops
SC41A	scallion	longer, taller; plant in fall

SC41A	shallots	bunches; plant in fall
NC25B	shallot	big bunch; branches out
NC56A	shallot	bunches
GA13A2	scallions	grow in clump
GA13A2	shallots	stress on second syllable; mildest, for potato soup
GA24A2	multiplying onion	eat tops cooked in frying pan with eggs added
GA432	onions	small)
SC11I2	scallions	eat tops and bottoms [also NC24N2]
SC12B2	white onion	eat top too; grow to large size
SC22B2	spring onions	eat top and bottom
SC25A2	onion	"didn't have no special name"
NC29B2	onions	young)
NC56A2	spring onions	= regular onions pulled early
NC69A2	spring onions	when thinned; *bermuda onion* when older
NC75B2	green onions	young regular onions

112. Lima Beans

1930s			*1990*	
butter bean	1		baby beans	1
butter beans	31		baby limas	1
lazy wife beans	1		butter bean	1
lima bean	1		butter beans	28
lima beans	18		calicos	1
NA	2		fordhooks	2
NR	2		lima beans	16
sallet beans	1		lima grands	1
sewee beans	5		limas	1
sewees	3		NR	1
sieva beans	9		Pennsylvania butter bean	1
			shell bean	1
			shell beans	1
			shelly	1
			sieva beans	3

Appendix 4

GA1F!	lima beans	large; green
GA1F!	butter beans	smaller; greenish white
GA1F!	sieva beans	as a child for lima beans
GA3A	lima beans	larger; rare [also GA13A]
GA4N	sieva beans	as a child
GA4N	lima beans	large [also GA10A, SC12B]
GA13A	sieva beans	old name
SC11I!	sieva beans	small [also SC12B]
SC11I!	sewee beans	small
SC11I!	lima beans	big; green
SC14A	sewee beans	running; spotted; medium-sized; [same comment for *sieva beans*]
SC14A	lima beans	bush-small; pole-running, white
SC14A	butter beans	older term for lima beans
SC25A	sallet beans	when tiny pods of butter beans & English peas
SC30A	butter bean	*running bean, bush bean* [same comment for *lima bean*]
SC41A	lima beans	so-called when dried and used for winter
SC41A	butter beans	when nearly ripe
GA1F2	sieva beans	faintly colored: lavender and green
GA3A2	butter beans	dark, speckled; easier to grow than white ones
GA3A2	lima	green ones
GA4N2	lima beans	speckled and white
GA10A2	lima grands	= fordhooks; commercial term
GA10A2	fordhooks	"one of them would make a mouthful"; = Pennsylvania butter bean
GA10A2	sieva beans	small; colored/speckled or green/white
GA13A2	sieva beans	kind of a primitive butter bean
GA13A2	calicos	colored
GA15A2	butter beans	green, flat, smaller than lima beans
GA24A2	butter beans	"a white 'un and a calico"
GA34A2	butter beans	white or colored (speckled) [also GA432, SC22N2, SC14A2]
SC1A2	butter beans	speckled
SC11I2	lima beans	Northern term
SC11I2	butter beans	= lima beans; light green; small ones better
SC11I2	sieva beans	white ones
SC12B2	butter beans	green
SC12B2	sieva beans	speckled; black juice; never hear anymore

SC14A2	lima beans	"all look the same to me" (as butter beans)
SC14A2	sieva beans	white, similar to butter bean
SC19N2	butter beans	2 types: low bush and high bush
SC22B2	lima beans	green, white, or speckled (any from pod)
SC25A2	butter beans	speckledy ones (= colored) [also SC41A2]
SC30A2	butter beans	white, small
NC23B2	lima beans	larger than butter beans; white are dried, green are fresh
NC23B2	butter beans	greenish
NC24N2	butter beans	speckled or white
NC24N2	sieva beans	in butter bean family
NC24B2	butter beans	also blue butter beans and speckled butter beans
NC25A2	butter beans	big, white or green
NC25B2	butter beans	= baby limas
NC25B2	baby limas	= butter beans
NC29B2	butter beans	green) = green lima beans; also speckled)
NC46B2	butter beans	some green; bigger ones white
NC52B2	lima beans	green, smaller than butter beans
NC52B2	butter beans	bigger than lima beans, colored
NC56A2	lima beans	white, speckled, or green
NC62B2	limas	smaller than butter beans
NC62B2	butter beans	big, light green
NC69A2	lima beans	different colors, speckled are popular
NC69A2	Lima beans	(pron. like the city)
NC71B2	lima beans	green
NC71B2	butter beans	white or yellow, bigger than lima beans
NC71C2	lima beans	white, large
NC75A2	butter beans	didn't have them as a child

114. Shell (beans)

1930s			*1990*	
hull		5	get rid of the shell	1
NA		2	hull	2
NR		1	NA	3
shell		34	NR	1
			remove the shell	1
			shell	29
			trash it	1

GA1F!	shell	natural
GA10A	hull	thrashing with a stick
NC75A	hull	rare
GA24A2	shell	*hull* is noun [also GA34A2, NC75A2]
SC19N2	trash it	dried beans in bag, hit with stick

115. Potatoes

1930s			*1990*	
Irish potato	1		baking potatoes	2
Irish potatoes	31		Idaho potatoes	5
Irish taters	3		Irish potatoes	28
NA	2		NA	1
potatoes	1		new potatoes	6
			potato	1
			potatoes	12
			spuds	1

GA34A2	Idaho potatoes	[-di-]; bought at store
SC22B2	Irish potatoes	from "Mammy"
SC25A2	Idaho potatoes	[-i-], [r] at end
SC41A2	Irish potatoes	[r] at end
NC62B2	taters	m. says
NC75B2	potatoes	general term

116. Sweet Potatoes

1930s		1990	
NA	2	barbido	1
potatoes	18	potato	1
pumpkin potato	1	potatoes	9
sweet potato	1	Puerto Rican yams	1
sweet potatoes	22	seed potato	1
sweet taters	2	sweet potato	1
taters	3	sweet potatoes	35
yam	1	sweet totters	1
yam potatoes	1	taters	2
yam taters	1	totters	1
yams	2	yam	2
		yams	4

SC11N	sweet potatoes	particular
SC11N	yam	enormous yellow ones [same comment for *pumpkin potato*]
SC11I!	yams	yellow variety
SC12B	taters	whitish [same comment for *yam taters*]
SC14A	demry	heard 15 miles west on forks of Salthatcher [?] River
NC25B	yams	deep yellow type
GA13A2	barbido	[Barbados?]
GA24A2	yams	old-fashioned; GA reds; type of sweet potato
SC1A2	potatoes	used in context of a pie
SC14A2	potatoes	FW suspects this more commonly means Irish potato
SC22B2	potatoes	from "Mammy"
SC22B2	yam	(was not a word we used
SC41A2	sweet potatoes	[r] at end
NC23B2	yams	f. said
NC24A2	yams	candied)
NC46C2	yams	don't know difference between yam and sweet potato; one may be darker
NC62B2	yams	m. says
NC75B2	yam	different from sweet potato

117. Woodpecker

1930s

henwood	1
NA	2
NR	1
peckerwood	10
redhead	1
sapsucker	5
wet-hen	1
woodcock	1
woodknocker	1
woodpeck	1
woodpecker	23
woodpicker	1

1990

downy woodpecker	2
flicker	2
hammerhead	1
Indian woodhen	1
NA	5
pecker	1
peckerwood	2
peckerwoods	1
pileated woodpecker	2
red pecker	1
red-bellied woodpecker	1
redhead woodpecker	1
redheaded peckerwood	2
redheaded woodpecker	9
sapsucker	2
sapsuckers	3
shirttail	2
tommytit	1
woodcocks	1
woodhens	1
woodpecker	22
woodpeckers	9
yellow bellied sapsucker	1
yellow hammer	4
yellow hammers	1

SC1A	woodpecker	larger than sapsucker
GA4N2	yellow hammers	big ones
GA10A2	redhead woodpecker	red, white, and blue
GA10A2	sapsuckers	3 or 4 different varieties
GA13A2	redheaded woodpecker	one here not true *red pecker* but cockaded one
SC14A2	sapsucker	he's got a red head
SC14A2	shirttail	green with black feathers and a white tail

SC14A2	woodhens	big, with long tail
NC25A2	tommytit	little bitty old woodpecker
NC25A2	shirttail	white and black
NC56A2	red-bellied woodpecker	= red-headed woodpecker
NC75B2	peckerwood	was corrected by f. when she used this term

118. Skunk

1930s			*1990*	
civet cat		1	civet cat	1
NA		2	civet cats	1
pole cat		37	kitty	1
skunk		12	NA	3
			pole cat	13
			pole cats	2
			skunk	27

SC11N	skunk	= mink; rarely used
NC25B	pole cat	natural
NC46B	pole cat	rare
GA3A2	pole cats	"there ain't not many of them things anymore"
GA4N2	pole cat	thus called because of its stripe
GA432	civet cats	/-vi#/
SC14A2	skunk	very few
NC24B2	skunk	I always say
NC24B2	pole cat	a lot of people call them
NC69A2	civet cat	technical term

119. Chipmunk

1930s		*1990*	
ground squirrel	13	chipmunk	6
NA	2	chipmunks	2
NR	24	ground squirrel	4
		NA	5
		NR	18

NC46C2	gopher	like chipmunk
NC71B2	ground squirrel	more common than chipmunk

120. Bullfrog

1930s		*1990*	
bloody noun	7	bullfrog	21
bullfrog	35	bullfrogs	8
frog	1	frog	2
NA	2	NA	3
pond chicken	1	NR	1
		rain frog	1
		toad frog	1

GA1F!	bloody noun	hrd. from sister
GA3A	bloody noun	larger than bullfrog
GA4N	bullfrog	around the house
GA4N	bloody noun	only out in water
SC11N	bloody noun	fresh water, 8" high, shot with rifle, eaten
SC14A	pond chicken	restaurant

GA4N2	bullfrog	not large kind
SC11N2	bullfrog	male
NC52N2	bullfrog	comes from tadpole

121. Treefrog

1930s		*1990*	
frog	1	baby frogs	1
frogs	5	frog	3
green frog	2	green frog	4
green frogs	1	green frogs	2
knee-deeps	1	NA	4
meddimo	1	NR	3
NA	2	rain frog	3
NR	5	rain frogs	4
pee-dee	1	spring frog	6
peep frog	1	treefrog	11
rain frog	1	treefrogs	3
shad frog	1		
shad frogs	1		
spring frog	12		
spring frogs	5		

NC23B	shad frog	smallest
GA13A2	spring frog	long, lanky
GA24A2	treefrog	they *holler*
SC14A2	spring frog	wet areas; different from treefrog
SC14A2	treefrog	"he's green": different from spring frog; love cornfields
SC22B2	frog	green and shiny, lives in water
SC30A2	rain frogs	"look like it wants to rain, he'll go to hollerin'"
NC23B2	rain frogs	green
NC25A2	treefrog	different from spring frog
NC25A2	spring frog	bigger than toad frog, green; makes long leaps
NC56A2	treefrog	little, changes color
NC71B2	treefrogs	hollers in the spring of the year
NC71C2	treefrog	color of tree bark
NC75A2	treefrog	kind that hung up on the tree; changes colors

122. Toad

1930s			*1990*	
bull toady	1		frog	6
bullfrog	2		frogs	2
frog	1		hoppy toad	1
hop toad	1		hoppy toads	1
NA	2		NA	2
toad	3		sandhill frog	1
toad frog	31		toad	6
toad frogs	5		toad frog	17
toady	2		toad frogs	6
toady frog	1		toads	1

GA1F!	toad	small ones
SC11N	bullfrog	rough skin, larger
GA13A2	toad	lives in yards
GA24A2	toad frog	around the house
SC22N2	sandhill frog	slim, brownish
NC46B2	frog	water
NC52N2	toad frog	come from cloud

123. Earthworm

1930s		*1990*	
angleworm	1	angle worm	1
bait	4	blood worm	2
bait worm	3	blood worms	1
earthworm	24	blue bait	1
fish worm	2	blue worms	2
fishing worm	2	earthworm	15
fishing worms	1	earthworms	5
mud worm	3	eel worm	1
NA	2	fish worms	1
red worm	7	fishing worm	2
red worms	1	fishing worms	2
		Georgia wiggler	1
		jumping jacks	1
		NA	2
		night crawler	2
		night crawlers	4
		night worm	1
		red wiggler	1
		red wigglers	3
		red worm	7
		red worms	3
		swamp wiggler	1
		wiggler	3
		wigglers	1
		worm	4
		worms	2

GA3A	earthworm	modern
GA3A	angleworm	always as a boy
GA4N	earthworm	not very long
GA15A	mud worm	black, in swamps
GA34A	stretchers	in the branches for fishing
SC12B	mud worm	rare, same as earthworm
NC52N	earthworm	= grub worm: white, curled
NC56A	baits	Negroes says
NC62B	red worm	rare

Appendix 4

GA4N2	worms	"I don't want him [fish] if he swallowed a worm"
GA10A2	red wigglers	from bait beds
GA13A2	red wiggler	*catawba worm* from *fish bait tree*
GA13A2	blue worms	in mud
GA13A2	eel worm	fast; in drier dirt
GA24A2	swamp wiggler	long, fast
GA24A2	worm	*ground puppies* = salamanders
SC11N2	worm	also one that snaps
SC25A2	earthworm	tiny, white; different from red worm
SC30A2	red worm	type of earthworm [same comment for *wiggler*]
NC52N2	baits	come out after rain
NC69A2	red worm	= angle worm
NC69A2	night crawlers	big

124. Minnows

1930s			*1990*	
little perch	1		krill	1
live bait	1		live bait	1
mineral fish	1		minnow	5
minerals	1		minnow fish	1
minnow	3		minnows	22
minnow fish	2		NA	4
minnows	32		NR	3
mud fish	1		roaches	1
NA	3		shiners	4
silver fish	2		silvers	3

SC11N	minnows	long, straight; young of some larger type
SC11N	silver fish	never larger, silver-gold streak
SC11N	mud fish	big stomach, never larger
SC14A	silver fish	never grows larger
SC14A	minnow fish	young fish [same comment for *minnow*]
GA10A2	minnows	/-r/; also *Baltimore minnows* (/-r/)
SC11N2	NR	don't know; "I don't miss the water"
NC24A2	minnows	/-r/ [also NC29B2]

246   *Appendix 4*

NC24A2 shiners	for salt water
NC24B2 minnows	at first /-r/, corrected to /-o/; also flat head minnow
NC24B2 roaches	larger than minnow [same comment for *shiners* and *silvers*]
NC46C2 minnows	[o]
NC69A2 minnow	varieties of minnows (a.k.a. *creek minnows*): chub, red horses
NC71C2 krill	on coast

125. Terrapin

1930s		*1990*	
cooter	11	alligator cooter	1
gopher	5	box turtle	1
NA	2	box turtles	1
NR	1	boxmouth cooter	1
terrapin	32	cooter	4
		cooters	1
		diamond back	1
		dry-land terrapin	1
		dry-land tortoise	2
		gopher	1
		gophers	2
		land turtle	1
		loggerhead	1
		NA	2
		NR	5
		snapping turtle	4
		speckleback	1
		stinkpot	1
		stripe head	1
		terrapin	10
		terrapins	2
		turtle	3
		turtles	4
		yellow land turtle	1

Appendix 4

GA3A	gopher	on highlands [also GA4N, GA10A]
GA15A	cooter	higher holes on land
GA15A	gopher	in piney woods; dig holes
SC12B	terrapin	big cooter
SC12B	gopher	buries in ground [also SC30A]
SC14A	gopher	a land cooter, burrowing
SC25A	cooter	big ones in water, small on the land
SC25A	terrapin	little ones, land, long tail
SC25A	gopher	black all over, burrow in ground
NC24N	cooter	large [also NC24B]
NC52B	cooter	used for either turtle or terrapin
GA1F2	cooter	"spelled c-u-d-d-e-r"
GA4N2	alligator cooter	"won't turn you loose until the thunder rolls"
GA4N2	cooters	we call them; = snapping turtle, will jump on you
GA10A2	gophers	dig holes
GA13A2	dry-land tortoise	tortoise 3 syllables
GA13A2	gopher	burrows
GA15A2	gophers	few
GA24A2	terrapin	small, "not fit to eat"
GA432	terrapin	[a], 2 syllables
SC11N2	cooter	once most common term, now half and half [alongside *turtle*]
SC11I2	turtles	hrd. *cooters* for ones that live in water
SC19N2	cooter	smaller than terrapin, same turtle family
SC30A2	snapping turtle	can eat them, grow up to 20–25 lbs.
SC41A2	terrapin	[a]
NC24A2	diamond back	land or water: in marshes
NC24B2	box turtles	live on land
NC25A2	yellow land turtle	/-r/ on *yellow*
NC25B2	terrapin	on land or water
NC46B2	turtles	just call them all)
NC52N2	terrapin	to cook, just throw in fire
NC57B2	terrapin	shell is domed: turtle has flat shell; get in your garden, eat your tomatoes
NC75B2	terrapins	small

126. Lightning Bug

1930s		1990	
firefly	1	fireflies	4
lighten bug	3	firefly	1
lightning bug	33	light bug	2
NA	2	lighten bug	1
		lighten bugs	1
		lightning bug	25
		lightning bugs	8
		NA	2

NC24B2	firefly	we don't call them
NC52N2	lightning bug	flying low = no rain; higher than 2 ft. = rain
NC71C2	firefly	used equally often as *lightning bug*
NC75B2	firefly	daughter (age 12) says

127. Dragonfly

1930s		1990	
dragonfly	4	big mosquito	2
mosquito hawk	14	dragonflies	1
NA	2	dragonfly	8
skeeter hawk	9	dragons	1
snake doctor	5	hawks	1
snake feeder	8	mosquito	1
snake skeeter	1	mosquito hawk	7
snake waiter	1	NA	5
		NR	3
		skeeter hawk	1
		snake doctor	5
		snake feeder	1
		snake feeders	1
		water bug	1

GA24A	snake doctor	a little larger kind
SC11I!	mosquito hawk	different than dragonfly: not bright colored
SC12B	skeeter hawk	3 inches, black

Appendix 4

SC12B	dragonfly	grey, shorter than skeeter hawk: 2 inches
SC14A	mosquito hawk	greenish
SC22B	mosquito hawk	smaller than dragonfly
SC22B	dragonfly	dark
SC25A	dragonfly	larger wings than skeeter hawk; a tobacco fly
GA4N2	dragonfly	he was something different
GA4N2	mosquito hawk	in yard; all we ever called 'em
GA10A2	mosquito hawk	"I don't know what the right name is"
GA13A2	skeeter hawk	double set of wings and big "fusillage"
GA24A2	NR	"can't call his name"
SC12B2	mosquito	doesn't bite, eats insects

128. Grasshopper

1930s			1990	
grasshopper	4		crickets	1
grasshoppers	31		grasshopper	20
hoppergrass	3		grasshoppers	10
locust	4		July fly	1
locusts	12		locusts	1
NA	3		NA	4
			NR	1

GA1F!	locust	collective, on trees
GA10A	locusts	on trees
GA13A	locusts	big bug on trees
SC11I!	locusts	on trees
SC14A	hoppergrass	rare
SC30A	locusts	on trees
GA10A2	July fly	holler "July"; bait; small, green; caught at night
SC14A2	grasshopper	green or grey: changes color like lizard
NC52B2	crickets	big and little: "call them all crickets"
NC69A2	locusts	in the West

129. Spiderweb

1930s		*1990*	
cobweb	9	cobweb	2
cobwebs	8	cobwebs	1
NA	2	NA	3
spiderweb	19	NR	1
spiderwebs	14	spider's web	1
		spiderweb	20
		spiderwebs	1
		web	25
		webs	1

GA1F!	spiderweb	outside only
SC11I!	cobweb	not by spiders
SC25A	cobwebs	especially if dusty

GA15A2	web	inside or out
GA34A2	cobweb	bigger than spiderweb
SC12B2	webs	"a mess"
SC22B2	spiderweb	outdoors or indoors [also SC30A2, NC24A2]
SC22B2	cobwebs	in the house only

130. Toadstool

1930s		*1990*	
frogstool	13	frogstool	1
frogstools	1	mushroom	19
NA	2	mushrooms	11
NR	12	NA	5
toad frog umbrella	2	toadstool	10
toad tables	1	toadstools	6
toadstool	10		

| NC25A | frogstools | on stumps |
| NC62B | frogstool | hard kind on stumps and rocks |

| GA13A2 | mushroom | gathered by youngsters for a tea |

SC14A2	mushroom	small or "big as a pie plate"; = toadstool	
NC52N2	mushroom	/-i-/, 3 syllables	
NC69A2	toadstool	different from mushroom but similar	
NC75B2	toadstools	thinks they're bigger than mushrooms	
NC75B2	mushrooms	*fairy ring* = circle of them	

131. Sycamore

1930s		*1990*	
NA	2	elm	1
NR	19	NA	19
sycamore	18	NR	1
		plane tree	3
		sycamore	8

GA4N2	Zaccheus tree	from Bible, but Zaccheus was short and sycamore has high limbs
GA10A2	sycamore	said they caused consumption (= lung cancer)
GA13A2	sycamore	/-ɪ-/
SC22B2	plane tree	in Europe
NC71C2	plane tree	from French

132. Husband

1930s		*1990*	
husband	1	(by first name)	1
me old man	1	(by name)	1
my husband	36	her husband	1
my old man	3	hubby	1
NA	1	husband	9
NR	1	mate	1
		my husband	12
		NA	13
		spouse	1

NC52N2	my husband	called him Mister John
NC69A2	husband	*old man* if living together (usually not if married)

133. Wife

1930s		1990	
a wife	1	(by name)	1
my old lady	2	better half	2
my wife	35	helpmate	1
NA	1	his wife	1
NR	1	my treasure	1
old lady	1	my wife	14
old woman	1	NA	11
the wife	1	the warden	1
wife	1	wife	9

SC1A2	old lady	as a joke
NC52B2	old lady	sometimes: "I'd try not to use it too much"
NC56A2	old woman	f. said
NC69A2	wife	*old lady* if living together but not married
NC69A2	the madam	fairly common
NC69A2	the warden	jokingly
NC75B2	old lady	m. didn't like

134. Widow

1930s		1990	
NA	1	NA	17
NR	1	widow	19
widow	34	widow woman	2
widow woman	8	widow-in-deed	1

GA4N2   widow-in-deed   Biblical term, = no husband or children

135. Father (term of address)

1930s		*1990*	
dad	3	dad	3
daddy	12	daddy	26
father	1	father	1
foddy	1	pa	2
NA	1	papa	7
NR	1	uncle	1
pa	12		
pae	8		
paepa	4		
pap	6		
papa	13		
papae	3		
pappy	5		
paw	2		
pop	2		

GA1F!	daddy	originally used for addressing old colored folk
SC1A	pappy	as a child
SC14A	pae	as a boy
SC22B	pae	when small
NC52B	pa	some said
NC52B	daddy	used by children now
NC71C!	daddy	modern only
GA10A2	pop	most people called them
SC11N2	uncle	uses *father* and *daddy* as term of reference
NC24A2	daddy	his children to him
NC75B2	daddy	as a child
NC75B2	dad	as an adult

136. Mother (term of address)

1930s		*1990*	
ma	11	ma	2
ma'am	1	mama	25
mae	8	mom	2
maema	3	mommy	1
maemae	1	mother	9
mama	14		
mamae	3		
mammy	10		
maw	4		
mother	5		
mums	1		
mumsy	1		
NA	1		

GA43	ma'am	little children [same comment for *mammy*]
SC14A	mae	as a boy
SC22B	mae	when small
GA4N2	mama	other families
NC24A2	mama	by his children

137. Grandfather (term of address)

1930s		*1990*	
dad	1	(by first name)	1
grand	1	granddad	2
granddad	1	granddaddy	9
granddaddy	3	grandfather	3
grandfather	30	grandpa	12
grandpa	19	grandpapa	3
grandpae	7	Mr. Mose	1
grandpaepa	1	NA	3
grandpap	4	NR	3
grandpapa	2	pa	3
grandpapae	1	paepaw	1
grandpappy	1	papa	3
grandpaw	6	pawpaw	1
NA	2	pop	1
pa	3		

GA1F2	papa	+ first name
GA4N2	Mr. Mose	step-MGF
GA34A2	pawpaw	by grandchildren [also GA432, NC71B2]
SC14A2	nandy	from his grandchildren
NC24B2	granddaddy	+ first name to distinguish as term of reference
NC71C2	(by first name)	for more formal side of family

138. Grandmother (term of address)

1930s		*1990*	
grandma	18	(by first name)	1
grandmae	10	grandma	16
grandmaema	1	grandmae	1
grandmama	1	grandmama	3
grandmamae	1	grandmaw	1
grandmammy	1	grandmother	11
grandmaw	7	granny	4
grandmother	16	ma	1
granny	6	mae	1
ma	2	maemaw	1
maw	1	mama	3
mother	1	mommy	1
NA	2	mother	2
		NA	1
		nanny	1

GA34A2	grandma	+ last name; PGM
GA34A2	mother	MGM: said not old enough to be *grandmother*
GA34A2	nanny	herself by grandchildren [also SC41A2]
SC12B2	grandmae	*grands* = grandchildren
SC41A2	grandmother	from grandchildren
NC23B2	grandmother	+ last name
NC24B2	grandma	+ first name to distinguish as term of reference
NC71C2	(by first name)	for more formal side of family

139. Relatives

1930s			1990	
blood kin	1		ancestors	1
connection	1		cousins	1
kin	8		family	7
kin people	2		kin	1
kindred	4		kinpeople	1
kinfolks	28		mama and them	1
kinnery	1		NA	17
kinsmen	1		people	8
NA	2		relations	1
people	1		relatives	8
relation	2			
relations	4			
relative	1			
relatives	12			

SC12B	relation	collective
GA24A2	people	called elderly blacks *aunt* and *uncle*
NC75B2	kinfolks	m. and f. said

140. Baby Carriage

1930s			1990	
baby carriage	35		baby buggy	2
baby wagon	3		baby carriage	9
go cart	1		baby stroller	1
NA	2		buggy	3
			carriage	22
			carriages	1
			go cart	1
			NA	4
			perambulator	1
			stroller	17
			strollers	2
			wagon	3

SC22B	go cart	sit up
SC14A2	baby carriage	"toted 'em" mostly
SC22B2	go cart	term for stroller
NC46B2	carriage	more elaborate than stroller
NC46B2	stroller	sit up in
NC75B2	baby buggy	m. said

141. Pregnant

1930s

big	2
broke a leg	1
broke foot	1
expecting	5
expecting to be sick	1
family way	1
in a family way	7
in delicate health	1
in family way	7
in the family way	1
looking to be down	1
looking to get down	1
NA	2
NR	4
pregnant	14
to be confined	3
with child	3

1990

bearing a cross	1
big	3
bigged up	1
expecting	13
fixing to deliver	1
going to find a little baby	1
going to have a baby	2
in a motherly way	1
in the family way	3
in the shade	1
knocked up	2
mother-to-be	1
NA	1
NR	1
pregnant	28
swallowed a seed	1
warming the oven	1
with child	3

SC14A	she broke a foot	Negroes
NC25B	broke a leg	means illegitimate expected
GA1F2	pregnant	secret, indelicate subject
GA3A2	pregnant	hardly ever see her out in public
GA4N2	got a answer from the letter she wrote	seldom used

Appendix 4

GA13A2	NR	didn't talk about it
SC11I2	expecting	more polite than *pregnant*
SC12B2	pregnant	didn't use term in old days
SC14A2	in the family way	hrd. from blacks
SC19N2	pregnant	"let it go at that"
SC22B2	going to find a little baby	found "in the cabbage patch"
NC23B2	expecting	more polite
NC24A2	big	also verb
NC25A2	pregnant	used to didn't hear nothing about nothing like that
NC25B2	expecting	in a low voice
NC29B2	pregnant	bad word
NC52N2	she broke her leg	m. said
NC56A2	pregnant	taboo
NC57B2	with child	rare
NC69A2	pregnant	never used formerly, now common
NC71C2	expecting	preferred term
NC75B2	going to have a baby	taboo

142. Midwife

1930s		*1990*	
granny	17	baby catcher	1
granny-woman	12	grandmother	1
midwife	29	granny	7
midwoman	1	granny woman	2
monthly	1	granny women	1
NA	2	midwife	30
old granny-woman	1	midwives	2
sheriff	1	NA	3

GA4N2	midwife	ggm. was one
GA13A2	midwife	for blacks [also NC52B2]
GA15A2	midwife	Aunt Sue—black, mostly served blacks; done played out
GA34A2	granny	maybe the ones who'd delivered a great many
SC12B2	midwife	black
SC14A2	midwife	*Aunt*
SC22B2	granny	black women, served both black and white outside town
SC25A2	midwife	black, "Aunt Sylvia"
NC24A2	midwife	*Granny*: term of address
NC25B2	midwife	aged Negroes; *Aunt* + first and last name

143. Looks Like

1930s

favor	5
favors	25
is the image of	3
is the spit of	1
is the very spirit and image of	1
look like	2
looks like	17
NA	2
resembles	4
spit image	1
take after	1
takes after	2
the image of	1
the spit of	1

1990

act just like	1
acts like	1
chip off the old block	3
closely related	1
dead ringer	1
exactly like	1
family resemblance	1
favor	3
favors	7
got ways like	1
has her features	1
has ways like	1
have all that person's ways	1
have ways like	1
image	1
is a lot like	1
is just like	1
is the spitting image of	3
just like	4
just like two peas in a pod	1
like father, like son	1
look like	1
looks just like	3
looks like	2
looks like she spit him out of her mouth	1
NA	4
similar	1
spitting image	2
take after	1
take back after	1
takes after	3
the image of	1
the spit image	1
the spitting image of	1
they look alike	1
typing out like	1

GA1F!	is the spit of	hrd. from colored people
GA13A	is the spit of	rare
SC14A	takes after	in ways
SC12B2	favor	seldom heard now
SC22N2	act just like	one of the twins)
SC22B2	takes after	in looks
SC22B2	is a lot like	in actions
NC52B2	favors	in looks
NC69A2	chip off the old block	similar children are like "two peas in a pod"

144. (Named) For

1930s		*1990*	
after	37	after	22
at	1	for	5
for	9	NA	11
NR	1		

SC14A	after	uncommon

145. Bastard

1930s		*1990*	
bastard	32	bastard	24
broomgrass colt	1	bastard child	1
bushwhacker	1	bastards	2
field colt	1	born out of wedlock	1
grass colt	2	illegitimate	6
illegitimate	1	illegitimate child	3
NA	2	NA	4
NR	3	other child	1
woods chicken	1	out of wedlock	2
woods colt	23	outside children	1
		six-month baby	1
		woods chicken	1
		woods colt	4
		woods colts	1
		yard child	1

Appendix 4

GA4N	bastard	other words used only by white people
SC11N	illegitimate	noun
GA1F2	illegitimate child	"didn't happen"
GA10A2	bastards	the Bible speaks of)
GA10A2	born out of wedlock	they're all got the same way, married or unmarried
GA13A2	bastard	looked down on it
GA34A2	NA	"it was a disgrace"
GA432	illegitimate kid	"I can't pronounce it" [first 2 syllables deleted]
SC11I2	yard child	also name of a dress shop she knows
SC19N2	bastard	reluctantly
SC22B2	bastard	"intellectually", not commonly used
NC23B2	bastard	"I don't like that term"
NC29B2	bastard	ugly word
NC52N2	outside children	husband's by another woman
NC52B2	bastard	might slip up and say
NC56A2	bastard	taboo
NC56A2	six-month baby	claimed it was premature
NC62B2	woods chicken	doesn't like to use
NC69A2	illegitimate	doesn't like: no illegitimate children, it's illegitimate parents
NC71C2	bastard	wouldn't use; wouldn't make that distinction
NC75B2	NA	taboo

146. Orphan

1930s

mother and fatherless	1
mother and fatherless child	1
motherless and fatherless child	2
NA	2
orphan	26
orphan child	5
orphanage	1
orphanage child	1
orphaned child	1

1990

adopted	1
daddyless	1
fatherless	2
half-orphan	1
motherless	2
motherless and fatherless	1
motherless and fatherless children	1
NA	8
NR	1
orphan	21
orphan child	2
orphan children	2
orphans	1

GA4N2	orphan	even if adopted
GA13A2	orphan	I was never called an orphan to my face but my m. died
GA34A2	orphan children	not used if they had some family
SC11I2	orphan	not if taken in by someone [also NC23B2, NC71C]
SC19N2	orphan	not used, usually raised by other family members
SC22N2	orphan child	only if intentionally abandoned by parents
SC22B2	orphans	even if taken in by family [also NC52B2, NC71B2, NC75B2]
SC22B2	half-orphan	lost one parent
SC30A2	orphan	technically right, not used if they had some family

147. Children

1930s		1990	
NA	2	children	32
our children	35	kid	1
our childrens	2	kids	9
young ones	1	NA	3
younguns	20	young people	1
		youngsters	1
		youngun	1
		younguns	2
		youths	1

GA43	childers	from "Dutchmen" in neighborhood
GA10A2	children	also pron. with /-dr-/ omitted [also SC22N2]
GA34A2	children	also pron. with /-dr-/ omitted: amused, doubtful
SC41A2	children	also metathesized pron.

148. Lets Out (school, at the end of the day)

1930s		1990	
break up	1	be through	1
breaks up	1	get out	3
closes	1	get through	1
lets out	6	gets out	2
NA	2	got out	3
out	1	is out	1
turns out	30	let out	1
		let us out	1
		NA	25
		turn out	2

GA15A2 got out   *took in* in morning

149. Starts (school, following vacation)

1930s		1990	
begin	12	NA	22
commence	3	opened	1
NA	2	start	10
open	8	start back	1
start	2	started	3
starts	19	starts	1
take in	2		
take up	1		

GA1F!	take in	each morning
NC25B	take in	each day
NC52N2	start	school)

150. Played Hookey

1930s		1990	
bolted his class	1	cut school	1
burnt school	1	cutting school	1
cut hookey	1	delinquent	1
laid out of school	6	laid out	4
lay out	4	lay out	1
lay out of school	10	misbehaving	1
lay out of school on purpose	1	NA	5
missed school	1	NR	2
NA	2	play hookey	1
NR	2	played hookey	9
play truant	1	playing hookey	3
played hookey	7	skipped class	1
played rookie	1	skipped school	3
played truant	2	truant	7
skip school	1		
skipped class	1		
skipped his class	1		
skipped school	3		
snapped school	2		

SC19N2	NR	not on the island	
NC25B2	truant	usually working	

151. Tattletale

1930s		*1990*	
NA	3	blabber mouth	1
taletattler	1	liar	1
taleteller	3	mockingbird	1
tattle box	3	NA	4
tattler	23	NR	3
tattletale	12	old refrigerator	1
tattletell	1	ratfink	1
telltale	4	snitch	3
tongue tattler	1	snitcher	1
traitor	1	squealer	1
		stool pigeon	1
		tattler	6
		tattletale	25

GA4N2	old refrigerator	just like an) (can't keep nothing
SC11N2	mockingbird	also *rats on*
SC11I2	tattletale	also *ratted on*: new
SC19N2	tattletale	stress on third syllable

152. Horseshoes (game)

1930s		*1990*	
horseshoes	28	horseshoe	1
NA	1	horseshoes	20
NR	6	NA	14
quoits	10	NR	2
		ring toss	1
		rings	1

GA1F!	quoits	with rings, read about only
GA3A	quoits	rings [also SC11N, SC22B, NC46B]
NC46B	quoits	rings

| GA13A2 | rings | rings used instead of horseshoes |
| SC19N2 | horseshoes | didn't play too much at) |

153. Teacher (female)

1930s			*1990*	
lady teacher	1		governess	1
ma'am	1		NA	15
marm	1		school teacher	2
mistress	1		school teachers	1
NA	2		teacher	14
school marm	4		teachers	5
school miss	1			
school mistress	7			
school teacher	26			
teacher	7			
woman teacher	1			

GA24A	school miss	rare
GA13A2	school marm	m. was called that (she taught)
NC62B2	teacher	lived in informant's home; taught grades 1–7
NC75B2	school marm	f. said

154. Student (elementary age)

1930s		*1990*	
NA	2	brats	1
scholar	15	classmates	1
student	32	NA	12
		pupil	2
		pupils	5
		schoolchildren	1
		schoolkids	2
		schoolmates	1
		student	5
		students	7

SC41A	scholar	older; as a girl
SC25A2	student	in high school

155. Rheumatism

1930s		*1990*	
NA	2	arthritis	14
rheumatic	2	arthuritis	14
rheumatism	34	bursitis	9
rheumatiz	9	gout	3
		lumbago	1
		NA	3
		neuritis	3
		old people troubles	1
		rheumatism	23
		rheumatiz	3
		the rheumatics	1
		the ritus boys	1
		them boys	1

SC41A	the pains	word as girl
GA4N2	the ritus boys	"Arthur's the worst one"

Appendix 4

GA10A2	gout	in ankle
GA10A2	gout-arthuritis	Dr. called it
GA13A2	arthritis	possibly the same as rheumatism
GA34A2	rheumatism	in back
GA34A2	arthritis	in feet and hands
GA34A2	bursitis	in shoulders and hips
SC19N2	rheumatism	stress on third syllable
NC24A2	rheumatism	in fingers; the worst kind
NC24A2	arthritis	general
NC24A2	bursitis	in shoulders and neck
NC46B2	arthritis	more severe than rheumatism
NC46C2	arthritis	anywhere
NC46C2	bursitis	in joints
NC52B2	rheumatism	a lot of people still call it
NC52B2	arthuritis	term used by people under 60
NC56A2	rheumatism	different from arthritis
NC57B2	arthritis	same as rheumatism and lumbago
NC75B2	misery	gm. said

157. Vomit

1930s			*1990*	
cascade	1		barf	1
fling up	2		being nauseated	1
heave	1		brought it up	1
heave up	2		got the colic	1
NA	2		have an upset stomach	1
puke	18		heaving	1
puked	1		NA	5
spew	17		nausea	1
spew up	1		nauseated	2
spewed	1		puke	7
throw up	24		puking	1
vomick	9		regurgitate	2
vomick up	2		throw up	15
vomit	21		throwed up	1
womick	2		throwing up	3
womit	2		toss up	1
			upchuck	5
			upset stomach	1
			vomick	4
			vomit	20
			vomiting	1

GA1F!	puke	babies
GA3A	womick	rare
SC11N	heave	country
SC11I!	vomit	rare
NC24N	throw up	initial [sr-]
NC52B	heave	hrd. from Negroes
GA13A2	throwed up	"ain't no nice way"
GA34A2	puke	"such an ugly thing to say"
SC11I2	puke	"there's a time and place for everything"
SC11I2	barf	in college
SC22B2	vomit	"I despise the word"
NC23B2	vomit	sounds terrible
NC75B2	puke	"there's an awful word"
NC75B2	upchuck	worse than *puke*

159. Died

1930s

dead	2
died	36
died out	1
fell asleep	1
left us	2
NA	2
pass away	1
passed away	26
passed on	2
passed out	8
was taken away	1

1990

bit the dust	1
come face to face with the Lord	1
croaked	1
crossed Jordan	1
crossed over	1
dead	1
dead and gone	1
deceased	4
departed	1
died	28
expired	3
fire up in hell	1
gave up the spirit	1
gone	2
gone beyond the sunset	1
gone on	1
gone on to glory	1
gone on to the great beyond	1
good thing he's gone	1
got what he deserved	1
kicked the bucket	9
left this earth	1
left us for glory	1
left us for good	1
make the transition	1
met their maker	1
NA	4
passed	5
passed away	15
passed on	10
passed on to the great beyond	1
spent his final days here on Earth	1
the Lord called them	1
toes turned up	1
went to the other side	1

Appendix 4

GA4N	passed out	politer
GA4N	left us	veiled
NC25B	was taken away	veiled

SC19N2	kicked the bucket	slang
NC24B2	deceased	not many say
NC52B2	passed on	to family members or of friends
NC62B2	passed on	on radio; makes her mad
NC69A2	passed	from blacks

161. Ghosts

1930s			*1990*	
boogers	1		apparition	1
fraids	1		boogers	2
ghost	2		evil spirit	1
ghosts	30		evil spirits	1
hant	1		ghost	7
hants	32		ghosts	13
NA	3		hag	1
spirit	2		haints	6
spirits	11		hant	1
spooks	4		haunts	1
stooks	1		Mister Bloody Bone	1
			Mister Cabus	1
			NA	9
			spirits	8
			spooks	2

GA1F!	hants	uneducated
SC14A	old hag	hrd. from blacks
SC14A	pooky spots	= scary places

GA13A2	hant	*hanted*: verb
SC11I2	haints	hrd. from blacks [also NC52B2]
NC24B2	Mister Cabus	[ke]
NC62B2	hants	gm. said

162. Devil

1930s		1990	
booger man	1	bad boy	1
bugbear	1	bad man	4
devil	36	booger	1
dragoon	1	booger man	9
NA	2	boogey man	2
Satan	8	devil	19
the old devil	1	devourer	1
the old Harry	1	evil one	2
		evil spirit	1
		forked tongue	1
		Lucifer	2
		man with the forked tail	1
		man with the pitchfork	1
		man with the red horns	1
		NA	4
		old boy	2
		old raw head and bloody bones	1
		old Satan	1
		Satan	20
		slew foot	1
		third in line in the host of heaven	1

GA3A2	bad man	got "hell in him"
GA13A2	bad man	the); to scare children
GA13A2	old split foot	fr. Baptist preachers; refers to foot like a cow
GA13A2	boogey man	not necessarily the devil
SC41A2	devil	he's busy all the time
NC24A2	forked tongue	3 syllables
NC52N2	devil	bad word
NC62B2	old raw head and bloody bones	that old)
NC71C2	Lucifer	fundamentalists

164. Attendants (at wedding)

1930s		*1990*	
best man	11	attendant	1
boss-man	1	attendants	5
bridemaid	1	best man	17
bridemaids	1	bridemaid	2
bridesmaid	8	bridemaids	1
bridesmaids	2	bridesmaid	10
groomsman	5	bridesmaids	8
groomsmen	1	groomsman	4
maid of honor	2	groomsmen	2
NA	2	maid of honor	13
waiter	7	matron of honor	8
waiters	19	NA	6
		NR	2
		ushers	13
		waiter	1
		witnesses	1

SC22B	best man	chief
SC22B	waiter	all [also NC46C]
SC22B	maid of honor	chief woman
NC25B	waiter	if several at home wedding: no chief one
GA3A2	groomsman	"someone to stand for them"
GA432	NR	only been to one wedding; don't know
SC19N2	NA	*flowers girl*
SC22B2	bridesmaid	also *junior bridesmaid*
NC75A2	NR	no weddings

166. Serenade (following wedding)

1930s		1990	
a belling	3	big blowout	1
beating the saw	1	cake-cutting	1
infare	1	dance	2
NA	2	dinner	2
NR	1	feed	1
serenade	29	fixing up the car	1
serenading	6	NA	2
		NR	1
		party	1
		reception	24
		receptionist	1
		refreshment	1
		serenade	8
		social	1
		wedding supper	1

SC25A	infare	= wedding party after the supper
GA3A2	serenading	heard as a small boy
SC14A2	dance	just called it having fun
NC24N2	serenade	pron. "sir-nade"
NC56A2	shivaree	in movies

167. Funeral

1930s		*1990*	
burying	3	Charleston burial	1
funeral	37	funeral	24
NA	2	funeral service	3
		funeral services	2
		funerals	1
		graveside	1
		graveside service	1
		memorial service	1
		NA	9
		service	2
		services	1

GA1F!	burying	in country
SC11I2	Charleston burial	stay to watch casket lowered and covered with dirt
NC71C2	memorial service	in case of cremation

168. Coffin

1930s		*1990*	
casket	19	box	3
coffin	34	boxes	1
NA	2	casket	25
		caskets	1
		coffin	16
		final box	1
		NA	2
		pine box	2
		piney box	1

GA1F!	casket	modern shape [also GA3A, GA13A, SC22B]
GA10A	coffin	old style
GA43	coffin	as a boy

278   *Appendix 4*

GA15A2 casket   same as coffin
NC24A2 coffin   homemade)
NC24A2 casket   store-bought)
NC52B2 casket   *vault*: wealthy only

169. Cemetery

1930s		*1990*	
burying ground	5	burial ground	2
cemetery	27	burial plot	1
God's acre	1	cemeteries	1
graveyard	36	cemetery	32
NA	2	church plot	1
potter's field	1	family plot	2
		family plots	1
		graveyard	14
		mausoleum	1
		memorial graveyard	1
		NA	1
		perpetual cemetery	1
		place of final rest	1
		private plot	1

GA1F!   graveyard   round a church
SC11N   potter's field   for poor
SC11I! graveyard   natural as child
SC22B   graveyard   country [also NC46C, NC71C]
NC25B   cemetery   in village
NC71C! burying ground   country

GA4N2   cemetery   community); originally for members of
                               burial society
GA13A2 cemetery   at church [also GA24A2, SC30A2]
SC19N2 graveyard   stress on second syllable
SC25A2 burial plot   family
SC41A2 burial ground   = plot
NC24B2 mausoleum   not many
NC25A2 cemetery   mostly family plots on property
NC46C2 cemetery   larger than graveyard

170. Vest

1930s | | *1990* |
---|---|---|---
jacket | 12 | jacket | 1
NR | 12 | NA | 12
vest | 14 | vest | 23
vests | 1 | |
weskit | 2 | |

GA4N vest   [w] not [v] [also SC12B]
NC23B weskit   [v] not [w]

SC1A2   jacket   *coat* went over it
NC56A2 vest   men's
NC56A2 weskit   ladies'

171. Pants

1930s | | *1990* |
---|---|---|---
britches | 12 | britches | 1
pantaloon | 1 | button pants | 1
pantaloons | 2 | dress pants | 1
pants | 37 | NA | 6
trousers | 9 | pants | 29
 | | trousers | 4

SC22N trousers   [sr-] not [tr-]

SC1A2   button pants   for boys: pants buttoned to the shirt
SC11I2 trousers   with a suit

173. Stranger

1930s		*1990*	
an off-fellow	1	damn Yankees	1
foreigner	24	drifters	1
NA	2	flatlander	2
stranger	35	Floridians	1
		foreigner	12
		foreigners	3
		goddamn Yankees	1
		migrated flatlanders	1
		NA	6
		newcomer	1
		Northerner	1
		Northerners	1
		nosy	1
		out-of-towner	1
		outsider	5
		outsiders	1
		stranger	5
		strangers	1
		visitor	3
		Yankee	6
		Yankees	4

GA13A	foreigner	natural
GA15A	foreigner	several states off
GA43	foreigner	from NC or TN
SC11N	stranger	if in Charleston
SC11N	foreigner	if from GA, etc.
SC11I!	foreigner	formerly used to = stranger, now of anyone not from surrounding states
SC12B	foreigner	old only
SC14A	foreigner	if not of this locality
SC25A	foreigner	= almost same as stranger
SC41A	foreigner	as a girl, someone from 100 mi. or so away
NC52N	foreigner	few hundred miles
GA13A2	foreigner	even said of father from Savannah (next co.)
GA15A2	foreigner	from another country

Appendix 4 281

GA15A2	Yankee	from up North
GA24A2	foreigner	doesn't apply to someone from another part of state
GA34A2	foreigner	even if from different part of same state
GA432	foreigners	from another country
SC12B2	Northerners	them old); now we're glad for them to come
SC12B2	Yankees	used to call them
SC19N2	nosy	just) [directed at field worker]
SC22N2	visitor	at church
SC22B2	Yankee	if they pronounce their r's and g's
SC22B2	foreigner	wouldn't say
SC30A2	damn Yankees	stress on first word
NC24A2	foreigners	old pron. like "fur"
NC24B2	foreigner	both prons.
NC24B2	goddamn Yankees	them)
NC29B2	foreigner	from overseas
NC46C2	Yankee	if from the North
NC52N2	tramp	"nothing BUT tramps now"
NC52B2	foreigner	both prons.
NC52B2	tramp	if a drifter, dirty
NC62B2	foreigner	only from overseas
NC69A2	flatlander	depends on which direction they came from
NC69A2	Yankee	depends on which direction they came from

175. Train Station

1930s			*1990*	
depot	19		Amtrak station	1
NA	20		depot	21
railroad station	6		depots	1
station	6		NA	6
			NR	2
			railroad station	1
			station	5
			train depot	2
			train station	6

Appendix 4

GA3A	railroad station	modern only, rare
GA3A	station	modern only, rare
SC22B2	station	acceptable, not preferred term
NC23B2	train depot	[ɛ] not [i]
NC56A2	station	also *train stop*: no building, only sign

176. County Seat

1930s

capital	2
county capital	1
county seat	32
county site	3
courthouse	1
NA	3
NR	2

1990

county seat	20
NA	10
seat	1

GA3A	capital	rare

177. Civil War

1930s

Civil War	24
Confederate	1
Confederate War	24
NA	3
our war	1
the Slave War	1
war	1
War between the North and South	1
War between the States	8

1990

Civil War	21
Confederate War	3
NA	8
NR	1
Rebel War	1
the War	3
War between the North and the South	1
War Between the States	12
War for Freedom	1
War of Northern Agression	2
War of the South	1

Appendix 4

SC11N	Civil War		rare
GA13A2	Civil War		gm. saw it, said there was nothing civil about it
SC11I2	War of Northern Agression		jokingly
SC22B2	Civil War		I actually find myself saying)
SC22B2	War between the States		used to be common
SC22B2	Confederate War		term of choice
NC52B2	War of Secession		term used by elite, educated people
NC71C2	War of the Northern Aggression		heard in Charleston

178. Merry Christmas

1930s
Christmas Gift	28
Christmas Treat	1
Merry Christmas	12
NA	3

1990
Christmas Eve	1
Christmas Gift	9
Happy Christmas	1
Merry Christmas	30
NA	3

GA1F!	Christmas Gift	darkies only
GA3A	Christmas Gift	used only by Negroes expecting a gift
GA4N	Christmas Gift	to own family: one who says it first gets a gift
GA10A	Christmas Gift	rare
GA10A	Merry Christmas	rare [also SC25A]
SC11I!	Christmas Gift	used by Negroes only
SC14A	Christmas Gift	often among common people
NC52B	Christmas Gift	first in morning, especially Negroes
GA1F2	Christmas Gift	"slaves used to say"
GA1F2	Christmas Treat	Negroes to boss, first thing Christmas morning; given liqour, sweets, money
SC11I2	Christmas Gift	f. said; doesn't know meaning
SC19N2	Merry Christmas	*Christmas Gift* a reply
SC22B2	Merry Christmas	used by grandchildren

SC22B2	Christmas Gift	probably of black origin, my family sticks to it
NC52N2	Christmas Gift	"hand it here!"
NC62B2	Christmas Gift	first to say it is supposed to get a present
NC69A2	Christmas Gift	any time of year if irritated by someone
NC71B2	Christmas Gift	heard, but didn't know meaning

179. Happy New Year

1930s

Happy New Year	19
Happy New Year's	2
NA	3
New Year's Gift	13
New Year's Present	1
NR	1

1990

Happy New Year	28
Happy New Year's	1
NA	3
New Year's Gift	1
NR	5

GA13A2	NR	didn't celebrate [also NC25B2]
NC69A2	NR	just another day

Appendix 5: Index of Variants by Question Number

Parentheses indicate that a feature sometimes occurs in the data. (x) denotes that a variety of terms occurred in this context. Curly braces denote an obligatory choice of variant features.

a belling, 166
after, 144
alley(s), 40
andirons, 2
armoire, 12
arth(u)ritis, 155
attendant(s), 164
attic(s), 13
automobile(s), 62
avenue, 65
baby carriage, 140
baby wagon, 140
back (x), 22
back house, 41
bacon, 101
bacon, 99
bacon rind(s), 100
bad man, 162
(x) bad weather, 78
bag(s), 37
bag(s), 36
bait, 123
baitworm, 123
baker's bread, 92
bakery bread, 92
barn lot, 46
barnyard, 46
bastard(s), 145

battercakes, 95
bawl, 75
bawl, 76
be still, 22
be(come) fresh, 68
bedspread, 7
begin, 149
bellow(s), 75
bellow(s), 76
bench, 5
best man, 164
biddie, 32
big, 141
big house, 1
big rain, 79
bin(s), 42
bite, 96
blate, 75
blinds, 6
blood worm(s), 123
bloody noun, 120
boar, 70
boar hog, 70
board(s), 38
boil(ed), 97
boogey(-r) man, 162
bought bread, 92
box(es), 168

bread, 91
breakfast bacon, 101
breakfast strip(s), 101
breaking, 77
breast bone, 102
bridemaid(s), 164
bridesmaid(s), 164
bridle reins, 57
bridle(s), 57
bring a calf, 68
britches, 171
buck, 69
bucket, 21
buggy, 140
bull, 67
bullfrog(s), 120
bureau(s), 10
burlap bag(s), 37
burlap sack, 37
bursitis, 155
burying, 167
burying ground, 169
butter bean(s), 112
butts meat, 99
(by name), 25
calve, 68
car, 62
carriage(s), 140
casket(s), 168
cemetery(-ies), 169
changing, 77
changing, 78
chest of drawer(s), 10
chest(s), 10
chick, 32
chick chickie, 32
chickie, 32
chifforobe, 12
children, 147
chip off the old block, 143

chipmunk(s), 119
Christmas Gift, 178
Civil War, 177
clabber, 18
clabber cheese, 19
clabber milk, 18
clabbered milk, 18
clapboard(s), 38
clearing, 77
clearing off, 77
clearing(-s) up, 77
clearseed (peach), 108
clearstone, 108
cling (peaches), 107
clingstone (peach), 107
clobber, 18
closet, 17
closet, 11
closet, 41
clothes closet, 11
cloud(ing, s) up, 78
cloudburst, 79
(cluck), 26
co(o)-nannie, 31
co(o)-sheep, 31
co-(w){e,a}nch, 23
co-eh, 23
cobbler(s), 109
cobweb(s), 129
coffin, 168
come (in) fresh, 68
come up, 26
come(-ing) in, 68
commence, 149
Confederate War, 177
cook room, 16
cooter(s), 125
corn barn(s), 42
corn bin, 42
corn crib(s), 42

Appendix 5

corn dodger, 86
corn house, 42
corn mush, 90
corn on the cob, 83
corn pone(s), 86
corn silk, 85
cornbread, 86
cottage cheese, 19
cotton (picking) sack, 37
couch, 5
counterp{in,ane}, 7
county seat, 176
county site, 176
coverl{et,id}(s), 7
cowpen, 44
crib(s), 42
crocus bag, 37
crocus sack, 37
croker sack, 37
cruller, 94
cry(-ies), 75
cur, 66
cur dog, 66
curd(s), 19
curtain(s), 6
cush, 90
dad, 135
daddy, 135
deceased, 159
deep dish (x) pie, 109
den, 1
depot(s), 175
devil, 162
died, 159
dish cloth, 35
dish cloth(s), 34
dish rag, 35
dish rag(s), 34
dish towel, 35
ditch, 81

dog irons, 2
dog(s), 66
dogs, 2
double singletree, 61
doubletree, 61
doughnut(s), 94
downpour, 79
dragonfly(-ies), 127
draw, 97
drawing room, 1
dresser(s), 10
drive, 65
driveway, 65
drop a calf, 68
dry(ing) cloth, 35
dry(ing) rag, 35
earthworm(s), 123
eave(s) trough(s), 39
electric storm, 80
electrical storm, 80
entrails, 103
expecting, 141
expired, 159
fair(-ing,-s) up, 77
fairing off, 77
(x) falling weather, 78
family, 139
family pie, 109
family plot(s), 169
(in {the, a}) family way, 141
fat lighter(d), 4
fat meat, 99
fatback, 99
fatwood, 4
favor(s), 143
feist, 66
fence(s), 48
fills, 59
find a calf, 68

fireboard, 3
firedogs, 2
firefly(-ies), 126
fishing worm(s), 123
flannel cakes, 95
flapjacks, 95
(migrated) flatlander(s), 173
flitters, 95
flood(s), 79
for, 144
foreigner(s), 173
fowl, 72
fowls, 72
freestone (peach), 108
freshen (in, -ing), 68
fritter(s), 94
fritters, 95
frog(s), 121
frog(s), 122
frogstool(s), 130
front room, 1
fry pan, 33
frying pan(s), 33
funeral service(s), 167
funeral(s), 167
garden house, 41
garret, 13
gee, 29
gee or haw, 28
gee or haw, 29
gentleman cow, 67
{get(s), got} out, 148
get up, 26
getting cloudy, 78
ghost(s), 161
giddy up, 26
go along, 26
go on, 26
gone on (x), 159

goober peas, 98
goober(s), 98
goop, 30
gopher(s), 125
{got, has, have} ways like, 143
gout, 155
granddaddy, 137
grandfather, 137
grandma(w), 138
grandmae, 138
grandmama, 138
grandmother, 138
grandpa(w), 137
grandpae, 137
grandpap, 137
grandpapa, 137
granny, 138
granny(-ies), 142
(old) granny-wom{e,a}n, 142
grasshopper(s), 128
graveyard, 169
green corn, 83
green onion(s), 110
greenfrog(s), 121
grinding stone, 52
grindrock(s), 52
grindstone, 52
grocery bag, 36
groomsm{a,e}n, 164
ground peas, 98
ground squirrel, 119
groundnut(s), 98
gully washer(s), 79
gully(-ies), 81
gutter, 40
gutter(s), 39
Happy New Year(s), 179
hard rain, 79
haslet(s), 103

Appendix 5

have a calf, 68
haw, 28
hayloft, 43
heavy rain, 79
heinz (57), 66
hen, 73
here chick, 32
hogpen(s), 45
homemade bread, 91
homemade cheese, 19
hoppergrass, 128
horse(s), 71
horseshoes, 152
hull, 114
hum, 76
hurricane, 79
husband, 132
husk(s), 82
h{a,ai}nt(s), 161
Idaho potatoes, 115
illegitimate (child, kid), 145
(is) the image of, 143
Irish potato(es), 115
Irish taters, 115
jacket, 170
john, 41
johnny house, 41
junk, 14
kernel, 105
kernel, 106
kicked the bucket, 159
kid(s), 147
kin, 139
kindling, 4
kindred, 139
kinfolks, 139
kitchen, 16
kw{o,ʊ}p, 25
k{o,ʊ,u}p, 25

lane, 65
lap siding (board), 38
lay(-id) out, 150
lay(-id) out of school, 150
lay(ing) the worm, 48
let(s) out, 148
light bread, 91
light bread, 92
lighten bug, 126
lighter wood, 4
lighterd, 4
lighterd splinters, 4
lightning bug, 126
lightwood, 4
(is) (exactly, a lot, just) like, 143
lima bean(s), 112
line(s), 57
line(s), 56
liver and lights, 103
living room, 1
loaf bread, 92
loaf bread, 91
locust(s), 128
lodging, 9
loft, 13
loft, 43
look(s) (just) like, 143
lot, 46
lot, 45
lounge, 5
low(ing), 76
lunch, 96
ma, 136
maa, 75
mae, 136
maema, 136
maid of honor, 164
make(-de), 97
making up for a storm, 78

male, 67
male beast, 67
male hog, 70
male horse, 71
mama, 136
mama, 138
mama hen, 73
mamae, 136
mammy, 136
mantel, 3
mantelboard, 3
mantelpiece, 3
marvelle(s), 94
matron of honor, 164
maw, 136
meat skin(s), 100
Merry Christmas, 178
middling meat, 99
middling(s), 99
midwife, 142
milk bucket, 21
milk pail, 21
milkgap, 44
minnow(s), 124
mixed breed, 66
mongrel, 66
moo(s), 76
mosquito hawk, 127
mother, 136
mother(less) and
  fatherless (child), 146
mud worm, 123
multiplying onion(s), 110
mush, 90
mutt, 66
mutton corn, 83
(being) nauseated, 157
nest onion(s), 110
neuritis, 155
new potatoes, 115

New Year's Gift, 179
night crawler(s), 123
old man, 132
onion(s), 110
open, 149
open (peach), 108
openstone, 108
orphan child(ren), 146
orphan(s), 146
outdoor toilet, 41
outhouse, 41
(born) out of wedlock, 145
outside toilet, 41
outsider(s), 173
pa, 135
pa, 137
pae, 135
paepa, 135
pail(s), 21
pallet, 9
pancake(s), 95
pantaloons, 171
pantry(-ies), 17
pants, 171
pap, 135
papa, 137
papa, 135
papae, 135
paper bag(s), 36
paper poke, 36
paper sack(s), 36
pappy, 135
(back, front) parlor, 1
pass(ed) away, 159
passed, 159
passed on (x), 159
passed out, 159
peach(es), 108
peach(es), 107
peanuts, 98

(redheaded)
   peckerwood(s), 117
pen, 44
pen(s), 45
people, 139
perk, 97
pie(s), 109
piecemeal, 96
pig, 30
pig lot, 45
piggie, 30
piggin, 21
pigoo(p), 30
pigpen, 45
pinder(s), 98
pine(y) box(es), 168
pit, 106
pit, 105
plane tree, 131
play(-ed,-ing) hookey, 150
play(ed) truant, 150
plum peach, 107
plunder, 14
poke, 36
pole cat(s), 118
pone bread, 86
pone of bread, 86
pone of cornbread, 86
pone(s), 86
pot pie, 109
potato(es), 115
potatoes, 116
poultry, 72
pourdown, 79
pregnant, 141
press (peach(es)), 107
privy, 41
puke(d,-ing), 157
pull bone, 102

pulley bone, 102
pupil(s), 154
quoits, 152
rail fence(s), 48
railroad station, 175
rain frog(s), 121
ram, 69
reception, 166
red wiggler(s), 123
red worm(s), 123
rein(s), 57
rein(s), 56
relation(s), 139
relative(s), 139
resembles, 143
rheumatis(m), 155
rich pine, 4
rind, 100
roasting ear corn, 83
roasting ear(s), 83
rope, 56
rubbish, 14
sack, 36
sack(s), 37
sallet ingan, 110
(yellow-bellied)
   sapsucker(s), 117
Satan, 162
sa{w,h}, 22
scallion(s), 110
scholar, 154
school marm, 153
school mistress, 153
school teacher(s), 153
seed, 106
seed, 105
serenade, 166
serenading, 166
service(s), 167
(onion) sets, 110

settee, 5
s{e,i}tting (hen), 73
sewee (beans), 112
shade(s), 6
shallot(s), 110
shav(s), 59
sheep, 31
sheepie, 31
shell, 114
shiners, 124
shuck(s), 82
side meat, 99
siding, 38
sieva beans, 112
silk(s), 85
silvers, 124
singletree, 60
s{i,e}tting room, 1
skeeter hawk, 127
skillet, 33
skin, 100
skip(ped) school, 150
skunk, 118
slapjacks, 95
smoke meat, 99
snack(s), 96
snake doctor(s), 127
snake feeder, 127
snapping turtle, 125
snitch, 151
so, 22
sofa, 5
soft (peach), 108
soo(k)-calf, 24
soo(k)-cow, 23
sooey, 30
sook, 23
sook, 24
sookie, 24
sooner(s), 66

sourdough bread, 91
spew(ed), 157
spider(s), 33
spiderweb(s), 129
spirit(s), 161
((is) the) spitting image (of), 143
split rail fence, 48
spooks, 161
spread(s), 7
spring frog(s), 121
spring onion(s), 110
stallion(s), 71
start(s, ed), 149
station, 175
stone, 105
stone, 106
store bread, 92
store-bought bread, 92
stove room, 16
stranger(s), 173
streak o' lean, 99
stroller(s), 140
stud horse, 71
stud(s), 71
student(s), 154
(sucking sound), 30
sweet corn, 83
sweet potato(es), 116
swingletree, 60
sycamore, 131
take(s) after, 143
taleteller, 151
tart, 109
taters, 116
tattlebox, 151
tattler, 151
tattletale, 151
teacher(s), 153
telltale, 151

Appendix 5

terrapin(s), 125
the War, 177
threatening, 78
throw(ed, ing) up, 157
thunder cloud, 80
thunder shower, 80
thunder squall, 80
thunderstorm(s), 80
to be confined, 141
toad frog(s), 122
toad(s), 122
toadstool(s), 130
toilet, 41
tongue, 58
tow bag(s), 37
tow sack(s), 37
train station, 175
trash, 14
tree frog(s), 121
trousers, 171
truant, 150
turn(s) out, 148
turtle(s), 125
upchuck, 157
upstairs, 13
ushers, 164
valley(s), 40
vest(s), 170
visitor, 173
vomick, 157
vomit(ing), 157
waffle(s), 95
wagon, 140
waiter(s), 164
War between the States, 177
wardrobe(s), 12
wash cloth(s), 34
wash stand, 10
washout, 81

water bucket, 21
weatherboard(s), 38
weatherboarding, 38
web(s), 129
(whistling), 25
white meat, 99
widow, 134
widow woman, 134
(his, my) wife, 133
wiggler(s), 123
window curtain(s), 6
window shades, 6
wipe(-ing) rag, 35
wishbone, 102
with child, 141
(x) woodpecker, 117
woods colt(s), 145
worm fence, 48
worm(s), 123
yam(s), 116
(damn, goddamn) Yankee(s), 173
yard dog, 66
yeast bread, 91
yellow hammer(s), 117
youngun(s), 147

References

Aitchison, Jean. 1991. *Language Change: Progress or Decay?* 2nd ed. Cambridge: Cambridge University Press.

Algeo, John. 1989. British-American Lexical Differences: A Typology of Interdialectal Variation. In *English across Cultures—Cultures across English*, eds. Ofelia García and Ricardo Otheguy. New York: Mouton de Gruyter.

Algeo, John, and Adele Algeo. 1988–92. Among the New Words. *American Speech*.

Allen, Harold B. 1985. Sex-Linked Variation in the Response of Dialect Informants. Part 1: Lexicon. *Journal of English Linguistics* 18:97–123.

———. 1986a. Sex-Linked Variation in the Response of Dialect Informants. Part 2: Pronunciation. *Journal of English Linguistics* 19:4–24.

———. 1986b. Sex-Linked Variation in the Response of Dialect Informants. Part 3: Grammar. *Journal of English Linguistics* 19:149–76.

———. 1989. New or Old-Fashioned? Informant Awareness of Chronological Status. *American Speech* 64:3–11.

Anttila, Raimo. 1972. *An Introduction to Historical and Comparative Linguistics*. New York: Macmillan.

Bachtel, Douglas C., and Susan R. Boatright. 1992. *The Georgia County Guide*. 11th ed. Athens: Cooperative Extension Service and Dept. of Housing and Consumer Economics, University of Georgia.

Bailey, Guy, and Cynthia Bernstein. 1989. Methodology for a Phonological Survey of Texas. In *Computer Methods in Dialectology*, eds. William A. Kretzschmar, Jr., Edgar W. Schneider, and Ellen Johnson. *Journal of English Linguistics* 22:6–16.

Bailey, Guy, and Natalie Maynor. 1989. The Divergence Controversy. *American Speech* 64:12–39.

Bailey, Guy, Thomas Wikle, and Lori Sand. 1991. The Focus of Linguistic Innovation in Texas. *English Worldwide* 12:195–214.

Bailey, Guy, Tom Wikle, Jan Tillery, and Lori Sand. 1991. The Apparent Time Construct. *Language Variation and Change* 3:241-64.

Bartley, Numan V. 1990. *The Creation of Modern Georgia*. 2nd ed. Athens: University of Georgia Press.

Baugh, John. 1983. *Black Street Speech*. Austin: University of Texas Press.

———. 1991. The Politicization of Changing Terms of Self-Reference among American Slave Descendants. *American Speech* 66: 133-46.

Bell, Allan. 1984. Language Style as Audience Design. *Language in Society* 13:145-204.

Berlin, Brent. 1972. Speculations on the Growth of Ethnobotanical Nomenclature. *Language in Society* 1:51-86.

Bernstein, Cynthia. 1993. Measuring Social Causes of Phonological Variation in Texas. *American Speech* 68:227-40.

Bréal, Michel. 1964 [1897]. *Semantics: Studies in the Science of Meaning*, trans. Nina Cust. New York: Dover.

Butters, Ronald. 1989a. *The Death of Black English*. New York: Verlag Peter Lang.

———. 1989b. Linguistic Profit. Paper presented at the Southeastern Conference on Linguistics XL, Norfolk, VA.

Cameron, Deborah, and Jennifer Coates. 1988. Some Problems in the Sociolinguistic Explanation of Sex Differences. In *Women in Their Speech Communities*, eds. Jennifer Coates and Deborah Cameron. London: Longman.

Carver, Craig M. 1987. *American Regional Dialects: A Word Geography*. Ann Arbor: University of Michigan Press.

Chambers, J. K. 1992. Dialect Acquisition. *Language* 68:673-705.

———. 1993. Sociolinguistic Dialectology. In *American Dialect Research*, ed. Dennis R. Preston. Amsterdam: John Benjamins.

Chambers, J. K., and Peter Trudgill. 1980. *Dialectology*. Cambridge: Cambridge University Press.

Christian, Donna, Walt Wolfram, and Nanjo Dube. 1988. *Variation and Change in Geographically Isolated Communities: Appalachian and Ozark English*. Tuscaloosa, AL: Publication of the American Dialect Society Number 74.

Coates, Jennifer. 1993. *Women, Men, and Language: A Sociolinguistic Account of Gender Differences in Language*. London: Longman.

Crozier, Alan. 1984. The Scotch-Irish Influence on American English. *American Speech* 59:310-31.

Daniel, Pete. 1986. *Standing at the Crossroads: Southern Life in the Twentieth Century*. New York: Hill and Wang.

Davis, Alva L., Raven I. McDavid, Jr., and Virginia G. McDavid. 1969. *A Compilation of the Work Sheets of the Linguistic Atlas of the United States and Canada and Associated Projects*. Chicago: University of Chicago Press.

Davis, Lawrence M. 1983. *English Dialectology: An Introduction*. University: University of Alabama Press.

———. 1990. *Statistics in Dialectology*. Tuscaloosa: University of Alabama Press.

Davis, Lawrence M., and Charles L. Houck. 1992. Is There a Midland Dialect Area?—Again. *American Speech* 67:61–70.

Doe, John. 1988. *Speak into the Mirror: A Story of Linguistic Anthropology*. Lanham, MD: University Press of America.

Doyle, Rodger. 1993. No-Phone Homes. *Atlantic Monthly* (June):77.

Eckert, Penelope. 1989a. *Jocks and Burnouts: Social Identity in the High School*. New York: Teachers College Press.

———. 1989b. The Whole Woman: Sex and Gender Differences in Variation. *Language Variation and Change* 1:245–68.

———. 1991. Social Polarization and the Choice of Linguistic Variants. In *New Ways of Analyzing Sound Change*, ed. Penelope Eckert. New York: Academic Press.

Eckert, Penny, and Sally McConnell-Ginet. 1992. Gender in Sociolinguistic Research: Time for a Paradigm Shift. Presented at New Ways of Analyzing Variation (NWAV) 21.

Feagin, Crawford. 1979. *Variation and Change in Alabama English*. Washington: Georgetown University Press.

Fischer, David Hackett. 1989. *Albion's Seed: Four British Folkways in America*. Oxford: Oxford University Press.

Gilliéron, Jules. 1902–1910. *Atlas Linguistique de la France*. Paris: Champion.

Görlach, Manfred. 1990. Heteronymy in International English. *English World-Wide* 11:239–74.

Grantham, Dewey W., Jr. 1963. *The Democratic South*. Athens: University of Georgia Press.

Guy, Gregory R. 1988. Language and Social Class. In *Language: The Socio-Cultural Context*, vol. 4 of *Linguistics: The Cambridge Survey*, ed. Frederick J. Newmeyer. Cambridge: Cambridge University Press.

Holland, Dorothy, and Naomi Quinn. 1987. *Cultural Models in Language and Thought*. Cambridge: Cambridge University Press.

Hudson, R. A. 1980. *Sociolinguistics*. Cambridge: Cambridge University Press.

Hymes, Dell H. 1972. Models of the Interaction of Language and Social Life. In *Directions in Sociolinguistics: The Ethnography of Communication*, eds. John J. Gumperz and Dell H. Hymes. New York: Holt, Rinehart, and Winston.

Jaberg, Karl, and Jakob Jud. 1928–40. *Sprach- und Sachatlas des Italiens und der Südschweiz*. Zofingen: Ringier.

Johnson, Ellen. 1993. The Relationship between Lexical Variation and Lexical Change. *Language Variation and Change* 5:285–304.

———. 1994a. The Distribution of Variants of /aɪ/ in the Middle and South Atlantic States. In *Verhandlungen des Internationalen Dialektologenkongresses Bamberg 1990*, vol. 3, ed. Wolfgang Viereck. Stuttgart: Franz Steiner Verlag.

———. 1994b. Yet Again: The Midland Dialect. *American Speech* 69: 419-30.

———. a, (in press). Gender Differences in Spoken American English. *Signos: Estudios de Lengua y Literatura* 26.33.

———. b, (in press). Geographical Influence on Lexical Choice: Changes in the Twentieth Century. In *Language Variety in the South II*, eds. Cynthia Bernstein, Thomas Nunnally, and Robin Sabino. Tuscaloosa: University of Alabama Press.

Johnson, Samuel. 1979 [1755]. *A Dictionary of the English Language*. London: Times Press.

Johnstone, Barbara. (in press). Southern Speech and Self-Expression in an African-American Woman's Story. In *Language Variety in the South II*, eds. Cynthia Bernstein, Tom Nunnally, and Robin Sabino. Tuscaloosa: University of Alabama Press.

Jubera, Drew. 1990. The Military Hitch. *The Atlanta Journal*, Sept. 16.

Kretzschmar, William A., Jr. 1992a. Isoglosses and Predictive Modeling. *American Speech* 67:227–49.

———. 1992b. Quantitative Methods in a Qualitative Paradigm. Paper presented at NWAV 21.

Kretzschmar, William A., Jr., and Jay Lee. 1991. Quantitative Methods for Word Geography. Paper presented at NWAV 20.

Kretzschmar, William A., Jr., Virginia G. McDavid, Theodore K. Lerud, and Ellen Johnson, eds. 1994. *Handbook of the Linguistic*

Atlas of the Middle and South Atlantic States. Chicago: University of Chicago Press.
Kretzschmar, William A., Jr., and Edgar W. Schneider. (in press). Atlas by the Numbers. Los Angeles: Sage.
Kroch, Anthony S. 1978. Toward a Theory of Social Dialect Variation. Language in Society 7:17–36.
——. 1989. Reflexes of Grammar in Patterns of Language Change. Language Variation and Change 1:199–244.
Kurath, Hans. 1949. A Word Geography of the Eastern United States. Ann Arbor: University of Michigan Press.
Labov, William. 1972. Sociolinguistic Patterns. Philadelphia: University of Pennsylvania Press.
——. 1981. What Can Be Learned about Change in Progress from Synchronic Description? In Variation Omnibus, eds. David Sankoff and Henrietta Cedergren. Edmonton, Alberta: Linguistic Research.
——. 1989. Exact Description of the Speech Community: Short A in Philadephia. In Language Change and Variation, eds. Ralph W. Fasold and Deborah Schiffrin. Amsterdam: John Benjamins.
——. 1990. The Intersection of Sex and Social Class in the Course of Linguistic Change. Language Variation and Change 2:205–54.
——. 1991. The Three Dialects of English. In New Ways of Analyzing Sound Change, ed. Penelope Eckert. New York: Academic Press.
Lakoff, George. 1987. Women, Fire, and Dangerous Things. Chicago: University of Chicago Press.
Lakoff, George, and Mark Johnson. 1980. Metaphors We Live by. Chicago: University of Chicago Press.
Lavandera, Beatriz R. 1978. Where Does the Sociolinguistic Variable Stop? Language in Society 7:171–82.
Lee, Jay, and William A. Kretzschmar, Jr. 1993. Spatial Analysis of Linguistic Data with GIS Functions. International Journal of Geographical Information Systems 7:541–60.
Lehmann, E. L. 1975. Nonparametrics: Statistical Methods Based on Ranks. San Francisco: Holden-Day.
LePage, Robert, and A. Tabouret-Keller. 1985. Acts of Identity. Cambridge: Cambridge University Press.
Light, Deanna. Ms. Who Gives a Damn and Who Doesn't: Women, Men, and Profanity.

McDaniel, Susan Leas, ed. 1981. The Conduct of an Atlas Interview in the Gulf States. *Linguistic Atlas of the Gulf States.* Working Paper no. 2. [From a recording done by R. McDavid in 1970.]

McDavid, Raven I., Jr. 1948. Postvocalic /-r/ in South Carolina: A Social Analysis. In *Dialects in Culture: Essays in General Dialectology* (1979, ed. William A. Kretzschmar, Jr.). University: University of Alabama Press.

———. 1955. The Position of the Charleston Dialect. In *Dialects in Culture: Essays in General Dialectology* (1979, ed. by William A. Kretzschmar, Jr.). University: University of Alabama Press.

———. 1970. Changing Patterns of Southern Dialects. In *Dialects in Culture: Essays in General Dialectology* (1979, ed. William A. Kretzschmar, Jr.). University: University of Alabama Press.

———. 1979. *Dialects in Culture: Essays in General Dialectology*, ed. by William A. Kretzschmar, Jr. University: University of Alabama Press.

McDavid, Virginia G. 1989. Grammatical Items in the North Central States and the Upper Midwest. Paper presented at the annual meeting of the American Dialect Society, Washington, DC.

McGill, Ralph. 1992 [1963]. *The South and the Southerner.* Athens: University of Georgia Press.

McLanahan, Sara S., Annemette Sorensen, and Dorothy Watson. 1989. Sex Differences in Poverty, 1950–1980. *Signs: Journal of Women in Culture and Society* 15:102–22.

Mead, George Herbert. 1974 [1936]. The Problem of Society: How We Become Selves. In *Language, Culture, and Society*, ed. Ben G. Blount. Cambridge, MA: Winthrop Publishers.

Meillet, Antoine. 1921. *Linguistique Historique et Linguistique Générale.* Paris: Champion.

Miller, George A. 1978. Practical and Lexical Knowledge. In *Cognition and Categorization*, eds. E. Rosch and B. Lloyd. Hillsdale, N.J.: Lawrence Erlbaum Assoc.

Miller, Michael I. 1978. *Inflectional Morphology in Augusta, Georgia: A Sociolinguistic Description.* University of Chicago dissertation.

Miller, Michael I. In press. Nonparametric Techniques for Analyzing Linguistic Survey Data. In *Proceedings of the International Congress of Dialectologists* [1990], ed. Wolfgang Viereck.

Milroy, James. 1992a. *Linguistic Variation and Change.* Oxford: Basil Blackwell.

———. 1992b. Toward a Social Model for the Interpretation of Language Change. Presented at NWAV 21.
Milroy, Lesley. 1987. *Language and Social Networks*. 2nd ed. Oxford: Basil Blackwell.
Montgomery, Michael. 1990. The Scotch-Irish Element in Appalachian English: How Broad? How Deep? Paper presented at the Ulster American Heritage Symposium, Johnson City, TN.
———. 1991. The Roots of Appalachian English: Scotch-Irish or British Southern? In *Southern Appalachia and the South: A Region within a Region*, ed. John C. Inscoe (*Journal of the Appalachian Studies Association*, Vol. 3). Johnson City, TN: East Tennessee State University Center for Appalachian Studies and Services.
———. Ms. How Scotch-Irish is Appalachian English?
Mufwene, Salikoko S. 1986. Les Langues Créoles Peuvent-Elles être Définies sans Allusion à Leur Histoire? *Études Créoles* 9:135-50.
Nerlich, Brigitte. 1992. *Semantic Theories in Europe 1830–1930: From Etymology to Contextuality*. Amsterdam: John Benjamins.
Newmeyer, Frederick J. 1986. *The Politics of Linguistics*. Chicago: University of Chicago Press.
Nichols, Patricia C. 1983. Linguistic Options and Choices for Black Women in the Rural South. In *Language, Gender, and Society*, eds. Barrie Thorne, Cheris Kramarae, and Nancy Henley. Rowley, MA: Newbury House.
Payne, Arvilla C. 1980. Factors Controlling the Acquisition of the Philadelphia Dialect by Out-of-State Children. In *Locating Language in Time and Space*, ed. William Labov. New York: Academic Press.
Pederson, Lee, Raven I. McDavid, Jr., Charles W. Foster, and Charles E. Billiard, eds. 1974. *A Manual for Dialect Research in the Southern States*. University: University of Alabama Press.
Pederson, Lee, Susan Leas McDaniel, Guy Bailey, and Marvin Bassett, eds. 1986. *Handbook for the Linguistic Atlas of the Gulf States*. Athens: University of Georgia Press.
Pederson, Lee, Susan Leas McDaniel, and Carol M. Adams. 1988. *General Index for the Linguistic Atlas of the Gulf States*. Athens: University of Georgia Press.
Porter, Mrs. Carl. 1992. Roadside Scenes. *Jackson County (GA) Herald*, July 1.

Preston, Dennis R. 1989. *Perceptual Dialectology: Nonlinguists' Views of Areal Linguistics.* Dordrecht: Foris Publications.
———. 1991. Sorting Out the Variables in Sociolinguistic Theory. *American Speech* 66:33–56.
Reed, John Shelton. 1986. *Southern Folk Plain and Fancy: Native White Social Types.* Athens: University of Georgia Press.
Rosch, Eleanor, C. Mervis, W. Gray, D. Johnson, and P. Boyes-Braem. 1975. *Basic Objects in Natural Categories.* Working paper no. 43, Language Behavior Research Laboratory. Berkeley: University of California.
Ruhl, Charles. 1989. *On Monosemy: A Study in Linguistic Semantics.* Albany: State University of New York Press.
Ryan, Ellen Bouchard, Howard Giles, and Richard J. Sebastian. 1982. An Integrative Perspective for the Study of Attitudes toward Language Variation. In *Attitudes towards Language Variation: Social and Applied Contexts,* eds. Ellen Bouchard Ryan and Howard Giles. London: Edward Arnold.
Sapir, Edward. 1951. *Selected Writings in Language, Culture, and Personality,* ed. David G. Mandelbaum. Berkeley: University of California Press.
Schneider, Edgar W. 1989. *American Earlier Black English.* Tuscaloosa: University of Alabama Press.
Schneider, Edgar W., and William A. Kretzschmar, Jr. 1989. LAMSAS goes SASsy: Statistical Methods and Linguistic Atlas Data. In *Computer Methods in Dialectology,* ed. by William A. Kretzschmar, Jr., Edgar W. Schneider, and Ellen Johnson. *Journal of English Linguistics* 22:129–41.
Smitherman, Geneva. 1991. "What is Africa to Me?": Language, Ideology, and *African American. American Speech* 66: 115–32.
Southern Poll. *Atlanta Journal-Constitution,* February 16, 1992.
Spender, Dale. 1980. *Man Made Language.* London: Routledge and Kegan Paul.
Stern, Gustaf. 1931. *Meaning and Change of Meaning.* Bloomington: Indiana University Press.
Sweetser, Eve E. 1990. *From Etymology to Pragmatics: Metaphorical and Cultural Aspects of Semantic Structure.* New York: Cambridge University Press.
Thibault, Pierrette, and Michelle Daveluy. 1989. Quelques traces du passage du temps dans le parler des Montréalais, 1971–1984. *Language Variation and Change* 1:19–46.

Trudgill, Peter. 1983. *Sociolinguistics*. New York: Penguin.
Ullmann, Stephen. 1962. *Semantics, an Introduction to the Science of Meaning*. Oxford: Blackwell.
U.S. Geological Survey. 1984. *Fold and Thrust Belts of the United States*. Reston, VA.
Wagner, Max Leopold. Forthcoming [1920]. Die Beziehungen zwischen Wort- und Sachforschung. In *Classics in Dialect Theory: The European Background of American Dialectology*, eds. Edgar W. Schneider and Michael I. Miller.
Webster's Third New International Dictionary. 1971. Chicago: Encyclopedia Britannica.
Weinreich, Uriel. 1953. *Languages in Contact*. New York: Linguistic Circle.
Whorf, Benjamin Lee. 1956. *Language, Thought, and Reality*, ed. John B. Carroll. Cambridge, MA: MIT Press.
Wierzbicka, Anna. 1992. *Semantics, Culture, and Cognition: Universal Human Concepts in Culture-Specific Configurations*. Oxford: Oxford University Press.
Wilson, Charles Reagan, and William Ferris. 1989. *Encyclopedia of Southern Culture*. 4 vols. New York: Anchor [University of North Carolina Press].
Wolfram, Walt. 1991a. *Dialects and American English*. Englewood Cliffs, NJ: Center for Applied Linguistics.
———. 1991b. The Linguistic Variable: Fact and Fantasy. *American Speech* 66:22–32.

Index

A

Acid jeans, 91
Acquisition, 2, 20, 71, 73, 81, 91, 92
Adams, C., 12
Adjectives, 6, 91, 114
Advertising, 89, 91
Africa, 105, 106, 115
African Americans, 22, 24, 26, 58, 69, 70, 80, 94, 97, 98, 104, 106, 113. *See also* Blacks
Age, 19–21, 25, 112; and language contact, 99–100; as a variable, 1, 5, 15, 18, 23, 31–33, 49, 71, 72, 99, 110; classification by, 19–20; differences, 2, 70, 99; groups, 1, 11, 26, 40, 49, 57, 61, 70–72, 99, 113; of first language acquisition, 20; variation by, 70–72. *See also* Generation
Agricultural referents, 110
Agriculture, 79, 97. *See also* Farming
Air-conditioning, 111
Aitchison, J., 79
Alexander, GA, 15, 117
Algeo, A., 91
Algeo, J., 7, 8, 91
Allen, H., 33, 62, 69

Amount of variation, 1, 2, 29, 30, 32–36, 74, 76, 77, 92, 100, 102, 110–13
Anderson (Co.), SC, 16, 124, 125
Andirons, 6, 49, 59, 83
Anglicans, 104
Anson Co., NC, 17, 129, 130
Anthropological linguistics, 113
Anthropology, 83, 84
Anttila, R., 76, 87, 88
Appalachians, 13, 105
Apparent time, 2, 19, 20, 61, 70, 72, 81, 90, 99
Arsenault, R., 111
Arthritis, 75
Artifacts, 10, 85, 89, 99, 113
Ashe Co., NC, 17, 132
Asheville, NC, 17, 131, 133–35
Atlanta, GA, 22, 31, 66, 97, 105, 112, 128, 129
Attic, 56, 57, 59, 67, 68, 75, 86, 101, 108
Automobile, 101
Avenue, 76

B

Baby carriage, 9, 76
Bachtel, D., 89
Back house, 51, 52, 68, 108
Bacon, 76, 87, 90

Bad weather, 61
Bailey, G., 4, 33, 41, 70, 71, 84
Bakery bread, 71, 78, 99
Baldwin Co., GA, 16, 23, 117
Barnyard, 82
Bartley, N., 89, 95, 100, 106, 107, 111
Bassett, M., 22
Bastard, 59, 88, 96
Battercakes, 89
Baugh, J., 4, 22
Bawl, 51, 59, 66, 75
Beaufort Co., SC, 16, 122
Bell, A., 29
Bellow, 90
Bench, 38
Berlin, B., 85
Bernstein, C., 33, 41, 73, 82
Best man, 51, 101
Billiard, C., 10
Binomial principle, 62
Biographical sketches, 15, 18, 114
Black Mtn., NC, 17
Black Vernacular English, 2, 4, 33, 98
Blacks, 2, 4, 15, 17, 18, 21, 22, 24, 26, 27, 29, 33, 40, 52, 57, 59, 69, 70, 95, 97, 98, 107, 118, 120, 121, 134. See also African Americans
Blinds, 12
Blue Ridge, 23
Boar, 88
Boatright, S., 89
Bogart, GA, 16, 24, 118
Boogey man, 76

Borrowing, 74, 89, 93, 107
Boyes-Braem, P., 85
Breakfast bacon, 76
Bréal, M., 74
Bridemaid, 98
Bridles, 99
Bring a calf, 52
Britches, 9, 36, 89, 108
British Isles, 106
Brown v. the Board of Education, 97
Brunswick Co., NC, 16, 125, 126
Bull, 88, 96
Bullfrogs, 83
Buncombe Co., NC, 17, 118, 133–35
Bungee jumping, 91
Bureau, 70, 71, 75, 117, 124, 134
Burgess, SC, 16, 119
Burke Co., GA, 15, 117, 135
Burlap bag, 90
Bursitis, 75, 89
Bush bean, 7
Butters, R., 83, 84

C

Calve, 86, 88
Camden, SC, 16, 114, 122, 123
Cameron, D., 69
Candler, NC, 17, 133
Car, 92, 101, 128
Carriage, 9, 49, 66, 76
Carver, C., 50
Casket, 99
Chambers, J., 3, 50, 70, 81, 91, 92

Change: cognitive, 85;
cultural, 62, 78, 80, 84,
85, 99; in variation
patterns, 80; language,
2, 62, 65, 70, 72, 73,
76, 80, 85, 93, 99, 112,
113; onomasiological,
74; rapidity of, 70, 78;
semantic, 3, 62, 74, 85;
semasiological, 74, 76;
sound, 71, 83;
structural motivation for,
74; technological, 88;
vocabulary, 3, 76, 80,
84
Change from above, 67, 68
Change from below, 68
Chapel Hill, NC, 67, 128,
130, 132
Charleston, SC, 16, 67, 105,
106, 114, 116, 117,
119–21, 135
Charlotte, NC, 67, 105, 129,
131
Chatham Co., GA, 15, 114,
128
Cherokee Co., NC, 17, 134,
135
Chest of drawers, 75
Chick, 51, 99, 100
Chi-square, 36, 40
Children, 95, 96, 106, 121
Children, 83, 118
Chipmunk, 59, 66, 90, 109
Christian, D., 61, 126, 132
Civil rights, 98, 107
Civil War, 19, 86, 114
Clabber, 6, 50, 86, 89
Clabber cheese, 89
Clarke Co., GA, 16, 118

Claxton, GA, 15, 116
Clingstone, 12, 75, 86, 109
Clinton, NC, 17, 127
Clothes closet, 101
Clouding up, 8, 61, 75
Coastal, 13, 18, 23, 26, 27,
40, 42, 43, 50, 51, 53,
57-60, 66, 67, 94, 101,
104, 105, 107, 109, 110,
115
Coastal Plain, 13, 23
Coates, J., 69, 84
Cobbler, 76, 96
Cochran Restriction, 40
Coffin, 87
Cognitive associations, 60
Cognitive model, 8, 85
Cognitive processes, 85
College, 17, 18, 21, 25, 26,
89, 100, 104, 114, 117,
121–23, 128, 129,
133–35. *See also*
Education, higher
Colleton Co., SC, 16, 121,
122
Commentary, 8, 11, 28, 37,
62, 68, 75, 134
Commercialization, 89
Commercial term, 99
Communities, 3, 5, 13-15,
25, 28, 30, 35, 103, 106,
111
Comparability (of data sets),
7, 9, 10, 17, 25
Conflicts, 4, 104, 106, 107
Connotational meaning, 9
Context, 9, 10, 75, 82, 85,
112, 113
Continuum of usage, 42, 66,
68, 71

Convergence, 2, 33, 97
Conversation, 11, 35, 41, 81, 103
Cornbread, 8, 90
Corn crib, 86, 87
Cottage cheese, 52, 59, 75, 86, 101
Cotton, 97, 103, 104, 118, 135
Coverlet, 96
Covert prestige, 101
Cowpen, 49, 51, 59, 66, 86
Creolists, 84
Crescent, GA, 15, 115
Crosstabulations, 58
Crozier, A., 105
Cultural forces, 3, 79, 90
Cultural models, 85. *See also* Cognitive models
Curd, 75
Cush, 98
Customs, 85, 116

D

Daddy, 69, 98
Danbury, NC, 17, 132
Daniel, P., 79, 80, 86, 97, 120
Database, 5, 11, 12, 19, 21, 28, 35, 37, 40, 62, 74; codes, 40; column, 39, 40, 111
Daveluy, M., 72, 73
Davis, A., 6
Davis, L., 41, 50
DBase, 40
Demographics, 26, 33, 58, 80, 95, 111
Den, 75, 89

Denotational meaning, 8
Depression, 20, 97
Devil, 76, 88
Diachronic differences, 3
Dialect areas, 13, 42, 50
Dialect boundary, 6, 50, 84
Dialect contact, 3
Dialect systems, 112
Dialectologists, 29, 42, 59, 70, 83
Dialectology, 3, 4, 41, 83, 113
Die, 88
Dish cloth, 76, 89, 108
Distance, 92, 95, 98, 106, 110
Divergence, 2, 33, 97
Division of labor, 97
Doe, J., 83
Dog irons, 6
Dorchester Co., SC, 16, 121
Doubletree, 57, 59, 67–69, 86, 96, 98, 108
Doubtful responses, 11, 37, 63, 82
Doughnuts, 51
Doyle, R., 41
Dragonflies, 83
Dramedy, 91
Drawing room, 8, 108
Driveway, 75
Dube, N., 61
Durham, NC, 67, 134

E

Eckert, P., 22, 28, 58, 73, 112
Economy, 79, 85, 89, 95, 103, 111

Edgefield Co., SC, 16, 124
Edmont, E., 10
Education, 13, 20, 21, 27, 57, 85, 89, 91, 92, 99, 101, 104; access to, 89, 90, 92, 100, 104; and language contact, 100–101; and lexical change, 89–90; as a variable, 1, 5, 18, 21, 23, 26, 31, 32, 34, 42, 48, 49, 68, 94, 100, 110, 112; classification by, 20–21; compulsory 20, 100; higher, 56, 100, 104; public, 80, 100; variation by, 68–69. *See also* School; Schooling, years of
Educational groups, 21, 25, 26, 40, 49, 52, 56–58, 67, 68, 100, 101
Educational system, 85, 97
Effingham Co., GA, 15, 116
Ehrhardt, SC, 16, 122
Elderly, 99, 132
Electric(al) storm, 78, 89
Elementary school, 18, 20, 21, 25, 66, 100, 122, 128, 129, 131
England, 90, 104, 105, 114, 132
Ethnic origin, 104, 106
Ethnicity, 2, 33, 102
Etymological evidence, 60
Euphemisms, 76, 87, 88, 99
Europe, 10, 105, 128, 134
Evans Co., GA, 15, 116
Explanatory mechanism, 60, 80, 93, 112

Explanatory principles, 84, 95
Expletives, 96
Exurbs, 105

F

Falling weather, 76
Familiarity, 86, 89, 107. *See also* Knowledge
Family pie, 53, 66, 76
Farming, 86, 103. *See also* Agriculture
Feagin, C., 28
Feist, 82
Females, 7, 15, 18, 26, 27, 35, 40, 56–59, 68–70, 95, 96, 98, 118. *See also* Women
Feminine speech, 69
Femininity, 22
Feminists, 84
Ferris, W., 90, 95, 97, 98, 100, 103, 111
Fieldwork, 3, 7, 13, 15, 20, 35, 67
Fieldworker, 7, 8, 10–12, 36, 41, 58, 63, 82
Fire dogs, 6
Fireboard, 51, 66, 105
Firefly, 107, 108
Fischer, D., 105
Fishing worms, 96
Fleming, GA, 15, 115
Flemington, GA, 15, 115
Flitters, 89
Floored pen, 10
Focal areas, 50, 66
Folk etymologies, 60
Folk speakers, 13, 21
Foreigner, 57, 58, 98

Foster, C., 10
Freeland, NC, 16, 126
Freestone, 52, 57, 75, 86, 101
Frequency, 3, 35, 36, 40, 41, 49, 64, 69, 73, 77, 89, 110
Frequent words, 107
Frog, 53, 59, 66, 107, 108
Frogstool, 12
Front room, 8, 108
Frying pan, 75, 98

G

Gaddistown, GA, 16, 119
Galloway Hill, SC, 16, 122
Garret, 68, 99, 108
Gee, 69
Gender, 22, 58, 102. *See also* Sex
Generation, 49, 52, 102. *See also* Age
Gentleman cow, 88
Georgia, 5, 13, 23–26, 34, 63, 89, 97, 99, 100, 103, 106, 111, 114–21, 125, 131, 132, 135
Giddy up, 91
Giles, H., 102
Galliéron, J., 10
Girard, GA, 15, 117
Good Hope, SC, 16, 119
"Good old boy", 93
Görlach, M., 8
Grammar, 20, 30, 73, 80–82, 84, 131. *See also* Syntax
Grandpa, 12
Grandview, NC, 17, 134
Granny, 98

Grantham, D., 107
Gray, W., 85
Green bean, 7
Greensboro, NC, 17, 125, 129, 130
Greenville, SC, 67, 123, 125
Grimm, J., 79
Grindstone, 59, 69, 86, 96
Grits, 7
Group loyalty, 101
Guilford, NC, 17, 129
Gully, 49, 52, 109
Gutters, 88
Guy, G., 34, 84

H

Half runner, 7
Hapax legomenon, 36
Happy New Year, 56, 57, 59, 68, 71, 101
Haslet, 51, 57, 58, 66, 68, 86
Haw, 69
Hen, 75
Hendersonville, SC, 16, 121, 122
Here chick, 99, 100
Here kitty, 100
Heteronymy, 8
High school, 18, 20, 21, 25, 100, 104, 115, 118, 121, 123, 124, 126, 127, 129–34
Hilton Head, SC, 16, 122
Historians, 2, 60, 80, 84, 85, 110
Historical linguistics, 113
History, 9, 19, 34, 74, 79, 84, 95, 120, 123, 128
Hog pen, 10, 57, 99

Holland, D., 85, 131
Horry Co., SC, 16, 119
Houck, C., 50
Hudson, R., 30
Hull, 51, 101, 105
Hum, 8, 75
Huntersville, NC, 17, 131
Hymes, D., 30

I

Iconicity, 75
Idaho potatoes, 57
Idealized Cognitive Models, 85
Identity: cultural, 102; peer group, 61; psychological construction of, 30; regional, 112; sexual, 96; social, 23, 101
Illegitimate child, 90
Income, 21, 33, 100
Individual choice, 9, 34
Individual preference, 81
Industrialization, 86, 95, 97, 101, 103
Informality, 8
Informant: auxiliary, 11, 58; numbers, 15, 37
Information, 4, 9, 20–23, 28, 37, 39, 41, 63, 64, 74, 85, 90–92, 100, 125
Inner cities, 98, 106
Innovation, 61, 72, 92, 93, 111
Institutions, 79, 85, 89, 97
Interaction between categories/variables, 26–27, 41, 56–58, 69

Interjections, 7
Interviews, trial, 6
Ireland, 105, 115, 117, 124, 131, 133
Irish potato, 98
Isoglosses, 50, 53, 84

J

Jaberg, K., 10, 79
Jacket, 76
Jim Crow laws, 98
Johnson, D., 85
Johnson, E., 7, 10, 11, 15, 19, 23, 35, 36, 51, 58, 61, 68, 86, 100
Johnson, M., 85
Johnson, S., 79
Johnston, SC, 16, 124
Johnstone, B., 9, 34
Jubera, D., 103
Jud, J., 10, 79

K

Kernel, 43, 47, 53, 66, 109
Kershaw Co., SC, 16, 23, 122, 123
Key, 91
Kid, 75
Kindling, 75, 90
Knowledge, 7, 58, 62, 75, 84, 85, 87, 95, 96, 99, 118, 128, 130. *See also* Familiarity
Kope, 12, 67
Kretzschmar, W., 4, 10, 13, 14, 18, 23, 24, 35, 36, 40, 42, 50, 62, 65, 98
Kroch, A., 72, 99

Kruskal-Wallis statistic, 40
Kurath, H., 6, 30, 31, 42, 50, 70, 80, 84, 90, 91; comparison to, 51–55
Kwope, 12

L

Labor union, 107
Labov, W., 4, 19, 28, 30, 67-72, 93, 101
"Lady", 93, 120
Lakoff, G., 73, 85, 96
Lane, 76
Language attitudes, 28, 30
Language contact, 3, 81, 90, 92, 94, 95, 99
Language universals, 83
Language Variation in the South, 84
Lavandera, B., 9, 10, 96
Lee, J., 23, 35, 123
Lehmann, E., 40
Leicester, NC, 17, 133, 134
LePage, R., 30
Lerud, T., 10
Levels of language, 80, 81
Lexical choice, 32, 34, 41, 56, 98, 101
Lexical competence, 87
Lexical crowding, 77
Lexical meaning, 34, 83, 85
Liberty Co., GA, 15, 103, 115, 125
Lifestyles, 79, 107
Light, D., 96
Light bread, 9
Lightning bug, 107, 108
Lightwood, 75, 87, 96

Lines, 2, 67, 87, 99, 108
Linguistic Atlas of the Gulf States, 12, 22
Linguistic Atlas of the Middle and South Atlantic States, 5, 6, 7, 9–13, 15, 18–26, 29, 37, 42, 43, 50, 51, 53, 56, 59, 65, 79, 90, 96, 100
Linguistic behavior, 3, 28, 30, 69, 84
Linguistic choices, 28
Linguistic conservatism, 70
Linguistic geographers, 31
Linguistic homogeneity, 30
Linguistic inquiry, 84
Linguistic profit, 83
Linguistic rules, 34
Linguists, 34, 62, 74, 79, 83, 84, 91
Literacy, 90, 120
Literary criticism, 83
Living room, 8, 51, 57, 67, 68, 83, 90, 96, 108
Local elite, 112
Local norms, 81
Loft, 57, 67, 68, 74, 99, 108
Lonesome Cove, GA, 16, 118
Longwood, NC, 16, 126, 127
Loss: of dialect terms, 90; of vocabulary, 76; of words, 88
Lot, 82, 120, 133
Lounge, 38
Low Country, 106, 125
Lowman, G., 7, 10, 11, 13, 22, 23, 26, 34, 35, 58, 61, 86, 100, 102
Lumberton, NC, 17, 128
Lykesland, SC, 16, 123

M

Maintenance of linguistic differences, 111
Male animals, 88
Males, 7, 13, 18, 24, 26, 27, 35, 40, 56–58, 68–70, 88, 92, 95, 96, 99, 131, 133. *See also* Men
Manassas, GA, 15, 116
Mantel, 51, 66, 68, 76, 101
Masculinity, 22
Mass media, 85, 90, 91
Material culture, 79, 84, 107
Maynor, N., 33
McConnell-Ginet, S., 73
McDaniel, S., 10
McDavid, R., 10, 28, 29, 33, 69, 82, 98, 103, 106
McDavid, V., 10, 33, 69
McGill, R., 97, 100, 102
McIntosh Co., GA, 15, 115
McLanahan, S., 111
Mead, G., 112
Mecklenburg Co., NC, 17, 129, 131
Meillet, A., 62
Men, 11, 22, 35, 68, 69, 95–97, 102, 103. *See also* Males
Meridian, GA, 15, 115
Merry Christmas, 90
Mervis, C., 85
Metaphor, 74, 75
Methodology, 3, 5, 50, 73, 85
Middle (age group), 19, 20, 27, 49

Middle (educational group), 21, 49, 52, 56, 58, 67, 68, 100, 101
Middle class, 89, 93, 98, 100
Midland, 50-53, 90
Midwife, 8, 51, 52, 98
Militarization, 101
Military, 103, 104, 133
Milk pail, 99
Mill Springs, NC, 17, 133
Miller, G., 70, 85, 97
Miller, M., 40, 70
Milroy, J., 72, 73, 92, 93, 110
Milroy, L., 68, 92, 110
Missing data, 36–40, 63–65
Mongrel, 82
Montgomery, M., 105
Montréal, Que., 73
Moo, 52, 68, 75, 90
Morphological differences, 84, 98
Morven, NC, 17, 130, 131
Mosquito hawk, 9, 43, 45
Mountain, 18, 23, 26, 27, 40, 42, 43, 49-53, 66, 94, 98, 101, 104, 105, 109, 134
Movies, 91, 132
Mt. Pleasant, SC, 16, 117
Mufwene, S., 84
Multiple causality, 95
Multiple synonymy, 76
Multivariate testing, 26, 41, 69
Murphy, NC, 17, 135
Mush, 69, 86, 98
Myrtle Grove Sound, NC, 125

N

Named after, 35
Named for, 35, 96, 110
Nerlich, B., 62
Neuritis, 75
New Deal, 97
New England, 90, 114
New Hanover Co., NC, 16, 125, 126
New Ways of Analyzing Variation, 73
New York, 82
New York, NY, 19, 90
Newmeyer, F., 84, 96
Nichols, P., 21
"No Response", 30, 36, 37, 42, 58-60, 69, 70, 86, 87, 96
Nomination, 74, 85
Non-parametric test, 40, 64, 73
North, 13, 50; as dialect area, 50, 51, 90; as region, 97, 98, 106
North Carolina, 5, 13, 24-26, 34, 35, 52, 103, 115, 118, 121, 123, 124-35
Northern Cities Shift, 67
Nouns, 7, 12
Number of responses: per informant, 35; per question, 76-78, 90

O

Obsolete referents, 65, 110
Occupation, 19, 21, 86, 95, 100, 103, 107, 112
Oconee Co., GA., 16, 118

Old (age group), 13, 19, 20, 25, 26, 57, 60, 68, 70-72, 78, 88, 97, 99, 100
Older words, 61, 62, 65-70, 74, 76-78, 88
Olympia Village, SC, 16, 123, 124
Orphan, 101, 118
Orthography, 12
Outhouse, 90

P

P-value, 41, 48, 56, 64
Pa, 12, 123, 129, 131, 133
Pail, 52, 99
Paired data, 64
Paired sample, 65
Pantaloons, 36, 108
Pants, 9, 36, 83, 108
Paper poke, 51, 105
Participation, 22, 30, 50, 112
Payne, A., 92
Peaches, 75, 109
Peckerwood, 57, 96
Pederson, L., 10, 12, 22
Pennsylvania, 90, 105
Perceptual experiences, 85
Personal history, 9, 34
Personality, 9, 22, 114
Philosophy, 83
Phonetic differences, 67, 91
Phonological choices, 80, 81, 84, 98
Phonological differences, 12, 81, 84
Phonological Survey of Texas, 34
Phonology, 1, 3, 80

Piedmont, 13, 18, 23, 26, 27, 40, 42, 43, 49, 50, 52, 53, 66, 94, 101, 104–6, 109, 132
Pig parlors, 10
Pinders, 89
Pit, 52, 71, 75
Plantation culture, 105
Plum peach, 51, 66, 89, 109
Poke, 51, 105
Pole bean, 7
Polecat, 57, 67, 71, 107
Polk Co., NC, 17, 133
Polysemy, 8, 76
Population, 2, 17, 21, 23, 24, 41, 73, 89, 100, 106, 111; African American, 22, 98; asymmetry in, 26, 58, 68; comparison of sample to, 24–26; homogeneous, 111; Southern, 79, 80, 105, 113
Porter, Mrs. C., 111
Potato, 98
Power, 58, 89, 91, 99, 105, 106, 125
Pregnant, 88
Prejudice, 112
Presbyterians, 105
Press peach, 51, 66, 68, 89
Prestige, 93, 101, 102
Preston, D., 28, 29, 33
Privy, 86, 88, 108
Prototypes, 85
Psychology, 83
Pulpwood, 95, 103

Q

Questionnaire, 3, 5–7, 13, 34, 58, 81–83, 88, 123. *See also* Worksheet
Quinn, N., 85

R

R:Base, 40
Race, 11, 15, 22, 33, 95, 97, 98; as a variable, 1, 5, 15, 18, 23, 26, 27, 31, 32, 69, 70, 94, 95, 97, 98, 99, 110, 112; and language contact, 97–99; classification by, 22; variation by 69–70
Racial integration, 97
Racial relations, 98
Racial segregation, 80, 97
Radio, 90, 91
Rail fence, 57, 67, 68, 86, 108
Raleigh, NC, 67, 114, 122, 134
Ram, 86, 88
Real time, 20, 61, 70, 81
Reception, 89
Reconstruction, 19, 20, 80
Reed, J., 93
Referent, 7–9, 11, 36, 58, 74, 76, 81, 82, 87, 88, 96, 109. *See also* Agricultural referents; Obsolete referents
Referential meaning, 8, 96

Region, 13, 23, 29, 35, 50, 66, 101, 104, 106, 107, 112; as a variable 1, 5, 15, 18, 22, 23, 31, 32, 34, 42, 49, 50, 52, 66, 94, 100-102, 104, 106, 107, 109, 110; and language contact, 101-10; classification by, 22-23; variation by, 66
Regionalisms, 33, 112, 130
Reins, 99, 108
Relationship between variation and change, 1, 3, 34, 61, 68
Relatives, 53, 118, 130
Relic area, 105
Religious differences, 106
Religious origin, 104
Replication, 51
Rheumatism, 68, 75
Richland Co., SC, 16, 23, 123, 124
Rincon, GA, 15, 116
Robeson Co., NC, 17, 128
Rosch, E., 85
Ruhl, C., 73
Rural, 4, 13, 18, 23, 24, 26, 27, 31, 40, 56-59, 66, 67, 69, 70, 79, 87, 88, 90, 92, 97, 99, 101-8, 110, 111, 123, 130, 133
Rural terms, 87
Rurality, 23, 24, 94, 102, 104, 106, 107, 110; and language contact, 101-10; as a variable, 1, 5, 15, 18, 26, 27, 32, 34, 57, 66, 67, 94, 101,
106, 107, 108, 110; classification by, 23-24; variation by, 66-67
Ryan, E., 102
Rye bread, 9

S

Sample, 3, 10, 13, 15, 17, 20-22, 24-26, 29, 33, 35, 41, 42, 43, 56-58, 64, 65, 69, 100, 113
Sampling, 13, 17, 24, 26, 41, 58, 59; random, 41
Sampson Co., NC, 17, 127, 128
Sand, L., 70, 71, 119, 122
Sapir, E., 85
Saspan Neck, NC, 16, 126
Savannah, GA, 15, 114, 116, 117, 122
Schneider, E., 23, 36, 62, 105
Scholar, 53, 66
School, 6, 20, 89, 91, 97, 100, 101, 104
School gets out, 90
Schooling, years of, 20, 100
Schuchardt, H., 79
Scotland, 105, 129, 131
Sebastian, R., 102
Seed, 43, 46, 49, 66, 67, 75, 108, 109
Self-image, 112
Semantic differences, 10, 81
Semantic distinctions, 34
Semantic extension, 75
Semantic field, 5, 58, 74, 87
Semantic merger, 74, 75
Semantic range, 74

Semantic restriction, 74
Semantic split, 74
Serenade, 87
Settee, 38, 39
Setting hen, 75
Sewee beans, 89, 109
Sex, 15, 22, 56, 95–97, 112; as a variable, 1, 5, 15, 18, 22, 23, 26, 27, 31–33, 35, 56, 57, 68, 69, 94, 95, 96, 99; and language contact, 95–97; classification by, 22; variation by, 68–69
Sexual preference, 22
Shallots, 89
Shallotte, NC, 15, 16, 125–27
Sharecropper, 95, 130
Shav(s), 57, 67, 68, 71, 101, 108
Sheep, calls to, 86, 87
Shell, 48, 101
Shenandoah Valley, 105
Shortening, 74, 76
Siding, 9, 75, 89
Sieva beans, 53, 109
Sign Test, 63-65
Singletree, 6, 59, 86, 108
Skunk, 90, 108
Slapjacks, 89
Smitherman, G., 22
Snake feeder, 9, 43, 44, 51, 53, 55
Snap bean, 7
Social class, 19, 21, 60, 93, 100
Social meaning, 8, 96, 102
Social networks, 93, 110, 111
Social situations, 82
Social status, 4, 67, 100, 107

Sociolinguistics, 4, 41, 113
Sociolinguists, 2, 4, 34, 73, 84
Sociology, 41, 84
Sofa, 38-40
Soft peach, 89
Solidarity, 101
Soo-calf, 49, 51, 66, 105
Soo-cow, 49, 105
Sooey, 99
Sook, 53, 105
Sorensen, A., 111
Sourdough bread, 9
South, 13, 50; as dialect area, 50–52, 90, 112; as region, 22, 24, 30, 86, 93, 97, 98, 100, 101, 103, 104, 106, 107, 111, 112
South Carolina, 5, 13, 24–26, 34, 52, 103, 106, 114, 116, 117, 119, 120–26, 130–32, 134, 135
Southern English, 29, 30, 92
Southern Poll, 112
Southerners, 30, 79, 98, 103, 112
Spartanburg, SC, 67, 134
Speech community, 3, 30, 93
Spender, D., 59
Spew, 12, 76
Spider, 52, 98
Spin, 91
Spring frog(s), 53
Springfield, GA, 15, 116
SPSS, 40, 48
St. Marys, GA, 106, 114, 121
Stallion, 86, 88
Statistical analysis, 24, 28, 51

Statistical methods, 3, 30, 35, 62
Statistical tests, 12, 17, 29, 40, 48, 53
Stereotypes, 31
Stern, G., 74
Stigma, 112
Stigmatization, 81, 82
Stokes Co., NC, 17, 132
String bean, 7
Stroller, 9, 68, 89, 101
Strong ties, 93, 111
Structuralist, 8, 83
Stud, 12, 96
Student, 57, 101, 128
Style, 9, 74, 82
Suburban areas, 106
Suburbanization, 97
Supply, NC, 16, 126, 127
Sweet potatoes, 8
Sweetser, E., 73
Synonymity, 7
Synonyms, 5-8, 10, 11, 33, 76
Syntactic choices, 81
Syntax, 1, 3
System, 19, 20, 30, 40, 69, 71, 72, 83-85, 89, 97, 111, 112

T

T-test, 64
Taboo, 81, 87, 88, 96
Tabouret-Keller, A., 30
Tape recorder, 11
Taxonomies, 74
Teacher, 76
Technology, 80, 85, 86-89, 91, 92, 96

Television, 10, 81, 90, 91, 111; educational, 91
Terrapin, 59, 75
Texas, 33, 34, 41, 73
Texas Poll, 41
Textbooks, 89
Textile mills, 103
Thibault, P., 72, 73
Threatening, 53, 66, 75
Tillery, J., 70
Toad, 107, 108
Toad frog, 107
Toilet, 90
Topic, 2, 5-7, 11, 30, 33, 42, 62, 74, 75, 101
Traditions, 89, 107
Transition area, 49, 51
Transition zones, 42
Transportation, 6, 80, 96, 101, 102, 104, 106
Travel, 13, 101, 102, 121, 128
Tripartite variables, 42-51
Trousers, 9, 36, 107, 108
Trudgill, P., 3, 50, 56, 70, 101
Turkey, NC, 17, 127, 128, 133, 134
Turtle, 68, 75

U

United States Census, 23, 25
United States Geological Survey, 23
Ullmann, S., 74
Union Co., GA, 16, 107, 118, 124, 125
Univariate testing, 26, 41
Upcountry, 106, 107

Urban, 4, 15, 18, 23–27, 31, 40, 52, 56–59, 66, 67, 69, 70, 79, 83, 87, 97, 99, 101–8, 110, 112
Urbanization, 24, 86, 95, 103, 104, 111

V

Variable rules, 34
Variables: demographic, 2, 5, 30, 48, 52, 62, 81, 92, 102; imbalance of, 27; linguistic, 1, 2, 5, 7–12, 19, 29–32, 34, 39–41, 56, 58, 59, 61, 65, 66, 70, 73, 76, 77, 81, 86, 90, 92, 94, 104, 107; non-linguistic, 2, 19, 29–32, 39–41, 56, 58, 59, 65, 66, 73, 81, 92, 94, 104; regional, 1, 2, 5, 11, 13, 18, 35, 66, 110; relative importance of, 2, 3, 29, 30, 33; social, 5, 18, 22, 33, 52, 58, 98; standard, 33
Variation: amount of, 1, 2, 30, 32–36, 76, 77, 92, 100, 102, 110; decline in group-based, 111; diachronic, 7, 88; language, 1, 2, 29, 31, 42, 70, 83, 84, 91, 92, 97, 104, 110, 111; linguistic, 3, 32, 60, 92, 95, 100; patterns of, 1, 29, 31, 33, 94; synchronic, 3, 73

Verbal tasks, 82
Verbs, 7
Vest, 76
Vocabulary: growth of, 111; loss of, 76; size, 2
Vomick, 99
Vomit, 7, 76, 88, 99, 101

W

W. Jefferson, NC, 17, 132
Wadesboro, NC, 17, 130
Wagner, M., 79
Wagon, 9, 59, 67, 86
Waiter, 76
Walnut Cove, NC, 17, 132
Watson, D., 111
Weak ties, 93, 111
Weatherboarding, 67, 89
Webster's Third New International Dictionary, 12
Wedding attendant, 7, 76
Weinreich, U., 107
Whites, 13, 15, 18, 22, 24, 27, 40, 52, 57, 59, 60, 69, 70, 93, 95, 97–99, 115, 118–21, 130, 131, 133, 135
Whoa, 7
Whole wheat bread, 9
Whorf, B., 85
Wierzbicka, A., 73
Wikle, T., 70, 71
Wilcoxon Rank Sum Test, 40, 64
Williamston, SC, 16, 125
Wilson, C., 90, 95, 97, 98, 100, 103, 111
Wishbone, 8, 90

Wolfram, W., 8, 61, 67, 72, 81
Women, 21, 22, 35, 56, 57, 59, 68, 69, 80, 94–98, 104, 118, 121, 125, 126, 133, 134. *See also* Females
Woodpecker, 56, 57, 68, 88, 96, 101
Word Geography, 6, 30, 42, 51, 52, 90
Workplace, 86, 95
Worksheet, 8, 10, 34, 36. *See also* Questionnaire

World War I, 20
World War II, 95, 98, 100, 101, 103
Wörter und Sachen, 10, 79

Y

Yams, 8, 98
Year of birth, 19, 20
Young, 19, 26, 27, 57, 59, 69, 71, 104, 111, 115, 119, 121, 124, 125, 128, 130

About the Author

Ellen Johnson is an assistant professor of English, Western Kentucky University. She obtained a bachelor's degree from Rhodes College in Memphis and her doctorate from the University of Georgia. In 1990–1991, the American Association of University Women awarded her a fellowship. In 1993, she received a Fulbright Senior Scholar Award to teach in Chile and conducted graduate courses in American English and English Dialectology at the Universidad de Chile. She is an editor for the Linguistic Atlas of the Middle and South Atlantic States.